The Best of The Mailbox® Math—Book 2

Table of Contents

Number and Operations
Places, Everyone! place value...3–8
The Big Four: addition, subtraction, multiplication, and division.....................................9–13
The Times: multiplication 14–19
Divide and Conquer! division 20–25
Come to Order, Please! order of operations..26–28
Scoring Big With Fractions and Decimals: fractions and decimals..................................29–35
Taking Note of Mixed Numbers: adding and subtracting mixed numbers..........................36–41
Investigating Integers: integers 42–44
In "Purr-suit" of Percents: percents...45–47

Algebra
Taking a Bite out of Algebra! introducing algebra concepts..48–53

Geometry
Scouting Out Spacial Relationships: spatial reasoning...54–56
Conquering Transformations and Symmetry: transformations and symmetry 57–59
Serving Up Circles: circles 60–66
Take a "Geo-Journey"! real-world geometry 67–72
Geo-Trek…: real-world geometry 73–77

Measurement
Measurement Magic: linear measurement 78–83
Taking the Mystery out of Measurement: perimeter, area, and volume..............................84–88
Edible Explorations: two- and three-dimensional measurement.......................................89–95

Data Analysis and Probability
Graphing Activities That Hit the Spot! graphing 96–101
Graphs Under Construction: graphing...102–107
Dealing With Data: range, mean, median, and mode...108–113
Chances Are…: probability...114–116

Problem Solving
Lassoing Lists: organized lists 117–119
Mission: Possible! problem-solving skills 120–125
A Problem-Solving Party: problem-solving skills and strategies..126–131

Multiple Skills
Math on the Go! everyday math skills 132–138
Picture Books and Math—Another Dynamic Duo! using picture books with math 139–141
Making the Writing-in-Math Connection: writing with math...142–148
Diggin' Dominoes and Dice: using dominoes and dice with math.....................................149–153

Game Plans 154–155

Answer Keys 156–160

Energize your math curriculum with **The Best of** The Mailbox® **Math—Book 2**! The editors of *The Mailbox*® have compiled the best teacher-tested ideas published in the 1996–2000 intermediate edition of the magazine to bring you this valuable, time-saving resource. Inside you'll find a wealth of math units covering all of the major mathematical topics, plus a collection of games regularly featured in the magazine. Each activity is clearly labeled with a skill line so you can see how it fits with your curriculum, and a detailed table of contents makes it easy for you to locate the skills you want to teach. With dozens of fun, creative ideas that provide meaningful ways for you to strengthen students' math skills, **The Best of** The Mailbox® **Math—Book 2** is a resource you can really count on!

www.themailbox.com

Managing Editor: Kelli L. Gowdy
Editor at Large: Diane Badden
Copy Editors: Tazmen Carlisle, Karen Brewer Grossman, Amy Kirtley-Hill, Karen L. Mayworth, Kristy Parton, Debbie Shoffner, Cathy Edwards Simrell
Cover Artist: Clevell Harris
Art Coordinator: Theresa Lewis Goode
Artists: Pam Crane, Theresa Lewis Goode, Nick Greenwood, Clevell Harris, Ivy L. Koonce, Sheila Krill, Clint Moore, Greg D. Rieves, Rebecca Saunders, Barry Slate, Donna K. Teal
The Mailbox® Books.com: Jennifer Tipton Bennett (DESIGNER/ARTIST); Stuart Smith (PRODUCTION ARTIST); Karen White (EDITORIAL ASSISTANT); Paul Fleetwood, Xiaoyun Wu (SYSTEMS)

President, The Mailbox Book Company™: Joseph C. Bucci
Director of Book Planning and Development: Chris Poindexter
Curriculum Director: Karen P. Shelton
Book Development Managers: Cayce Guiliano, Elizabeth H. Lindsay, Thad McLaurin
Editorial Planning: Kimberley Bruck (MANAGER); Debra Liverman, Sharon Murphy, Susan Walker (TEAM LEADERS)
Editorial and Freelance Management: Karen A. Brudnak; Hope Rodgers (EDITORIAL ASSISTANT)
Editorial Production: Lisa K. Pitts (TRAFFIC MANAGER); Lynette Dickerson (TYPE SYSTEMS); Mark Rainey (TYPESETTER)
Librarian: Dorothy C. McKinney

Manufactured in the United States
10 9 8 7 6 5 4 3 2 1

Places, Everyone!

Creative Strategies for Teaching Place-Value Concepts

Putting numbers in their places—that's what place value is all about! Help students better understand this challenging math topic with the following hands-on games and learning activities.

by Irving P. Crump

This Must Be the Place!

Skill: Reviewing place value

Review basic place-value concepts and introduce new ones with this versatile, hands-on chart that students can make and keep. Provide each student with a 12" x 18" sheet of light-colored paper and a ruler. Also provide permanent markers for students to share. Then guide them through these steps:

1. With your sheet of paper lying horizontally, fold it in half and crease it. Then fold it in half and crease it again.
2. Open up your sheet. Using a permanent marker, draw lines along the three vertical creases.
3. Measure and draw a horizontal line one inch from the top edge of your sheet.
4. Beginning on the left side, label the four resulting boxes "billions," "millions," "thousands," and "ones."
5. Measure and draw another horizontal line one inch below the first one.
6. Beginning on the right side of your paper, measure and draw a vertical line 1½ inches from the edge. Extend this line from the first horizontal line down to the bottom edge of the paper.
7. Measure and draw another vertical line 1½ inches from the first one. Extend this line from the first horizontal line down to the bottom edge of the paper.
8. From left to right, label the three resulting small boxes "H" (hundreds), "T" (tens), and "O" (ones).
9. Continue measuring and drawing vertical lines (1½ inches apart) across the paper so that the thousands, millions, and billions sections are exactly like the ones section.
10. Label the three column headings ("H," "T," and "O") in each section.

Next, provide each student with a small (about 4" x 6") piece of construction paper in a color that contrasts with his chart. Have each student cut this sheet into small markers (about one square centimeter each). Share with students that our numeration system is based on groups, or multiples, of ten—thus it's a *decimal system.* Our numeration system is also known as a *place-value system.* In a place-value system, every digit in a numeral has two different values: the *value of the digit* and the *place value of the digit.* Students' charts show just some of the place values in our numeration system.

Then have students use their place-value charts and markers with the teacher-directed lessons on page 4.

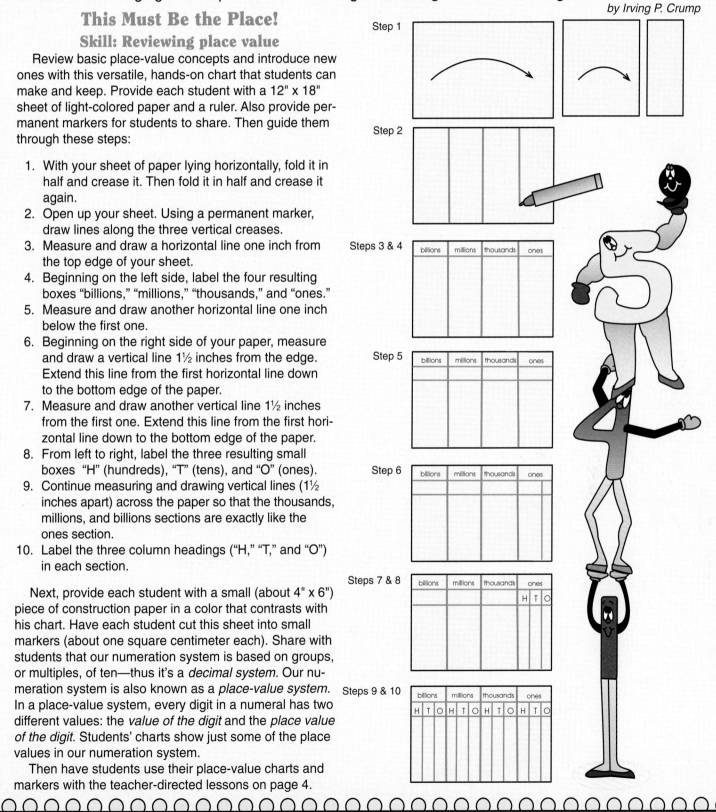

Introductory Activities

Number Families

Skills: Building vocabulary, basic skills

Write the numeral 123,456,789,246 on a chalkboard or transparency. Tell students to note that the digits are grouped in threes. Each group is called a *period.* (Students may wish to use the word *family* instead.) The periods are named—reading from left to right: *billions, millions, thousands,* and *ones.* Also have students observe that within each group the names are the same: *hundreds, tens,* and *ones.* Thus the *place value* of any digit is ones, tens, or hundreds followed by the group name. Ask students if the ones family is named when reading a numeral *(no).* Help students see that to read a numeral, it's necessary to consider the *values* of the digits and the *positions* they occupy.

Breaking Down Big Numerals

Skill: Simplifying large numerals

Cover all of the digits in the numeral written on the board (123,456,789,246) except for the 123 group. Ask a volunteer to read that group of digits *(one hundred twenty-three).* Next, cover all of the digits except the 456 group and ask a volunteer to read that group of digits *(four hundred fifty-six).* Repeat this procedure with the last two groups of digits. Guide students to see that in reading (or writing) a large numeral, it's helpful to break it down into its periods and read each period as a simple, three-digit numeral. Also help students see that the commas represent pauses when reading a numeral, just as they do in reading text. Whenever a student comes to a comma in reading or writing a large numeral, he knows to pause and say or write a period name. Ask volunteers to reread each group of three digits—this time adding the period name after each one.

In First Place

Skill: Naming the first place value

Beginning from the right, have each student place one marker in each of the first eight columns of his chart. Ask a volunteer to read the numeral that is formed *(11 million, 111 thousand, 111).* Next, have students clear their charts and place four markers in each of the first six columns. Ask a volunteer to read the numeral that is formed *(444 thousand, 444).* Have students observe that the first digit in a numeral represents the largest place value, and that it determines how to begin reading or writing the numeral. Continue with various other examples, extending all the way to the hundred billions place.

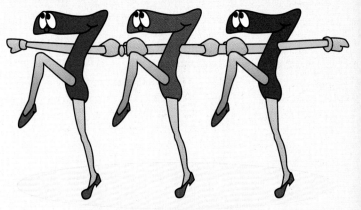

A Place for Nothing

Skill: Recognizing zeros as placeholders

Have each student place six markers in the one millions place, five in the hundred thousands place, three in the one thousands place, one in the hundreds place, and seven in the ones place. Then ask the class, "How many digits will this numeral have when you write it?" *(seven)* Ask a volunteer to write the numeral on the board *(6,503,107).* Remind students that the value of the first digit's place *(millions)* determines how large the numeral will be and that any empty place to the right of that digit must have a zero placeholder. Continue with other similar examples. Have students write their resulting numerals on paper.

Place-Value Games

Place-Value Matchup
Whole-Class Game

Now have students put away their place-value charts for this fun game of skill and chance. First have each student draw five blanks on a sheet of paper to represent a five-digit number. Next, pull ten cards from a deck of playing cards: one joker plus the 2–9 and an ace of any suit. The ace will represent *1* and the joker *0*. Also label five index cards as follows: "10,000s"; "1,000s"; "100s"; "10s"; and "1s."

To play, shuffle the ten playing cards. Draw a card and announce its value to the class. Each student writes that digit in one of his five blanks. After the digit is written, it cannot be moved. Lay that card aside, and continue drawing and announcing four more cards. Keep these cards together to use later. After you've drawn five cards, each student will have written a five-digit number.

Next, mix up the five discarded cards. Draw one playing card and one index card. Announce the value of the playing card and the place value on the index card. If a student's digit matches both the digit *and* the place value you announce, he earns one point. Have each student who has a match draw a circle around it. Continue drawing four more pairs of cards: one each of the discarded playing cards and one of the index cards. If all five of a student's digits match, he earns a bonus of five points for a total of ten altogether. Extend this game to include hundred thousands and millions by making additional matching place-value cards.

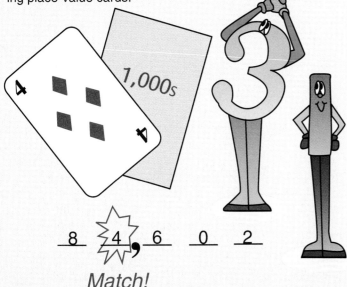

Match!

The Great Place-Value Race
Game For Two

Provide each pair of students with one copy of the gameboard on page 6, the directions on the top half of page 7, and a pair of dice. Give Player 1 ten markers (paper squares, buttons, checkers, etc.) of the same color; give his opponent ten markers of a different color. Read and discuss the directions with the entire class. Then have each pair of students determine who begins the game by rolling the dice. The student in each pair who rolls the larger number begins play.

Take a Chance!
Whole-Class Game

Provide each student with a copy of page 8. Have each student cut the sheet in half and save the bottom half to use later. Have students follow steps 1–3 in the directions to prepare for playing "Take a Chance!"

While students prepare, pull ten cards from a deck of playing cards: one joker plus the 2–9 and an ace (any suit). The ace will represent *1* and the joker *0*. Mix up the cards. When everyone is ready, draw a card and announce its value to the class. (Remind students that you have the digits 0–9, but will call out only nine of them.) Each student must decide in which of the nine places to write that digit. Continue play until you've drawn and announced nine digits. Then instruct each student to write the nine-digit numeral that results from matching each digit to its place value on the octagon. Determine who has the greatest numeral.

To play again, have each student move his octagon to a blank space on his paper. Mix up the cards and follow the same directions above, or try one of the following variations:

- Students must leave the center box blank until the ninth card is announced. Every student will write that digit in the box.
- After a card is drawn and its value announced, put the card back in the deck and reshuffle. Then draw a second card. Repeat this process until nine cards have been drawn.

The Great Place-Value Race

millions			thousands			ones		
H	T	O	H	T	O	H	T	O
								Start

Note to the teacher: Use with "The Great Place-Value Race" on pages 5 and 7.

The Great Place-Value Race

Materials needed:

for each pair of players: one gameboard (page 6), pair of dice
for each player: ten same-colored game markers, pencil and paper

Directions for two players:

1. Place your ten game markers beside the gameboard near *Start.*
2. Player 1 rolls the dice and moves one of his game markers that number of spaces.
   If he rolls a *10, 11,* or *12,* he follows the arrows and continues to the top half of the gameboard.
   Example: If *12* is rolled, the marker will land in the one millions space.
3. Player 2 then takes a turn.
4. Play continues until all ten of each player's markers have been moved onto the gameboard.
5. The object of the game is to build the largest number possible.
   —A player may have more than one marker in a space.
   —If a player lands in a space occupied by one or more of his opponent's markers, he may bump one
     marker and remove it from the gameboard. That marker is no longer in play.
6. BONUS ROLL! After all markers of both players are on the gameboard, each player gets one bonus
   roll of the dice. A player may move any one of his markers on the gameboard the same number of
   spaces as his roll. (If that marker reaches the ones place, it follows the arrow on into the
   bottom half of the gameboard.)
7. Each player writes the numeral he created by counting his markers in both halves of the gameboard.
   Be sure the player includes any zero placeholders. The winner is the student with the greater numeral.

©The Education Center, Inc. • *The Best of* The Mailbox® *Math • Book 2* • TEC1492

Note to the teacher: Use with "The Great Place-Value Race" on pages 5 and 6.

- -

Name _____ Patterns

Place-Value Patterns

Can you complete each pattern below? Pay close attention to place value—especially how each
numeral is different from the one to its left. Fill in each blank with the numeral that fits the pattern.

1. 148; 158; 168; _____; 188; 198; _____

2. 605; 705; 805; _____; _____; 1,105; 1,205

3. 6,734; 5,734; 4,734; _____; _____; 1,734; _____

4. 76,485; 81,485; 86,485; _____; 96,485; _____; 106,485

5. 18,000; _____; _____; 24,000; 26,000; 28,000; _____

6. 156; 166; 266; 276; 376; _____; _____; _____; 596

7. 85; 185; 285; 385; 1,385; 2,385; 3,385; _____; _____; 33,385

8. 12,612; 12,617; 12,667; 13,167; _____; 68,167

9. 1,487,329; 487,329; 387,329; 377,329; 376,329; _____; _____

10. 512,479; 512,478; 512,468; 512,368; _____; 501,368; _____

11. 614,375; 614,376; 614,386; 614,486; 615,486; _____; _____

BONUS CHALLENGE: 364,237; 364,240; 364,300; 365,000; _____; 400,000

©The Education Center, Inc. • *The Best of* The Mailbox® *Math • Book 2* • TEC1492

7

Name_____

Take a Chance!

Feeling lucky? See what happens in this game of skill and chance!

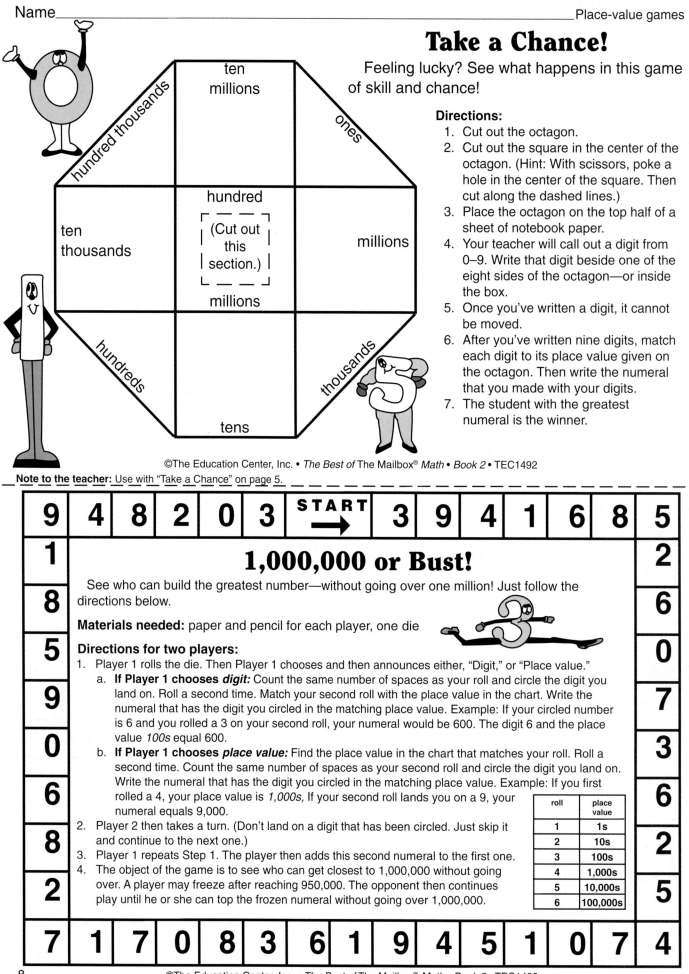

Directions:
1. Cut out the octagon.
2. Cut out the square in the center of the octagon. (Hint: With scissors, poke a hole in the center of the square. Then cut along the dashed lines.)
3. Place the octagon on the top half of a sheet of notebook paper.
4. Your teacher will call out a digit from 0–9. Write that digit beside one of the eight sides of the octagon—or inside the box.
5. Once you've written a digit, it cannot be moved.
6. After you've written nine digits, match each digit to its place value given on the octagon. Then write the numeral that you made with your digits.
7. The student with the greatest numeral is the winner.

Octagon labels: hundred thousands, ten millions, ones, ten thousands, hundred (Cut out this section.), millions, hundreds, millions, thousands, tens

©The Education Center, Inc. • *The Best of* The Mailbox® *Math* • *Book 2* • TEC1492

Note to the teacher: Use with "Take a Chance" on page 5.

Border digits (top): 9 4 8 2 0 3 START → 3 9 4 1 6 8 5
Border digits (right side): 2 6 0 7 3 6 2 5
Border digits (bottom): 7 1 7 0 8 3 6 1 9 4 5 1 0 7 4
Border digits (left side): 1 8 5 9 0 6 8 2

1,000,000 or Bust!

See who can build the greatest number—without going over one million! Just follow the directions below.

Materials needed: paper and pencil for each player, one die

Directions for two players:
1. Player 1 rolls the die. Then Player 1 chooses and then announces either, "Digit," or "Place value."
   a. **If Player 1 chooses *digit:*** Count the same number of spaces as your roll and circle the digit you land on. Roll a second time. Match your second roll with the place value in the chart. Write the numeral that has the digit you circled in the matching place value. Example: If your circled number is 6 and you rolled a 3 on your second roll, your numeral would be 600. The digit 6 and the place value *100s* equal 600.
   b. **If Player 1 chooses *place value:*** Find the place value in the chart that matches your roll. Roll a second time. Count the same number of spaces as your second roll and circle the digit you land on. Write the numeral that has the digit you circled in the matching place value. Example: If you first rolled a 4, your place value is *1,000s,* If your second roll lands you on a 9, your numeral equals 9,000.
2. Player 2 then takes a turn. (Don't land on a digit that has been circled. Just skip it and continue to the next one.)
3. Player 1 repeats Step 1. The player then adds this second numeral to the first one.
4. The object of the game is to see who can get closest to 1,000,000 without going over. A player may freeze after reaching 950,000. The opponent then continues play until he or she can top the frozen numeral without going over 1,000,000.

roll	place value
1	1s
2	10s
3	100s
4	1,000s
5	10,000s
6	100,000s

©The Education Center, Inc. • *The Best of* The Mailbox® *Math* • *Book 2* • TEC1492

The Big Four

Super Ideas to Reinforce Basic Math Operations

Faster than a speeding calculator...more powerful than the latest computer...able to leap a math problem in a single bound! Energize your teaching of the basic operations—and turn students into math superheroes—with the following hands-on activities, games, and reproducibles.

by Irving P. Crump

867
+927
1,794

Tic-Tac-Add!

Skill: Addition

Strengthen students' addition skills with this easy-to-play game. On a transparency out of students' sight, draw a tic-tac-toe grid and write the digits 1–9 in the sections (see the example). Circle any two rows, columns, or diagonals; then add the resulting three-digit numbers as shown. Next, have each student draw a tic-tac-toe grid on his own paper, write in the digits 1–9 in any arrangement, and circle any two rows, columns, or diagonals. Then have him add those two resulting three-digit numbers. When everyone has finished, turn on the overhead projector so students can see your work on the transparency. If anyone matched your sum, have him check his work. Then reward him with bonus points or a small prize. If no exact match is found, award the prize to the student who is closest to your sum. Play additional rounds, drawing larger grids to practice adding bigger numbers.

Four-by-Four Target

Skills: Subtraction, guess-and-check strategy

Reinforce subtraction skills with a fun game that also stresses the guess-and-check problem-solving strategy. On a chalkboard, draw a 4 x 4 grid similar to the one shown and write the digits 0–9 in its 16 sections. (You'll use some digits more than once.) Direct students to copy the grid and digits on their own papers. Next, write a target number above the grid, such as 48. Tell students that the object of this game is to find and circle two 2-digit numbers in the grid that, when subtracted, will result in a difference of the target 48. The digits in each circled pair must be adjacent or diagonal to each other, and the circles may overlap.

Next, direct each student to subtract the smaller number he has circled from the larger one. Award bonus points or a small prize to each student who matches the target or is close.

target: 48

0	5	3	2
8	1	7	6
9	7	2	3
4	4	0	5

72
-24
48

Variations:

- Have each student find pairs of two-digit numbers in the grid that, when subtracted, equal a difference in the range of 0–9, 10–19, 20–29, etc.

- See who can find the largest difference.

- See who can find the smallest difference (greater than 0).

- Play the game as described above, but use three-digit numbers.

Product Poker

Skills: Multiplication, place value

Ante up for a game of Product Poker! Draw a 3 x 3 grid on the chalkboard. Then write a two-digit number above each column and a single digit from 2 to 9 beside each row (see the example). Instruct students to copy the grid and numbers on their own papers. Then have each student fill in the grid by multiplying each two-digit number by each single digit and writing the product in the corresponding box as shown. Have students check their work as you write the products in the grid.

Next, have each student draw another grid. Have her write any two-digit number above each column and any single digit from 2 to 9 beside each row. Direct students to multiply as they did with the model. When everyone has finished, have each student look at her nine products and determine her best hand using the guidelines below. Award small prizes to the students with the best hands.

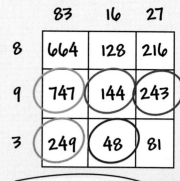

	83	16	27
8	664	128	216
9	747	144	243
3	249	48	81

Five of a kind! 20 points

Guidelines:

- 5 of a kind = 20 points. Examples:
  - five products with the same digit in the 10s place, such as **62**, 1**68**, **65**, 1**60**, and 5**66**
  - five products with the same digit in the 100s place, such as **4**98, **4**15, **4**22, **4**80, and **4**56
- 5-number straight = 15 points. Examples:
  - in the 10s place, such as **5**6, **6**2, 1**7**5, **88**, and 3**9**8
  - in the 100s place, such as **2**54, **3**54, **4**48, **5**56, and **6**78

- 4 of a kind = 10 points. Examples:
  - four products with the same digit in the 10s place, such as **85**, 1**80**, **82**, and 2**84**
  - four products with the same digit in the 100s place, such as **2**40, **2**68, **2**04, and **2**90
- 4-number straight = 5 points. Examples:
  - in the 10s place, such as **4**4, 2**5**6, **6**8, and 1**7**6
  - in the 100s place, such as **5**69, **6**75, **7**88, and **8**64

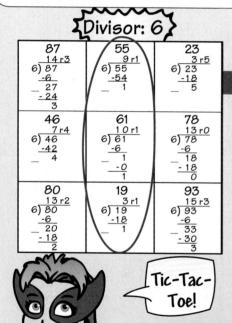

Divisor: 6

87	55	23
14 r3	9 r1	3 r5
6) 87	6) 55	6) 23
-6	-54	-18
27	1	5
-24		
3		

46	61	78
7 r4	10 r1	13 r0
6) 46	6) 61	6) 78
-42	-6	-6
4	1	18
	-0	-18
	1	0

80	19	93
13 r2	3 r1	15 r3
6) 80	6) 19	6) 93
-6	-18	-6
20	1	33
-18		-30
2		3

Tic-Tac-Toe!

Remainder Tic-Tac-Toe

Skill: Division

Try another version of tic-tac-toe with a game that makes it easy to divide and conquer! Have each student draw a large 3 x 3 grid on a sheet of paper. One at a time, call out nine 2-digit numbers. Direct each student to randomly write each number at the top of a box in his grid. Tell students that the simple object of this game is to win tic-tac-toe. How? By getting the same division remainder in all three boxes of a vertical, horizontal, or diagonal row. Remind students that they may work the problems in any order, and that the first student who gets three like remainders in a row should shout, "Tic-Tac-Toe."

To begin play, call out a single-digit divisor, such as 6. Direct students to begin dividing and to show all of their work in the boxes. If anyone gets tic-tac-toe, check his work for accuracy. If not, play another round.

Five in a Row

Skill: Review of all four basic operations

Encourage students to think creatively with this review of all four basic operations. First, write any three digits on the board, such as 2, 7, and 9. Direct students to combine the digits in any way, plus use any combination of the four basic operations, to come up with as many problems having different answers as possible. Invite volunteers to go to the board and write their number sentences. Examples:

$27 \div 9 = 3$ $(7 \times 2) - 9 = 5$ $(7 - 2) \times 9 = 45$ $92 + 7 = 99$ $(7 \times 9) - 2 = 61$ $(7 + 9) \times 2 = 32$

When the list of possible solutions seems to have dried up, provide each student with a copy of page 13. Direct students to look at the examples on the page. Next, have students read the directions for the game. When everyone is ready to play, call out three digits and tell students to begin. If no one is able to find five answers in a row after about ten minutes, call out three more digits. Play until someone calls, "Five in a row!"

What's Your Sign?

Directions: Follow the directions in each box to create true number sentences. Use a calculator to help you.

Example:
Add a + sign and an = sign:
3   4   2   8   6   2

Solution:
3   4 + 2   8 = 6   2

---

1. Add a + sign and an = sign.

a.   6   8   5   9   1

b.   1   7   9   2   6

c.   6   3   2   7   9   0

d.   5   8   2   7   8   5

e.   8   6   9   5   1   8   1

---

2. Add a – sign and an = sign.

a.   4   7   9   3   8

b.   6   2   7   5   5

c.   9   1   1   9   7   2

d.   1   0   6   8   9   8

e.   1   4   3   5   6   8   7

3. Add a x sign and an = sign.

a.   9   8   7   2

b.   1   6   5   8   0

c.   4   2   4   9   6

d.   5   4   7   3   7   8

e.   1   7   2   1   3   5   7

---

4. Add a ÷ sign and an = sign.

a.   1   8   6   3

b.   5   6   7   8

c.   6   0   4   1   5

d.   1   2   0   1   0   1   2

e.   4   3   5   1   5   2   9

5. Add either a +, –, x, or ÷ sign and an = sign.

a.   7   2   1   2   6

b.   4   6   3   9   7

c.   9   5   7   6   6

d.   7   1   4   9   8

e.   2   7   2   5   2

6. Add *two* signs and an = sign. Add parentheses if needed. The first one is done for you.

a.   (6 x 8) + 5 = 5   3

b.   7   3   6   6   0

c.   9   5   8   1   2

d.   2   0   5   3   7

e.   5   6   3   9   0

Bonus Box: On the back of this sheet, write a number sentence that could be added to one of the boxes above. Challenge a classmate to fill in your sentence with the correct sign (or signs).

Score the Big Four

Use a colored marker or pen to grade the Big Four's math test on…the big four! Mark a ✓ beside each correct answer; circle an answer if it is incorrect. On the back of this sheet, rework each incorrect problem. Then write a sentence that explains the Big Four's mistake. Since there are 20 problems in all, each one is worth five points. What is the Big Four's score? _____

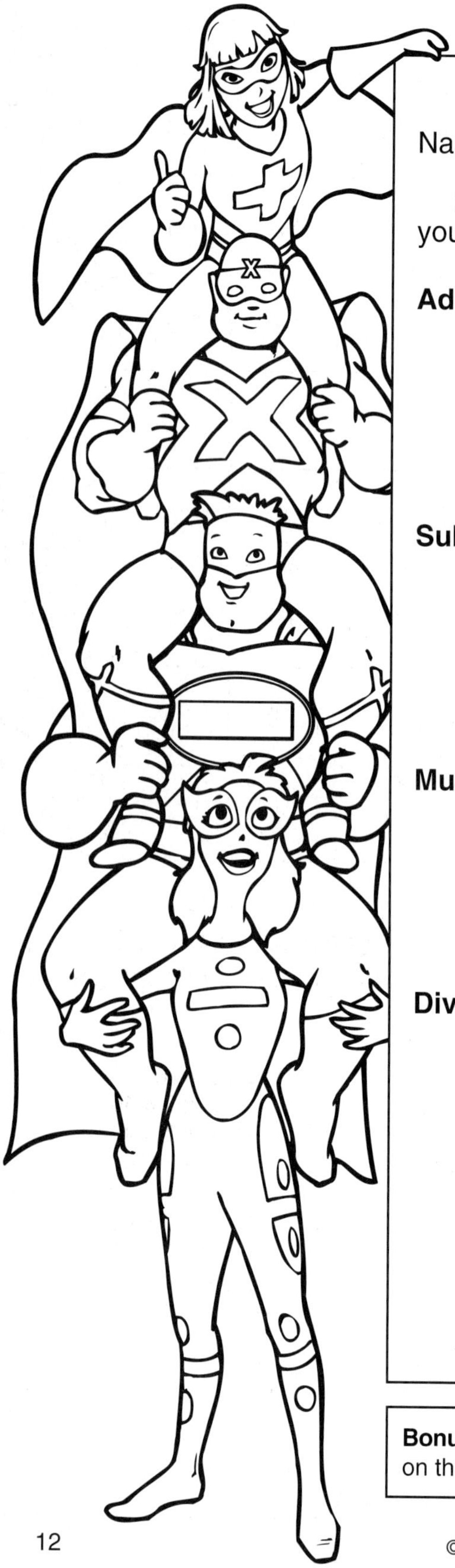

Name ___The Big Four_____ Test: basic operations

Follow the directions for each set of problems below. Show all of your work.

Add:

	$\overset{1\;1}{107}$	$\overset{1}{456}$	$\overset{1}{205}$	$\overset{1\;1}{398}$
65	107	456	205	398
+ 21	+ 95	+ 327	+ 806	+ 273
86	202	773	1,011	571

Subtract:

	$\overset{5\;1}{1\cancel{6}4}$	$\overset{1}{2}\overset{10}{\cancel{1}2}$	$\overset{0\;\;9\;10\;1}{1,\cancel{0}\cancel{1}\cancel{0}}$	$\overset{7\;\;5\;1}{8\cancel{6}2}$
73	164	212	1,010	862
− 20	− 25	− 96	− 253	− 149
53	39	116	757	613

Multiply:

$\overset{1\;\;12}{2\cancel{3}}$	63	$\overset{5}{17}$	$\overset{1}{86}$	$\overset{6}{107}$
x 8	x 10	x 7	x 3	x 9
92	630	126	258	903

Divide:

```
    14r0          13r9          20r1          157r3          1,517r3
  2) 28         6) 87         4) 81         5) 783         7) 1,062
                  −6            −8             −5              −7
                 ¹2¹7           01             28              36
                 −18            −0            −25             −35
                   9             1             38              12
                                             −35              −7
                                               3              52
                                                             −49
                                                               3
```

A Big Four Game: Five in a Row

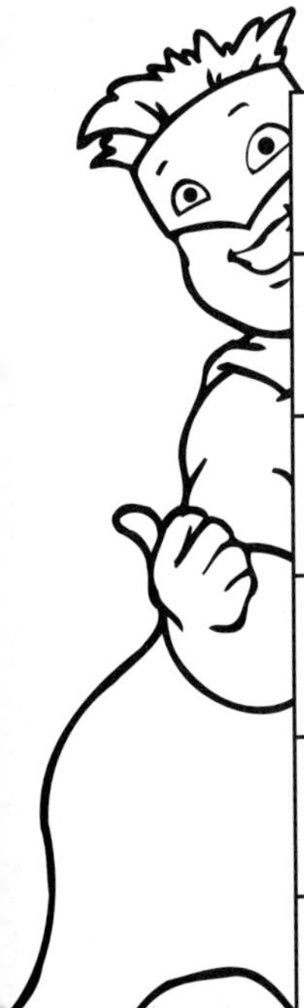

1	2	3	4	5	6	7	8	9	10
11	12	13	14	15	16	17	18	19	20
21	22	23	24	25	26	27	28	29	30
31	32	33	34	35	36	37	38	39	40
41	42	43	44	45	46	47	48	49	50
51	52	53	54	55	56	57	58	59	60
61	62	63	64	65	66	67	68	69	70
71	72	73	74	75	76	77	78	79	80
81	82	83	84	85	86	87	88	89	90
91	92	93	94	95	96	97	98	99	100

Directions:

The object of this game is to circle five numbers in a row in the grid, either vertically, horizontally, or diagonally. Here's how to play:

1. On another sheet of paper, write the three digits that your teacher calls out.
2. Combine or order the three digits in any way—and use any of the four basic operations—to get as many math problems that have different answers as you can. Show all of your work.
3. Circle each answer in the grid.
4. When you have circled five numbers in a row, call out, "Five in a row!"

Example:

Suppose your teacher called out 7, 2, and 9. The following number sentences are possible:

$(9 - 7) \div 2 = 1$
$27 \div 9 = 3$
$(9 - 7) + 2 = 4$
$(7 \times 2) - 9 = 5$
$(9 + 7) \div 2 = 8$
$(9 \times 2) - 7 = 11$
$(9 - 2) + 7 = 14$
$7 + 2 + 9 = 18$
$29 - 7 = 22$
$(7 \times 2) + 9 = 23$
$(9 \times 2) + 7 = 25$
$(7 + 9) \times 2 = 32$

$29 + 7 = 36$
$(7 - 2) \times 9 = 45$
$(9 - 2) \times 7 = 49$
$(7 \times 9) - 2 = 61$
$72 - 9 = 63$
$(7 \times 9) + 2 = 65$
$(9 + 2) \times 7 = 77$
$72 + 9 = 81$
$92 - 7 = 85$
$97 - 2 = 95$
$92 + 7 = 99$

Note to the teacher: Use with "Five in a Row" on page 10.

The TIMES

A Special Edition of Multiplication Ideas

Extra! Extra! Read all about it! Looking for some newsworthy ideas for teaching multiplication skills? Then check out the following creative activities, games, and reproducibles.

by Irving P. Crump

Four-Square Facts
Skill: Basic multiplication facts

Basic facts are in the headlines with this fun game! Divide students into groups of three or four and then provide each group with a deck of cards (all face cards are removed, ace equals one, and each number card equals its value). To begin, a dealer deals four cards in a 2 x 2 array to each player. He places the remaining cards in a stack and turns over the top card. He places this card beside the stack to begin a discard pile. The object of the game is to have the greatest product. To play:

1. Each player turns over any two of his four cards. The other two cards remain facedown.
2. Each player mentally multiplies the numbers on his two cards, as well as those on his opponents' cards.
3. The player to the dealer's left begins. If this player thinks he has the greatest product and no one can top it, he may "freeze." Each remaining player will then have one turn to try to beat that product. If the first player does not freeze, he draws the top card from either the deck or the discard pile. He then swaps one of his four cards with the one he drew. The card that is swapped is then placed faceup on the discard pile.
4. Play continues to the left. A player may freeze at any time when it's his turn if he thinks he has the greatest product.
5. After a player freezes and each of the other players has had one final turn, each player declares his product. A player may declare the product of the two cards showing, or he may choose any two of his cards and multiply them together. Thus, a player could pick up his two facedown cards, multiply them together, and possibly beat the current greatest product.
6. In case of a tie, players multiply their remaining two cards to see who has the greater product.

After a winner is determined, each player records his product (or products, if there's a tie) as his score for that round. Cards are then reshuffled to play another round.

Facts War
Skill: Basic multiplication facts

This fast-paced game is similar to the traditional card game War, but players compare products instead of single cards. Provide each pair of students with a deck of playing cards (ace equals one, number cards equal their values, and each face card equals ten). If needed, provide each pair of students with a multiplication table for checking. To play:

1. The dealer deals all of the cards facedown—half to her opponent and half to herself.
2. Each player turns over her first two cards, multiplies the two values, and announces the product.
3. The player with the higher product wins all four cards.
4. If the products are the same (8 x 5 = 4 x king), each player repeats Step 2. The winner keeps all eight cards.
5. If there's still a tie, then Step 2 is repeated. The player with the higher product keeps all of the cards that have been turned over.

Play continues until all of the cards have been used. The winner is the player who wins more cards.

Multiples Are in the Cards!

Skills: Basic multiplication facts, multiples

Help students recognize multiples and practice basic facts with this card game. Provide each team of three or four students with a deck of playing cards (ace equals one, number cards equal their values, jack equals 11, queen equals 12, and king equals 13). Have a team captain shuffle the cards and stack them facedown. Next, write a digit from 2 to 9 on the board. Tell students that the object of the game is to make the first ten multiples of that digit. For example, if the digit is 8, then the multiples to make are 8, 16, 24,…80.

At a signal, the captain of each team turns over the first two cards. The students in that team multiply the two card values together, then decide whether the product is a multiple of the digit on the board. Have each captain call out the two numbers and their product. If the product is a multiple of the target digit, then the team earns that number of points. (Example: $2 \times$ queen $= 24$; 24 is a multiple of 8.) Then have each team captain place the cards at the bottom of the stack. Continue play until all ten multiples of the target digit have been won.

9 x 8 = 72
72 is a multiple of 8!

Five-Factor Lotto

Skill: Recognizing factors of numbers

Factors are front-page news with this versatile grid game! Provide each student with a copy of the grid at the top of page 17. Direct each student to randomly fill in his grid with the numbers 2–10, writing each one four times. Also have each student make about 20 paper game chips. To play, call out a number that has factors in the grid, such as 30 (factors of 30: 1, 2, 3, 5, 6, 10, 15, 30). Direct each student to write 30 on a game chip and then place the chip on one of 30's factors, either 2, 3, 5, 6, or 10. Once a chip is placed, it can't be moved. Continue playing until a student has covered five factors in any row. To check, have the winner remove each game chip, announce its number, and name the factor under the chip.

Place Target

Skill: Multiplying by two-digit factors

Provide plenty of multiplication practice with this simple game! Have each student draw a 4 x 4 grid similar to the one shown. To the left of each row, have the student write a different digit from 2 to 9; at the top of each column, have the student write a different two-digit number. Each two-digit number should belong to a different tens family (10–19, 20–29, 30–39, etc.). When every student has finished, call out "Multiply!" At that signal, the student multiplies each single digit by each two-digit number and writes the products in the corresponding boxes. (See the example.)

After every student has completed all 16 problems, write a place target (a one-digit number) on the board. Tell students that each place target in the hundreds place of a product scores 20 points, each place target in the tens place scores ten points, and each place target in the ones place scores five points. Have each student find his total score.

1 6 6 9 6

16 x 6 = 96!

Where's the Sign?

Skills: Multiplying by two-, three-, and four-digit factors; estimating

Go on a search for missing math signs with this nifty activity! Write on the chalkboard a multiplication sentence with all of the signs omitted. The sentence will look like a string of single digits (see the sample on the board at left). Share with students that these digits make a multiplication sentence but that the sentence needs signs inserted in the appropriate places. Tell students how many multiplication signs the sentence needs and that it must have an equal sign. (In the sample, one multiplication sign is needed to make 16 x 6 = 96.) Have students first estimate and then check their estimates by working out the problem on paper. Repeat with the other examples shown or problems from your math textbook.

Other examples:

1 3 7 7 9 5 9 *(one: 137 x 7 = 959)*   1 6 4 2 1 2 8 *(two: 16 x 4 x 2 = 128)*
4 5 3 1 3 5 *(one: 45 x 3 = 135)*   5 0 5 7 1 7 5 0 *(two: 50 x 5 x 7 = 1,750)*
2 5 6 6 0 *(two: 2 x 5 x 6 = 60)*

---

19 x 13 = 247
I'm close to the target of 250!

247

Hit the Product!

Skills: Using a calculator, estimating

Estimation and calculator skills are the newsworthy topics of this challenging activity. First, write the following prime numbers on the chalkboard so that every student can easily see them: 2, 3, 5, 7, 11, 13, 17, 19, 23, 29, 31, 37, 41, 43, 47, and 53. Each student will need a calculator, paper, and pencil.

To play, announce a target number (example: 250) and the number of factors each student may use (example: 2). The object of the game is for each student to choose two factors from the board whose product he estimates is close to the target number. First, have the student perform his multiplication with pencil and paper. Then have him check his work with the calculator. Award points to the student(s) who come closest to the announced target. Play additional rounds with different target numbers, as well as rounds in which students must use three or four factors to arrive at a target.

Short Takes

Skill: Shortcuts in multiplication

Provide each student with a copy of the shortcuts guide on the bottom of page 17. Review each shortcut with students; then give additional problems for them to solve by using the shortcuts. Remind students that some shortcuts are helpful when computing mentally or when only estimates are needed.

Five-Factor Lotto

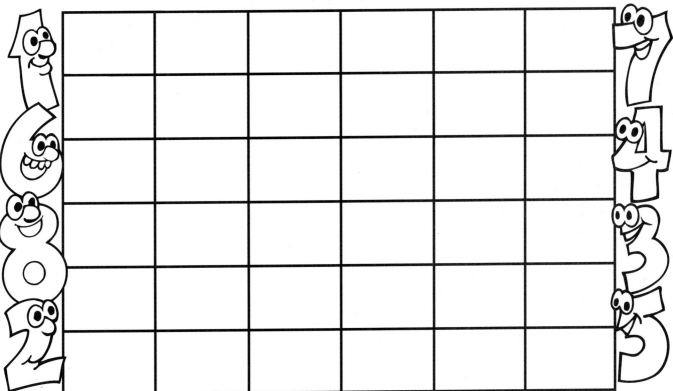

Note to the teacher: Use with "Five-Factor Lotto" on page 15.

Top 10 Shortcuts

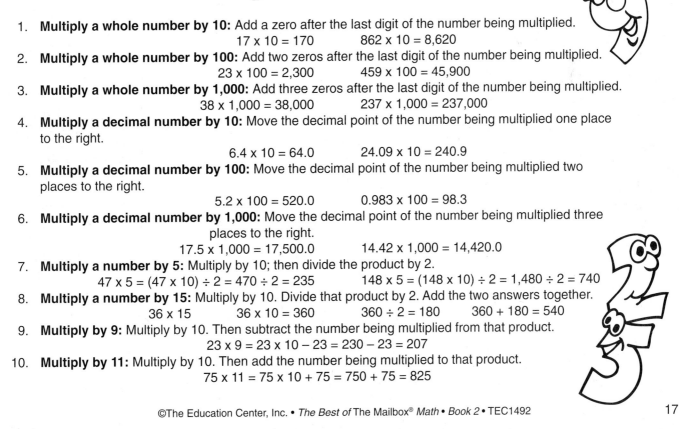

1. **Multiply a whole number by 10:** Add a zero after the last digit of the number being multiplied.

   $17 \times 10 = 170$ $862 \times 10 = 8{,}620$

2. **Multiply a whole number by 100:** Add two zeros after the last digit of the number being multiplied.

   $23 \times 100 = 2{,}300$ $459 \times 100 = 45{,}900$

3. **Multiply a whole number by 1,000:** Add three zeros after the last digit of the number being multiplied.

   $38 \times 1{,}000 = 38{,}000$ $237 \times 1{,}000 = 237{,}000$

4. **Multiply a decimal number by 10:** Move the decimal point of the number being multiplied one place to the right.

   $6.4 \times 10 = 64.0$ $24.09 \times 10 = 240.9$

5. **Multiply a decimal number by 100:** Move the decimal point of the number being multiplied two places to the right.

   $5.2 \times 100 = 520.0$ $0.983 \times 100 = 98.3$

6. **Multiply a decimal number by 1,000:** Move the decimal point of the number being multiplied three places to the right.

   $17.5 \times 1{,}000 = 17{,}500.0$ $14.42 \times 1{,}000 = 14{,}420.0$

7. **Multiply a number by 5:** Multiply by 10; then divide the product by 2.

   $47 \times 5 = (47 \times 10) \div 2 = 470 \div 2 = 235$ $148 \times 5 = (148 \times 10) \div 2 = 1{,}480 \div 2 = 740$

8. **Multiply a number by 15:** Multiply by 10. Divide that product by 2. Add the two answers together.

   36×15 $36 \times 10 = 360$ $360 \div 2 = 180$ $360 + 180 = 540$

9. **Multiply by 9:** Multiply by 10. Then subtract the number being multiplied from that product.

   $23 \times 9 = 23 \times 10 - 23 = 230 - 23 = 207$

10. **Multiply by 11:** Multiply by 10. Then add the number being multiplied to that product.

   $75 \times 11 = 75 \times 10 + 75 = 750 + 75 = 825$

First in America

What was the name of the first regularly published newspaper in the American colonies? To find out, follow the directions below. Remember these properties of multiplication:

Order property: The order in which numbers are multiplied does not change the product.
$$5 \times 8 = 8 \times 5$$

Grouping property: The way in which numbers are grouped does not change the product.
$$(4 \times 5) \times 6 = 4 \times (5 \times 6)$$

Property of one: The product of any number and 1 is that number.
$$24 \times 1 = 24$$

Zero property: The product of any number and 0 is 0.
$$12 \times 0 = 0$$

Part I: The capital letter in each number sentence below stands for a missing number. Find the value for each letter. The first one has been done for you.

1. $N \times 13 = 13 \times 7$
   N = __7__

2. $E \times 1 = 24$
   E = _____

3. $(L \times 8) \times 3 = 9 \times (8 \times 3)$
   L = _____

4. $17 \times W = 0$
   W = _____

5. $B \times 20 = 20 \times 15$
   B = _____

6. $8 \times (R \times 10) = (8 \times 3) \times 10$
   R = _____

7. $5 \times 7 = 7 \times O$
   O = _____

8. $54 \times T = 54$
   T = _____

9. $(8 \times 7) \times T = 8 \times (7 \times 5)$
   T = _____

10. $17 \times S = 15 \times 17$
    S = _____

11. $(9 \times 5) \times 4 = E \times (5 \times 4)$
    E = _____

12. $E \times 21 = 0$
    E = _____

13. $37 \times 1 = H$
    H = _____

14. $0 \times 72 = S$
    S = _____

15. $6 \times (2 \times 15) = (6 \times T) \times 15$
    T = _____

16. $16 \times 23 = O \times 16$
    O = _____

17. $(10 \times 31) \times 5 = 10 \times (31 \times E)$
    E = _____

18. $33 \times N = 0$
    N = _____

19. $15 \times T = 51 \times 15$
    T = _____

Part II: If a letter is used in a number sentence that shows the
- property of one, write it here: ___ ___ ___
- order property, write it here: _N_ ___ ___ ___ ___ ___
- zero property, write it here: ___ ___ ___ ___
- grouping property, write it here: ___ ___ ___ ___ ___ ___ ___

Part III: Now unscramble the letters in each group to discover the name of the newspaper:

___ ___ ___   ___ ___ ___ ___ ___   ___ ___ ___ ___ ___ - ___ ___ ___ ___ ___ ___

Bonus Box: What year was this newspaper first published? Solve the following riddle to find out: The sum of the first two digits is twice as large as the last digit. The sum of all the digits is 12.

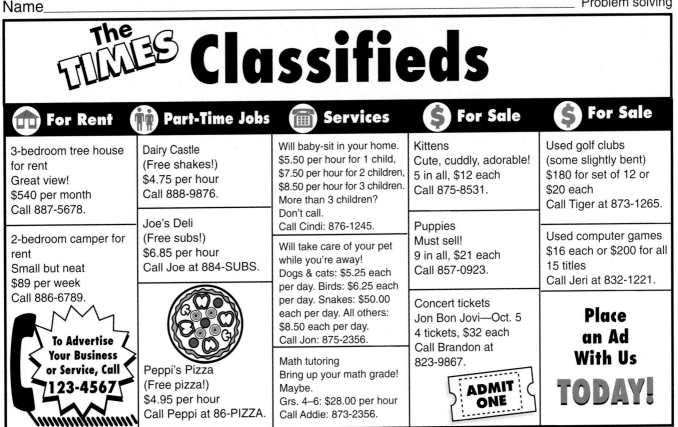

Use the information in the ads above to solve the following problems. Show your work on another sheet of paper; then write your answers in the blanks provided.

1. How much would 7 golf clubs cost? _____

2. What is the cost of 6 hours of math tutoring? _____

3. How much would you earn in an 8-hour day working at Dairy Castle? _____

4. How much would it cost to rent the camper for 4 weeks? _____

5. How much would all 5 kittens cost? _____

6. How much would you make working at Peppi's for 5 hours? _____

7. How much would 3 concert tickets cost? _____

8. How much would 6 puppies cost? _____

9. Employees at Joe's Deli earn an average of $7.50 per hour in tips on weekend nights. About how much would you expect to earn if you worked 5 hours on Saturday night? _____

10. If Cindi baby-sat 1 child on Friday night for 4 hours and then 2 children on Saturday night for 5 hours, how much money did she earn? _____

11. If 3 housemates shared the tree house, how much rent would each one pay per month? _____ How much rent would each person pay for 12 months? _____

12. How much would Jon charge to look after your dog and ferret for 7 days? _____

13. How much money would you save by buying all 15 computer games instead of buying each one individually? _____

14. How much rent would you pay in 12 months if you rented the tree house? _____

15. How much would Jon charge to look after your cat, dog, and bird for 3 days? _____

Bonus Box: The regular price for the concert tickets is $85 per pair. How much money would you save if you bought the 4 Brandon is selling? _____

Divide and Conquer!

Creative Activities to Strengthen Students' Division Skills

Does the mere mention of long division cause a collective moan to rise from your class? If so, include the following fun-filled games and reproducibles in your math plans. They're sure to help students conquer the division blues!

by Irving P. Crump

I've got a factor of 18.

Just a Faster Way to Subtract
Skill: Understanding division

Yep, that's what division is—a shortcut for subtraction! Help students understand this concept with a simple calculator activity. Provide each student with a calculator. Then write a division problem, such as $59 \div 7$, on the board. Remind the class that to divide 59 by 7 means to find out how many whole groups of 7 are in 59. One way to do that is by subtracting.

Direct each student to enter $59 - 7 =$ in his calculator and note the display *(52)*. This represents one group of 7. Next, tell students to press the = key again and note the display *(45)*. Two groups of 7 have now been subtracted from 59. Have students continue to press the = key (and count the number of times they press it) until 3 is displayed. Students should count eight whole groups of 7 subtracted from 59, with 3 left over. Repeat these same steps with other dividends and divisors. (This would be a perfect time to review the calculator's *constant function.* To repeat an operation, such as *subtract 7,* without reentering it, simply continue to press the = key the number of times that you want to perform the operation.)

Factor Frolic
Skill: Recognizing factors

Factors are numbers that multiply to give a product. So a factor of a number divides that number without a remainder—an important concept to grasp when doing long division. Provide practice with recognizing factors by playing this mental-math game. Give each student five index cards. Direct her to write a number from 2 to 10 on each card, without repeating a number (example: 2, 3, 6, 7, and 10). Have each student lay her cards faceup on her desk. Tell students that the object of this game is to determine factors of numbers that you call out. Here's how to play:

1. Call out any two-digit number, such as 20.
2. Each student checks her cards to see whether she has a factor of 20.
3. If a student has a card with a factor of 20, she holds it up so that you can check it.
4. If she is correct, she turns that card over. If not, she places the card back faceup on her desk.
5. Although a student may have more than one factor of the number you call, she can hold up only one card at a time. For example, if a student has cards with 2, 3, 6, 7, and 10, she may hold up either the 2 or the 10, since each is a factor of 20.

Continue play until a student wins by being the first to turn over all of her cards. Then have students swap cards and begin a new game. For a variation, allow students to hold up more than one card at a time. In the example above, the student could hold up the 2 and the 10 since they are both factors of 20. For more fun with factors, see the reproducible on page 22.

Stand Up and Divide
Skill: Long-division steps

Why does division often unnerve intermediate kids? Maybe it's because they must know their multiplication facts in order to have a good grasp of division—plus they must have good subtraction skills. Help students get the hang of the long-division process with this fun game. Gather 36 index cards; then divide them equally into two 18-card sets. In each set, label one card 0, one 9, and two cards each with the digits 1–8. Divide the class into two teams and give a set of cards to each team. Have a dealer deal his team's cards. Some players will have two cards, but make sure that no player has duplicates. Write a division problem, like the one shown, on the chalkboard. To play, follow these steps:

1. Say, "Divide," to Team 1. Each student on that team mentally divides 51 by 8 *(6)*.
2. Each student on Team 1 who has a 6 card stands and shows it to you to be checked.
3. After you check the cards, award each correct response a point.
4. Appoint one of the 6-card holders to go to the board and write 6 in the quotient.
5. Next, say, "Multiply," to Team 2. Each student mentally multiplies 6 times 8 *(48)*.
6. Each student on Team 2 who has a 4 or an 8 card (for the product 48) stands and shows it to you to be checked.
7. After you check the cards, award each correct response a point.
8. Appoint one of the 4- or 8-card holders to go to the board and write 48 in its position.
9. Next, say, "Subtract," to Team 1. Each student on Team 1 mentally subtracts 48 from 51 *(3)*.
10. Each student on Team 1 who has a 3 card stands and shows it to you to be checked.
11. After you check the cards, award each correct response a point.
12. Appoint a 3-card holder to go to the board and write 3 in its position. Also tell that player to bring down the 8 from the dividend's ones place.
13. Begin the cycle again by saying, "Divide," to Team 2. Each student mentally divides 38 by 8.

Continue the steps of the game until the problem is solved. Then erase the problem and write another one on the board. The team with the most points at the end of the game wins.

Right On Target!
Skills: Division and multiplication

More practice with long division is in store with this game of chance. First, remove the cards ace through 10 of two suits from a deck of playing cards. Shuffle these 20 cards; then have a volunteer draw four. Write the values of the four cards on the chalkboard (ace = 1; ten = 0). Next, have each student arrange the digits to make a four-digit number and write it on his paper. Direct students to divide their numbers by 2. Then instruct students to check their work by multiplying (quotient x divisor + remainder = dividend). Instruct students to put down their pencils when they are finished.

When every student has checked his work and is satisfied with his answer, call out a target number—any digit from 0 to 9. Tell students that if the target digit
- is in the ones place of the quotient, they score 5 points;
- is in the tens place of the quotient, they score 10 points;
- is in the hundreds place of the quotient, they score 15 points;
- is in the thousands place of the quotient, they score 20 points;
- matches the remainder, they score 50 points.

After teaching this game to the entire class, provide each pair of students with a copy of page 25. Each pair also needs 20 playing cards, so you'll need a deck of cards for every four students.

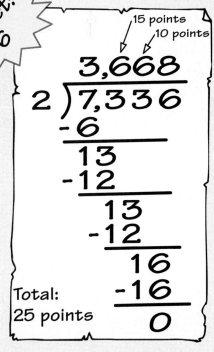

Target: 6

15 points
10 points

$$2\overline{)7{,}336}$$
3,668

Total: 25 points

Factor Face-Off

How well do you know the factors of numbers? Find out by challenging a friend to a game of Factor Face-Off!

Materials: 2 different-colored pencils, a die, a calculator

How to play:
1. Each player rolls the die. The player with the higher roll is Player 1.
2. Player 1 rolls the die and writes the number showing in the first blank of Game 1, Round 1. Player 1 rolls the die again and writes the number showing in the second blank.
3. Player 1 studies Game 1's factors and then circles each one that is a factor of his two-digit number.
4. If necessary, Player 2 checks Player 1's circled factors with the calculator. If Player 1 has circled an incorrect factor, Player 2 marks through it.
5. Player 2 repeats steps 2–4, with Player 1 checking. Player 2 cannot circle a factor that is already circled or marked out.
6. Play continues for four rounds. The winner of the game is the player who correctly circles more factors.
7. Special rule for Game 4: Add 2 to each roll of the die.*
8. Special rule for Game 5: Add 3 to each roll of the die.**

Player 1:	FACTORS					Player 2:
Rounds 1. ___ ___ 2. ___ ___ 3. ___ ___ 4. ___ ___	**Game 1**					Rounds 1. ___ ___ 2. ___ ___ 3. ___ ___ 4. ___ ___
	2 3 5 6 11					
	4 9 8 7					
Rounds 1. ___ ___ 2. ___ ___ 3. ___ ___ 4. ___ ___	**Game 2**					Rounds 1. ___ ___ 2. ___ ___ 3. ___ ___ 4. ___ ___
	2 3 5 7					
	4 6 8					
	12 13 9 11					
Rounds 1. ___ ___ 2. ___ ___ 3. ___ ___ 4. ___ ___	**Game 3**					Rounds 1. ___ ___ 2. ___ ___ 3. ___ ___ 4. ___ ___
	2 3 4 5					
	9 8 13 7 6					
	15 11 14 12					
Rounds 1. ___ ___ 2. ___ ___ 3. ___ ___ 4. ___ ___	***Game 4**					Rounds 1. ___ ___ 2. ___ ___ 3. ___ ___ 4. ___ ___
	7 6 3 2					
	8 5 9 4 11					
	14 13 15 18 12 16					
Rounds 1. ___ ___ 2. ___ ___ 3. ___ ___ 4. ___ ___	****Game 5**					Rounds 1. ___ ___ 2. ___ ___ 3. ___ ___ 4. ___ ___
	2 6 16 11					
	3 7 9 13 12					
	4 5 8 18 15 14					

"A-maze-ing" Division

Can you find your way through the maze? All you have to do is move from one number to the next by dividing the first number evenly by 2, 3, 4, or 5. Work through this example to get started:

1. Start at Enter. Divide 129,600 by 2. Check your work.
2. Is the quotient next to 129,600? No? Then divide 129,600 by 3.
3. Is the quotient next to 129,600? No? Then divide 129,600 by 4.
4. Is the quotient next to 129,600? No? Then divide 129,600 by 5.
5. Great! If you worked this problem correctly, you discovered that 129,600 divides evenly by 5 to get a quotient of 25,920—which is right next to 129,600! Use a colored pencil to connect 129,600 to 25,920.
6. Now divide 25,920 by 2, 3, 4, or 5 to discover the next number to draw a line to. Continue until you get all the way through the maze to the exit. Remember that you can't use a path more than once!

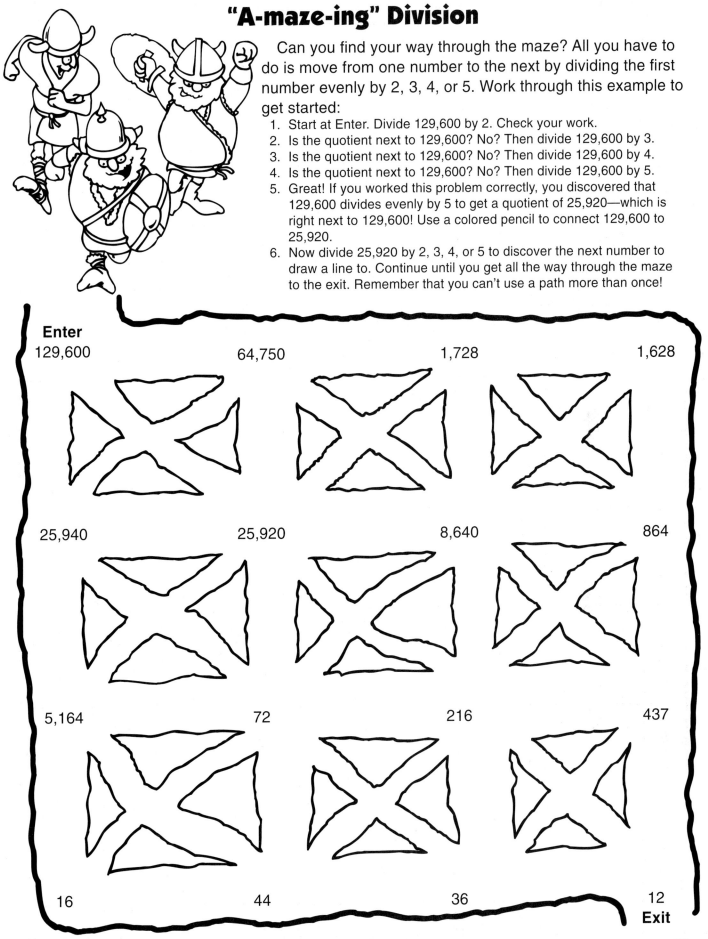

Enter
129,600   64,750   1,728   1,628

25,940   25,920   8,640   864

5,164   72   216   437

16   44   36   12
Exit

Remainder Relay

Go to battle with a friend as you divide by the divisors 6, 7, 8, and 9!

Materials: 4 index cards (numbered 6–9)   pencils and paper   calculator
9 playing cards (ace–9)   2 different-colored markers

Directions: The object of the game is to circle four numbers in a row in the grid—down, across, or diagonally. First, mix up the nine playing cards and stack them facedown. Mix up the four index cards and stack them facedown. To play:

1. Player 1 turns over the top three playing cards.
2. Player 1 makes any three-digit number with the three numbers showing (ace = 1) and writes it on his paper.
3. Player 1 turns over the top index card.
4. Player 1 divides his three-digit number by the number on the index card.
5. Player 2 checks Player 1's work with the calculator (quotient x divisor + remainder = dividend).

6. If Player 1 is correct, he chooses a number in the grid that matches his remainder and circles it with his marker. If he is incorrect, he does not circle a number.
7. Player 1 then mixes up each set of cards and stacks each set facedown.
8. Player 2 repeats steps 1–7, with Player 1 checking.
9. Continue play until a player circles four numbers in a row with his marker.

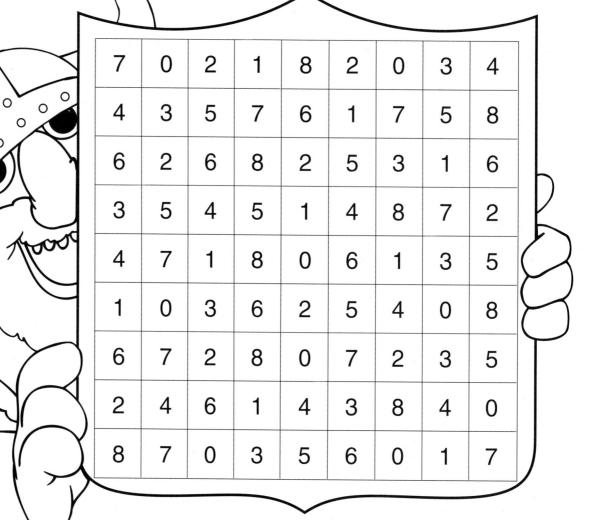

7	0	2	1	8	2	0	3	4
4	3	5	7	6	1	7	5	8
6	2	6	8	2	5	3	1	6
3	5	4	5	1	4	8	7	2
4	7	1	8	0	6	1	3	5
1	0	3	6	2	5	4	0	8
6	7	2	8	0	7	2	3	5
2	4	6	1	4	3	8	4	0
8	7	0	3	5	6	0	1	7

Right On Target!

With a little luck, maybe you can hit the target!

Materials: 20 playing cards, including 2 each of ace–10 (ace = 1; 10 = 0); pencils and paper; calculator

To play each round:

1. Shuffle the cards. Stack them facedown.
2. Player 1: Turn over the first four cards. Arrange them to form a four-digit number. Write it on your paper.
3. Player 2: Turn over the next four cards. Arrange them to form a four-digit number. Write it on your paper.
4. Divide your four-digit number by 2—the divisor for the first round. See the example below.
5. After dividing, check each other's work with the calculator. Remember that quotient x divisor + remainder = dividend. If your answer is incorrect, rework the problem.
6. Player 1 or Player 2: Turn over the next card in the deck—the target number. Write its value in the target space for Round 1.

To score:

If your quotient has the target number
- in the ones place, the score is 5 points;
- in the tens place, the score is 10 points;
- in the hundreds place, the score is 15 points;
- in the thousands place, the score is 20 points;
- as its remainder, score 50 points.

At the end of the game, add your total score. Write it in your box on the scorecard.

Example: A player draws 8, 10, ace, and 5. Then the player writes 5,108 and divides:

```
     2,554 r.0
2)5,108
    -4
    ──
     11
    -10
    ───
     10
    -10
    ───
     08
     -8
    ──
      0
```

If the target is 5, the player scores:
10 points for 5 in the tens place
+15 points for 5 in the hundreds place
25 points in all

Rounds			Player 1	Player 2
1	divide by **2**	target		
2	divide by **5**	target		
3	divide by **7**	target		
4	divide by **3**	target		
5	divide by **6**	target		
6	divide by **8**	target		
7	divide by **9**	target		
8	divide by **4**	target		
9	divide by **2**	target		
10	divide by **5**	target		
11	divide by **7**	target		
12	divide by **8**	target		
13	divide by **9**	target		
14	divide by **3**	target		
	Totals			

Note to the teacher: Use with "Right On Target!" on page 21.

Come to Order, Please!

Activities for Teaching the Order of Operations

Getting dressed, following a recipe, packing a suitcase—knowing what to do first can determine if the outcome of these activities is terrific or a mess! The same is true with math operations. Use the following activities to bring order to your students' confusion over problems that involve multiple operations.

ideas by Peggy W. Hambright

Gotta Have Order!
Skill: Computation

Begin to help students understand the need for having an order of operations by asking the following questions: What would happen if you put on your shoes before your socks? Frosted a cake before baking it? Packed small suitcases in a car trunk before the big ones? Guide students to conclude that the order in which such tasks are done can definitely affect the outcome.

Next, guide students to discover that the same is true when it comes to performing calculations that involve different operations. Copy the first set of problems below (without the italicized solutions) onto the board for students to solve. Check the answers together. Repeat with the second set of problems, directing students to do the operations in parentheses first. Repeat again with the third set, this time having students do the computations in order from left to right. Afterward, ask students how the sets are alike and different *(all three sets contain the same numbers and operations, the answers to the first and second sets are the same, the answers to the third set are different and incorrect).* Explain that to avoid such confusion and to be consistent, mathematicians agreed to follow a certain order—the order of operations. To help students remember the order, display the poster shown along with the two reminders given.

Set 1
$5 \times 2 + 3 = 10 + 3 = 13$
$12 \div 2 + 4 = 6 + 4 = 10$
$7 \times 2 + 6 = 14 + 6 = 20$
$150 \div 5 + 5 = 30 + 5 = 35$

Set 2
$3 + (2 \times 5) = 3 + 10 = 13$
$4 + (12 \div 2) = 4 + 6 = 10$
$6 + (7 \times 2) = 6 + 14 = 20$
$5 + (150 \div 5) = 5 + 30 = 35$

Set 3
$3 + 2 \times 5 = 5 \times 5 = 25$
$4 + 12 \div 2 = 16 \div 2 = 8$
$6 + 7 \times 2 = 13 \times 2 = 26$
$5 + 150 \div 5 = 155 \div 5 = 31$

Order of Operations

1. Parentheses (do the work inside these first)
2. Exponents (if there are no exponents, skip this step)
3. Multiplication and division (whichever comes first left to right)
4. Addition and subtraction (whichever comes first left to right)

Helpful Reminders: Remember the sentence "<u>P</u>lease <u>e</u>xcuse <u>my</u> <u>d</u>ear <u>A</u>unt <u>S</u>ally" or the word PEMDAS (p = parentheses, e = exponents, m = multiplication, d = division, a = addition, s = subtraction).

Problems	Answers
$8 \times 9 + 12$	x, 84
$7 \times (4 + 9)$	(+), 91
$45 - 25 \div 5$	÷, 40
$(5 + 4) \times (6 + 5)$	(+), 99
$86 - 7 \times 2$	x, 72
$64 - 72 \div 9$	÷, 56
$300 \div (22 - 7)$	(−), 20
$18 - 12 \div 3$	÷, 14
$4 \times 6 \div 8$	x, 3
$26 + 19 - 15$	+, 30

$26 + 19 - 15$

$+, 30$

Order Counts!

Skills: Recognizing which step to do first, solving problems

Put together an easy-to-make math center activity that will give pairs of students practice identifying which step to tackle first. Place a copy of the order of operations (see page 26) at the center as a helpful reminder. Next, program ten index cards with the problems listed on the right, writing a problem on the front of the card and its answer on the back. Direct the pair to stack the cards problem-side up in a pile between them. Have Student A take the top card and hold it so that the answer faces him and the problem faces Student B. Direct Student B to study the problem, identify which step to do first, and then solve the problem on paper. After Student A checks Student B's answer, have him put the card on the bottom of the pile. Then have Student B draw the top card and repeat the steps for his partner.

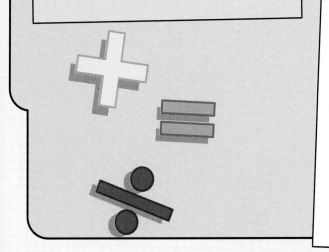

1. $27 + 45 - 31 = 41$
2. $889 - 200 \times 4 = 89$
3. $20 \times 6 \div 3 + 43 + 27 + 53 = 163$
4. $742 \div (7 \times 2) + 7 = 60$
5. $16 + (80 \div 4) + 6 \times (8 + 7) = 126$
6. $300 + 509 \times 12 \div 12 - 19 = 790$
7. $5 + 4 \times 9 - 12 \div 6 - 1(6 + 3) = 30$

The Case of the Odds Versus the Evens

Skills: Order of operations, numeration

Cast students into the roles of lawyers to play a fun order of operations game. Divide the class into two teams, the Prosecutors and the Defenders. Write a problem without the solution (see the examples) on the chalkboard. Have two players from each team work together to use the order of operations to solve the problem. As soon as the pair has its answer, have the twosome call out, "Order in the court!" Check the pair's answer. If correct, award the pair's team five points for an even-numbered answer or three points for an odd-numbered answer. If incorrect, give the opposing pair time to answer and earn points. If neither pair answers correctly, guide students to the correct solution but award no points. Continue in this manner until every student has had a turn.

To challenge students with another tough case, write four different numbers—such as 8, 3, 19, and 25—on the board. Have students use the numbers to write four problems that each have a different answer.

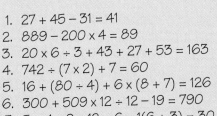

Ordering More Practice

Skills: Creating and solving problems using the order of operations

If you're looking for a ready-to-use activity to practice the order of operations, then you won't object to the reproducible on page 28! After each student completes a copy of this page, give him an index card. Challenge the student to label the front of the card with a problem similar to those on page 28. Have him write the answer to the problem on the back of the card. Collect the cards and check them for accuracy. Then use the cards as free-time fillers or as extra-credit problems on future math assignments.

Order, Please!

How well can you judge which operation to do first in a problem? Find out by following the directions below.

Directions: Use each number below four times and the order of operations to write a problem whose answer equals the number on the gavel. For example, if the number is 8 and the answer to reach is 152, you could write 88 + 8 x 8.

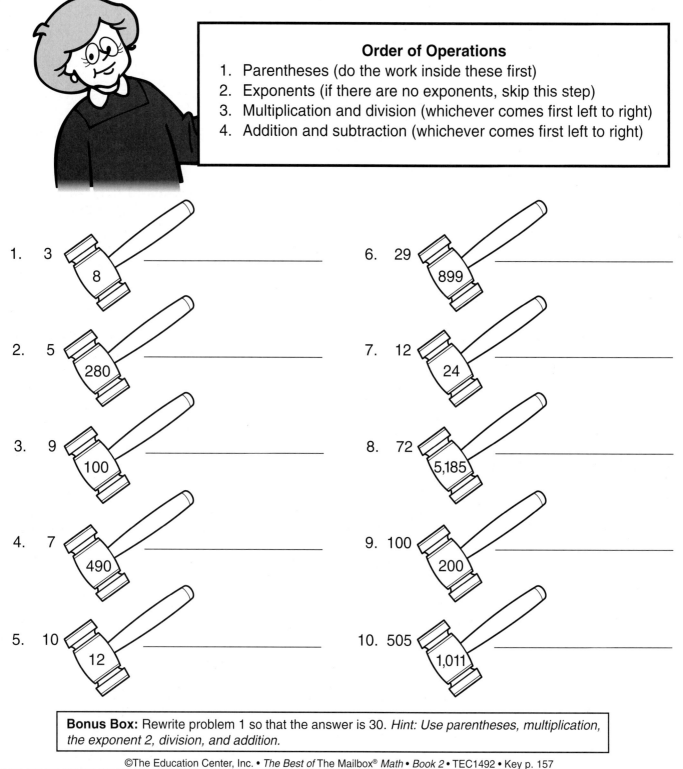

Order of Operations
1. Parentheses (do the work inside these first)
2. Exponents (if there are no exponents, skip this step)
3. Multiplication and division (whichever comes first left to right)
4. Addition and subtraction (whichever comes first left to right)

1. 3   8 _____

2. 5   280 _____

3. 9   100 _____

4. 7   490 _____

5. 10   12 _____

6. 29   899 _____

7. 12   24 _____

8. 72   5,185 _____

9. 100   200 _____

10. 505   1,011 _____

Bonus Box: Rewrite problem 1 so that the answer is 30. *Hint: Use parentheses, multiplication, the exponent 2, division, and addition.*

SCORING BIG WITH FRACTIONS AND DECIMALS

When students come up against fractions and decimals, they need a game plan that's loaded with can't-be-beat offensive and defensive strategies. As their coach, prepare them to take on these challenging opponents with the following creative ideas and reproducibles!

by Marsha Schmus

FIRST-HALF ACTION: FRACTIONS

GOING FOR ONE!
Skill: Identifying fractions

Tip off the unit with this hands-on activity on identifying fractions. Place 15 color tiles or paper squares—five blue, two red, three yellow, and five green—in a paper lunch bag. List the four colors in separate columns on the board; then select five students to help with the activity. Have four students take turns drawing one tile at a time from the bag while the other student tallies the tiles on the board by color. After the bag has been emptied, help students understand that the separate drawings represent the different parts of a *whole*, or the total contents of the bag. For example, since two of the 15 tiles are red, they represent $\frac{2}{15}$ of the bag's total tiles. As students identify the fractional parts by color, record the parts on the board as addends equaling one whole as shown. Repeat this activity several times, each time varying the number of tiles per color. Then place the materials in a free-time center for extra practice.

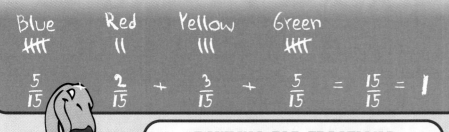

Blue	Red	Yellow	Green
$\cancel{||||}$	$||$	$|||$	$\cancel{||||}$

$$\frac{5}{15} + \frac{2}{15} + \frac{3}{15} + \frac{5}{15} = \frac{15}{15} = 1$$

BOWLING FOR FRACTIONS
Skill: Adding fractions

Looking for a winning way to practice addition of fractions? Take a shot at this super small-group game! Gather a small ball and an inexpensive set of plastic bowling pins (or use ten empty paper-towel tubes instead). Label each pin with a different fraction, using like or unlike fractions depending on students' abilities. Set up the pins; then have one student start by rolling the ball toward the pins. Have her add together the fractions from the knocked-down pins. Direct the other group members to check her sum. If correct, the player scores her sum for that frame. If the player adds incorrectly, she doesn't score. At the end of ten frames, have students total their scores to determine the winner. If desired, reprogram the pins to reinforce other important skills, such as adding decimals.

MYSTERY FRACTION OF THE DAY
Skill: Number sense

How can riddles rev up fraction skills? You'll soon see with this easy idea! Program large index cards with the following fractions (one fraction per card): $\frac{3}{4}$, $\frac{9}{10}$, $\frac{5}{6}$, $\frac{8}{12}$, $\frac{6}{12}$, $\frac{3}{8}$, $\frac{5}{10}$, $\frac{2}{3}$, $\frac{1}{3}$, $\frac{1}{4}$. Display the cards in your classroom. Each day write a different fraction riddle—such as those suggested below—on the board. Ask students to select the correct answer from the fraction cards. Challenge each student who solves the riddle to write another riddle for one or more of the other fractions displayed. With this idea, you'll always have a fresh supply of fraction riddles on hand!

- My numerator and denominator are both divisible by 3. I am equal to $\frac{1}{2}$. What fraction am I? *($\frac{6}{12}$)*

- My numerator is between 7 and 11. My denominator is less than 14 and is divisible by 3. What fraction am I? *($\frac{8}{12}$)*

- My numerator is less than 5. My denominator is a multiple of 2 that's greater than 6. I am less than $\frac{1}{2}$. What fraction am I? *($\frac{3}{8}$)*

- My numerator is the smallest odd number. My denominator is the next largest odd number. I am less than $\frac{1}{2}$. What fraction am I? *($\frac{1}{3}$)*

- Both my numerator and denominator are divisible by 2. I am less than $\frac{2}{3}$ and greater than $\frac{1}{3}$. What fraction am I? *($\frac{6}{12}$)*

- My denominator is a two-digit number divisible by 5. I am greater than $\frac{2}{3}$. My numerator is a one-digit number divisible by 3. What fraction am I? *($\frac{9}{10}$)*

29

FULL-COURT GRAPHIN'
Skill: Identifying fractions, graphing

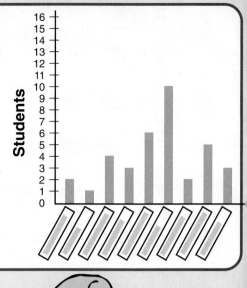

Provide your students with a perfect shot at learning more about one another *and* about fractions with this kid-pleasin' activity! Direct each student to choose a different topic—such as students who in-line skate, students who watch [name of TV show], or students who have home computers—and interview his classmates. Meanwhile, mount bulletin board paper on a board or wall. Draw a graph on the paper, as shown, labeling it with your number of students. Have each student write his interview topic on a sentence strip and post it on the graph's horizontal axis. Then assist students with compiling and plotting their data on the graph. Discuss the graph's information with students in terms of fractions: $^2/_{25}$ of the students live in apartments, $^5/_{25}$ watch game shows, etc. Follow up by having students write the graph's fractions in order from greatest to least.

FRACTION-ACTION BINGO
Skill: Fraction concepts

Coaches know that practice is the key to improving any skill. Use the familiar game of bingo to strengthen students' understanding of several fraction concepts. Give each student scissors and a copy of page 32. Review the sheet's directions with students; then give them time to program and cut out their gameboards. Next, distribute dried beans for students to use as markers. Read aloud one clue at a time from the list below until a student calls, "Bingo!" To play additional games, suggest that students trade gameboards.

Clues:

- the fraction equivalent to 1 *($^{18}/_{18}$)*
- the picture that shows $^3/_4$ (△)
- the fraction equivalent to $^4/_6$ *($^2/_3$)*
- a mixed number *($1^2/_3$)*
- an improper fraction *($^9/_7$)*
- the picture that shows tenths (▭)
- the fraction equivalent to $^1/_2$ *($^{10}/_{20}$)*
- the picture that shows $^2/_8$ of a set (⊙⊙⊙⊙)
- the fraction with 11 as its numerator *($^{11}/_{23}$)*
- the sum of these fractions is 1 *($^3/_8 + ^5/_8$)*
- $^3/_5$ is lowest terms for this fraction *($^{12}/_{20}$)*
- $^1/_5$ is lowest terms for this fraction *($^2/_{10}$)*
- this fraction is lowest terms for $^{14}/_{28}$ *($^1/_2$)*
- this fraction is lowest terms for $^4/_{12}$ *($^1/_3$)*
- the least common denominator of $^1/_{12}$ and $^1/_{24}$ *(24)*
- the difference between these fractions is $^5/_7$ *($^7/_7 - ^2/_7$)*
- the least common denominator of $^1/_3$ and $^1/_4$ *(12)*
- the picture that shows unequal parts (▱)

- the difference between $^7/_{11}$ and $^5/_{11}$ *($^2/_{11}$)*
- the fraction equivalent to $^6/_{14}$ *($^3/_7$)*
- the whole number equivalent of $^{20}/_5$ *(4)*
- the whole number for $^{12}/_6$ *(2)*
- $^4/_7$ is the sum of these fractions *($^3/_7 + ^1/_7$)*
- the picture that shows fourths (▦)

LCD RECIPES
Skill: Finding the lowest common denominator

Evaluating players' strengths and weaknesses is part of a coach's job. Quickly assess students' abilities for finding lowest common denominators with this easy task. Clip recipes from old newspapers and magazines; then give each student one recipe. Challenge the student to rewrite his recipe's ingredients so that all the fractions have common denominators. What a simple exercise for finding out exactly how much each student knows!

MIXING IT UP
Skill: Sequencing decimal numbers

Order up some terrific decimal practice with this beat-the-clock game! Write 30 decimal numbers on index cards, one number per card. Place any five cards on your chalkboard tray, arranging them so they're not in sequential order. Select one student to rearrange the cards from least to greatest as you time her. When she completes this task, record her time; then have the rest of the class check her arrangement. If she has ordered the cards correctly, announce her time as her score. If she has ordered them incorrectly, add ten seconds to her time to determine her score. Continue play by replacing the cards with five different ones and calling up another student. After everyone has had a turn, declare the student with the lowest score the winner.

SIZE 'EM UP!
Skill: Rounding decimals

Help students size up their decimal skills with this rounding activity! Draw a number line on the board as shown. Use the number line to review how to round several decimals to 0 or 1; then erase it. Next, ask each student to write a one- or two-digit decimal number that is less than 1 on the board. Have each student use the key (see the illustration) to draw a shape around his decimal. Then point to the decimals with squares around them. Have students help you order them from least to greatest. In the same manner, have students order the decimals with triangles around them. Use this activity and a number line divided into sixteenths to help students round fractions to 0 or 1!

| 0 | 0.1 | 0.2 | 0.3 | 0.4 | 0.5 | 0.6 | 0.7 | 0.8 | 0.9 | 1 |

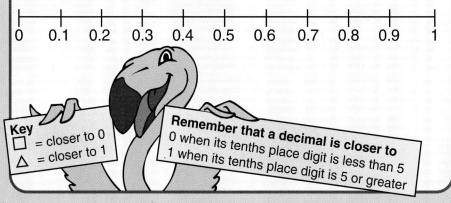

Key
☐ = closer to 0
△ = closer to 1

Remember that a decimal is closer to 0 when its tenths place digit is less than 5 1 when its tenths place digit is 5 or greater

SLAM-DUNKING DECIMALS
Skill: Decimal concepts

Watch decimal skills soar as high as Michael Jordan with this multipurpose activity! Make a transparency of a 10 x 10 grid; then use wipe-off markers to color a design on the grid as shown (or draw the grid on the chalkboard and use colored chalk). Have students tell you the decimal numbers that represent the colors on the grid (for example, .04 of the grid is black). Next, ask the class to add all the decimal numbers together to see that they equal one whole. Afterward, direct students to compare one color's decimal value with another and/or perform specific calculations, such as finding the sum of the decimal values of any three colors or the difference between the decimal values of any two colors. Lastly, have students order the decimal values of the colors from greatest to least or least to greatest. To follow up this activity, reach for the reproducible activity on page 35!

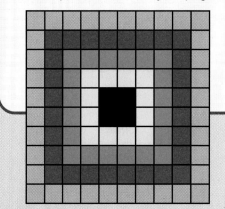

FRACTION-ACTION BINGO

Directions: Choose any 16 items from the box below. Write or draw each item in a different square on the gameboard at the bottom of the page. Then cut out the gameboard. Listen to the clues that your teacher gives you; then cover the square on the gameboard that matches a clue. When you've covered four squares in a row—horizontally, diagonally, or vertically—call out, "Bingo!"

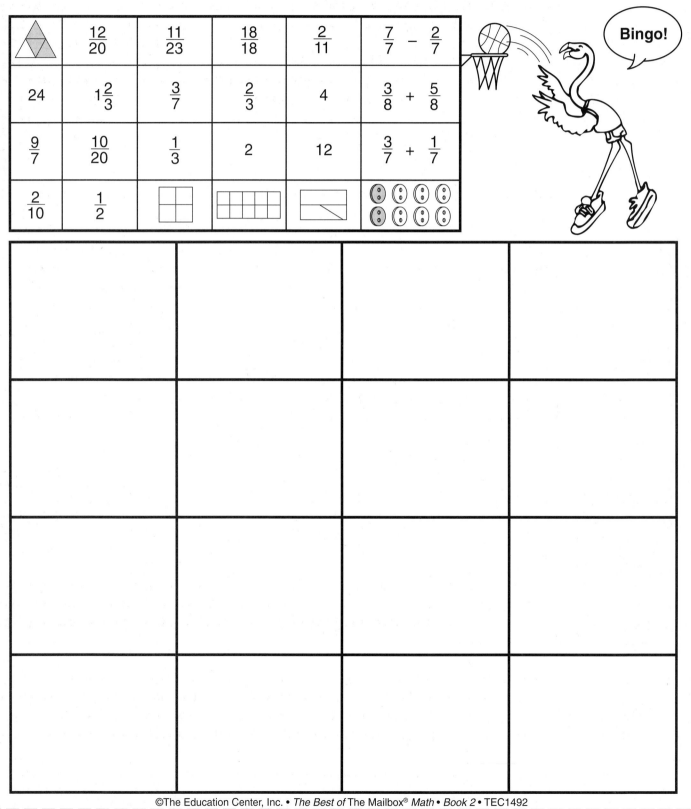

©The Education Center, Inc. • *The Best of* The Mailbox® *Math* • *Book 2* • TEC1492

32   **Note to the teacher:** Use with "Fraction-Action Bingo" on page 30.

GOING ONE-ON-ONE!
A Game for Four Players

Getting ready to play:
1. Cut out the box below. Glue it to tagboard; then cut the cards apart. Also cut out the key.
2. Shuffle the cards. Deal the same number of cards to each player.
3. If you have a fraction card and a decimal card that are equivalent, lay them faceup on the table. Use the key to check.

Playing the game (follow these steps when it's your turn):
1. Ask any player for a card you need to make a match. If you have a fraction card, ask for its matching decimal card ("Do you have a decimal card that matches $\frac{1}{5}$?"). If you have a decimal card, ask for its matching fraction card ("Do you have a fraction card that matches .33?").
2. If the player doesn't have a matching card, he or she says, "No match."
3. If the player has the card you want, he or she gives it to you. Check the match with the key. If it's correct, lay it faceup on the table. If the cards don't match, the player must give one of his matching pairs to the player on his left.

When all cards have been matched, count your matches. The player with the most matches wins.

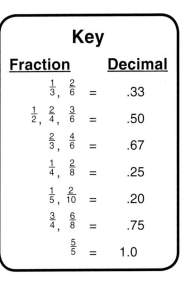

Key		
Fraction		**Decimal**
$\frac{1}{3}$, $\frac{2}{6}$	=	.33
$\frac{1}{2}$, $\frac{2}{4}$, $\frac{3}{6}$	=	.50
$\frac{2}{3}$, $\frac{4}{6}$	=	.67
$\frac{1}{4}$, $\frac{2}{8}$	=	.25
$\frac{1}{5}$, $\frac{2}{10}$	=	.20
$\frac{3}{4}$, $\frac{6}{8}$	=	.75
$\frac{5}{5}$	=	1.0

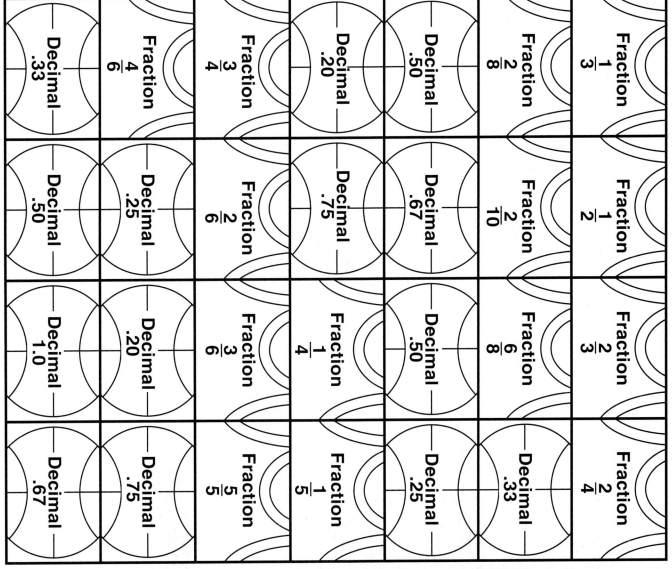

Decimal .33	Fraction $\frac{4}{6}$	Fraction $\frac{3}{4}$	Decimal .20	Decimal .50	Fraction $\frac{2}{8}$	Fraction $\frac{1}{3}$
Decimal .50	Decimal .25	Fraction $\frac{2}{6}$	Decimal .75	Decimal .67	Fraction $\frac{2}{10}$	Fraction $\frac{1}{2}$
Decimal 1.0	Decimal .20	Fraction $\frac{3}{6}$	Fraction $\frac{1}{4}$	Decimal .50	Fraction $\frac{6}{8}$	Fraction $\frac{2}{3}$
Decimal .67	Decimal .75	Fraction $\frac{5}{5}$	Fraction $\frac{1}{5}$	Decimal .25	Decimal .33	Fraction $\frac{2}{4}$

Note to the teacher: Give scissors, a sheet of tagboard, glue, and one copy of this page to each group of four students.

TIC-TAC-TOE FRACTIONS

Practice games are good for sharpening players' skills. Strengthen your ability to find equivalent fractions with this tic-tac-toe game. All you need is a partner, a die, and a winning effort!

Code:

$\boxed{\cdot} = \frac{1}{4}$ $\boxed{\cdot\cdot} = \frac{1}{3}$ $\boxed{\cdot\cdot} = \frac{1}{2}$ $\boxed{::} = \frac{1}{8}$ $\boxed{:\cdot:} = \frac{3}{4}$ $\boxed{:::} = \frac{2}{3}$

Directions for two players:

1. Roll the die. The player with the higher roll becomes Player 1.
2. Player 1 rolls the die and uses the code above to find the equivalent fraction on gameboard 1. If she finds a correct fraction, she writes her initials in that block.
3. Player 2 rolls and repeats Step 2.
4. Play continues until one player initials three blocks in a row—vertically, horizontally, or diagonally—to get the win. Record the winner's name on the line below the gameboard.
5. Repeat Steps 1–4 for the three remaining gameboards.

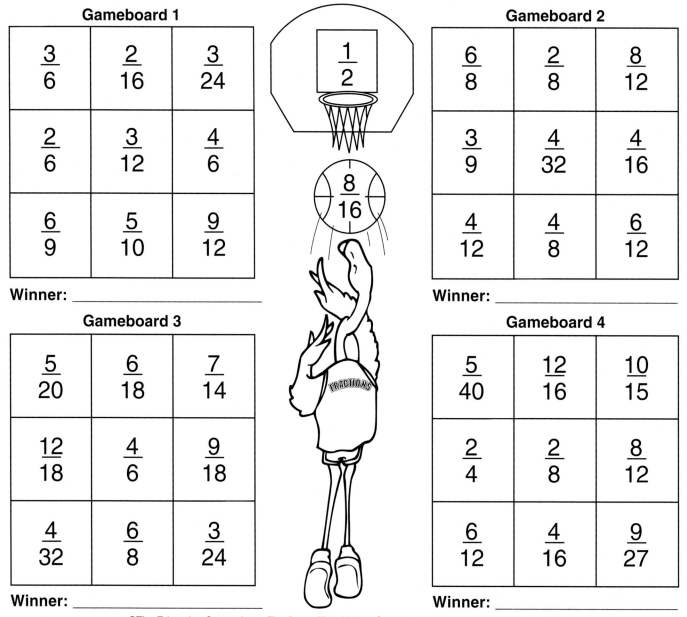

Gameboard 1

$\frac{3}{6}$	$\frac{2}{16}$	$\frac{3}{24}$
$\frac{2}{6}$	$\frac{3}{12}$	$\frac{4}{6}$
$\frac{6}{9}$	$\frac{5}{10}$	$\frac{9}{12}$

Winner: _____

Gameboard 2

$\frac{6}{8}$	$\frac{2}{8}$	$\frac{8}{12}$
$\frac{3}{9}$	$\frac{4}{32}$	$\frac{4}{16}$
$\frac{4}{12}$	$\frac{4}{8}$	$\frac{6}{12}$

Winner: _____

Gameboard 3

$\frac{5}{20}$	$\frac{6}{18}$	$\frac{7}{14}$
$\frac{12}{18}$	$\frac{4}{6}$	$\frac{9}{18}$
$\frac{4}{32}$	$\frac{6}{8}$	$\frac{3}{24}$

Winner: _____

Gameboard 4

$\frac{5}{40}$	$\frac{12}{16}$	$\frac{10}{15}$
$\frac{2}{4}$	$\frac{2}{8}$	$\frac{8}{12}$
$\frac{6}{12}$	$\frac{4}{16}$	$\frac{9}{27}$

Winner: _____

PUTTING NEW MOVES ON DECIMALS

During a basketball game, players guard each other and try to keep opponents from scoring. You can guard against confusion about decimal numbers with the help of this activity. Just follow the directions below, and you'll come out a winner!

Code:
R = red
Bl = blue
G = green
B = black
W = white

G	G	W	R	B	B	R	W	G	G
G	G	W	R	B	B	R	W	G	G
W	W	R	B	B	B	B	R	W	W
W	R	B	Bl	B	B	Bl	B	R	W
R	B	B	B	B	B	B	B	B	R
B	Bl	B	Bl	B	B	Bl	B	Bl	B
R	B	B	B	B	B	B	B	B	R
W	R	R	R	B	B	R	R	R	W
G	W	W	R	B	B	R	W	W	G
G	G	W	R	B	B	R	W	G	G

Directions:

1. Color the squares in the grid above according to the code. Don't color the squares marked with a *W.*

2. Record the number of squares for each color as a decimal number.

   R = _____ Bl = _____ G = _____ B = _____ W = _____

3. Find the sum of the decimals in Step 2.

   _____ + _____ + _____ + _____ + _____ = _____

   Explain the importance of this sum. _____

   _____

4. Calculate the sum or difference of each problem below. Use the back of this page to work the problems if you need more space.

   R + Bl = _____   G + B = _____   R + G + W = _____

   Bl + B = _____   B – W = _____   R – G = _____

   (B + Bl + G) – (R + W) = _____

5. Use <, >, or = to compare the following:

   B _____ R   R _____ W   G _____ W   G _____ Bl   W _____ Bl

Bonus Box: On the back of this page, order the decimal numbers in Step 2 from greatest to least.

Note to the teacher: Use after "Slam-Dunking Decimals" on page 31. Students will need crayons or colored markers to complete this activity.

Taking Note of Mixed Numbers

Noteworthy Ideas on Adding and Subtracting Mixed Numbers

A symphony of skills is needed to add and subtract mixed numbers: writing equivalent fractions, renaming whole numbers as fractions, reducing fractions, and—don't forget!—adding and subtracting. Help students better understand this challenging process with the following creative activities and reproducibles.

by Irving P. Crump, Contributing Editor

Noting Fraction Forms

Skills: Reviewing forms of fractions, simplifying fractions

Before students begin to add and subtract mixed numbers, use this game to review the different forms of fractions. Divide students into two teams; then draw the blank diagram on the chalkboard as shown. Have the first student on Team 1 roll a die three times and announce each number rolled as you write it in the diagram: the first number in the large whole-number box, the second number as the fraction's numerator, and the third number as the fraction's denominator. Then ask students to silently consider the following questions:

- Is this mixed number in its simplest form? (See Figure 1.)
- Does the fraction part need to be reduced? (See Figure 2.)
- Does the fraction part need to be changed to a whole number, then added to the existing whole number? (See Figure 3.)
- Does the fraction part need to be changed to a mixed number, then added to the existing whole number? (See Figure 4.)
- Does the fraction part need to be reduced, changed to a mixed number, then added to the existing whole number? (Or the fraction part can first be changed to a mixed number and then reduced; see Figure 5.)

Next, ask the student who rolled the die to evaluate the mixed number. If the mixed number is in its simplest form and the student correctly identifies it as such, award his team ten points. If the mixed number needs to be simplified and the student says so, award his team five points. If the student can then correctly simplify the mixed number, award his team a ten-point bonus. Then have the first player on Team 2 take a turn.

For more challenging rounds, have players roll two dice to determine each part of the mixed number.

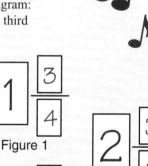

Figure 1

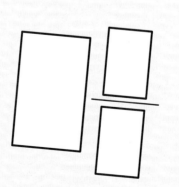

Figure 2

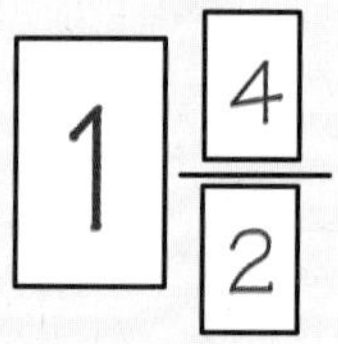

Figure 4

Figure 3

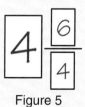

Figure 5

Mixed-Number Relay
Skill: Adding mixed numbers

Get students up and moving with this mixed-number relay! On each end of the chalkboard, draw a diagram like the one shown. Divide students into two teams and have the first player from each team go to a diagram. Next, roll a die, announce the number, and tell each student at the board to write it in a box of his diagram. Repeat five more times so that each player writes two mixed-number addends, switching numbers, if necessary, to make sure that each fraction's numerator is less than its denominator. To play the game:

1. Player 1 of each team sits down, and the second player goes to the board. If the fractions in the mixed numbers have like denominators, Player 2 may solve the problem. If one fraction needs to be rewritten so that its denominator is like the other's, Player 2 rewrites it. (Example: If $\frac{1}{2}$ and $\frac{3}{4}$ are the fractions, $\frac{1}{2}$ needs to be rewritten as $\frac{2}{4}$.) If both fractions need to be rewritten with like denominators, Player 2 may rewrite *one* of them. (Example: $\frac{2}{3}$ and $\frac{3}{4}$ need to be rewritten as $\frac{8}{12}$ and $\frac{9}{12}$.) Player 2 then sits down.
2. If necessary, Player 3 goes to the board. He either solves the problem if the fractions have like denominators or, if necessary, rewrites the second fraction. Player 3 then sits down.
3. If necessary, Player 4 approaches the board. Both fractions should now have like denominators, so Player 4 solves the problem.

Award each team ten points for a correct sum. Award the team that finishes first with a five-point bonus if its sum is correct. Continue with additional rounds. For more advanced play, roll a pair of dice to determine the diagrams' numbers.

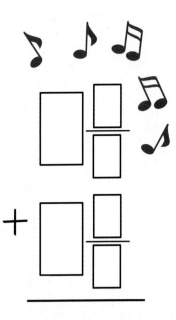

Red, White, and Blue Mixed Numbers
Skills: Measuring, adding mixed numbers

Give students lots of hands-on practice with measuring and adding mixed numbers with this partner activity. Provide each pair of students with four 9" x 12" sheets of construction paper (one red, one blue, two white), scissors, a ruler, and glue. Have each pair turn the red and blue sheets vertically and then measure and cut each into nine one-inch-wide strips. Next, write the following addition problems on the chalkboard:

$3\frac{1}{4}$ in. red + $4\frac{1}{2}$ in. blue
$5\frac{5}{8}$ in. red + $3\frac{7}{8}$ in. blue
$4\frac{3}{4}$ in. red + $2\frac{3}{8}$ in. blue
$6\frac{1}{8}$ in. red + $1\frac{1}{2}$ in. blue
$3\frac{3}{4}$ in. red + $4\frac{7}{8}$ in. blue

Have each student measure and then cut a $3\frac{1}{4}$-inch red paper strip and a $4\frac{1}{2}$-inch blue paper strip. Have the student label each strip with its measure, glue the two strips side by side, as shown, on a white sheet of construction paper, and then add the measures. Have the student repeat these steps with the other four problems.

When everyone has finished, have students exchange white sheets with their partners. Have each student measure his partner's combined red and blue strips to see whether their measures equal those written on the paper.

$$3\frac{1}{4} = 3\frac{1}{4}$$
$$+\ 4\frac{1}{2} = 4\frac{2}{4}$$
$$7\frac{3}{4}\text{ in.}$$

Pass It On!
Skills: Measuring, subtracting mixed numbers

Encourage accurate measuring and subtracting with this group activity. Divide students into rows of five students each. Provide each child with a ruler and scissors; give the first student in each row an 18" x 1" strip of light-colored construction paper. Direct the first student to measure and cut a $2\frac{1}{2}$-inch-long piece from his strip. Then have him pass the remainder of the strip to the next player. Have that child measure and cut a $3\frac{3}{4}$-inch-long piece from the strip and then pass the remainder of the strip to the next player. Continue with the remaining players measuring and cutting pieces of $2\frac{5}{8}$ inches, 3 inches, and $4\frac{1}{4}$ inches. Have the last student on each team write her name on the remainder of the strip and give it to you.

As you measure the teams' remaining strips, have the class subtract five times to determine how long each one should be: $18 - 2\frac{1}{2} - 3\frac{3}{4} - 2\frac{5}{8} - 3 - 4\frac{1}{4}$. *($1\frac{7}{8}$ inches)* Award 20 points to each team that has an exact measure, 15 points for a measure within $\frac{1}{8}$ inch, ten points for a measure within $\frac{1}{4}$ inch, and five points for a measure within $\frac{1}{2}$ inch.

Measure Twice, Cut Once!

Skills: Measuring, subtracting mixed numbers

Ask students why carpenters often say, "Measure twice, cut once." Then guide them through the following hands-on measuring and subtracting activity. Provide each pair of students with two 9" x 12" sheets of construction paper (one yellow and one green), scissors, a ruler, and glue. Have each pair turn the sheets of paper vertically and then measure and cut each into nine one-inch-wide strips. Next, write the following problems on the chalkboard:

1. $5^3/_8$ in. green – $3^1/_8$ in. yellow
2. $4^3/_4$ in. green – $2^5/_8$ in. yellow
3. $7^1/_2$ in. green – $3^5/_8$ in. yellow
4. $8^1/_8$ in. green – $4^1/_4$ in. yellow
5. $9^7/_8$ in. green – $5^3/_4$ in. yellow

Have each student cut a $5^3/_8$-inch green strip and a $3^1/_8$-inch yellow strip. Have the student write "1" on the yellow strip and then glue it onto the green one, making sure the ends are aligned. Have students repeat this process with problems 2–5. Next, invite volunteers to the board to solve the five problems as their classmates solve them at their desks. When everyone agrees that the answers are correct, have the students in each pair exchange paper strips with one another. Have each student measure only the green section of each strip, whose measure should match the difference shown on the board.

$$5 \frac{3}{8}$$
$$- 3 \frac{1}{8}$$
$$2 \frac{2}{8} = 2 \frac{1}{4}$$

Picture a Problem

Skills: Drawing diagrams, adding and subtracting mixed numbers

Invite students to put their visual-thinking skills to the test with this problem-solving activity. Have students listen carefully as you read the following story:

Marie left her campsite and hiked $4^7/_8$ miles south to the river. She then hiked $3^1/_2$ miles west to a cave. Then she turned north and hiked $3^1/_4$ miles to a deserted cabin. After she rests awhile, Marie plans to hike east to pick up the first trail. When she leaves the cabin, how far does Marie have to hike to reach the campsite?

Have each student draw a diagram to help him solve the problem as you reread it. (Solution: The trail from the cabin to the first trail completes a rectangle, so it measures $3^1/_2$ miles. The distance from that point back to the tent is $1^5/_8$ miles: $4^7/_8$ miles – $3^1/_4$ miles. The distance from the cabin to the campsite is $5^1/_8$ miles: $3^1/_2$ miles + $1^5/_8$ miles.) Use the diagram to generate other questions that involve adding and subtracting mixed numbers. For example:

• How far will Marie hike all together?
• If Marie hiked to the river and then back to the campsite, how far would she hike?
• Marie hiked $2^3/_4$ miles toward the river and stopped to take a break. How much farther does she have to go before reaching the river?

Follow up by giving each student a large index card. On one side of the card, have the student write a story that includes at least three mixed numbers with a question to answer. Instruct him to draw a diagram that would help solve the problem on the opposite side. Have students exchange cards and solve each other's problems *without* looking at the diagrams.

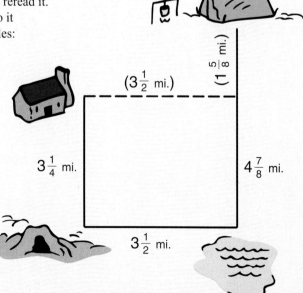

38

Do, Re, Mi: A Pattern I See!

Make sweet music when you complete these patterns! First, figure out the next two numbers that go in the notes of each pattern. Then describe the rule on the line that follows. The first one has been done for you.

1. $2\frac{1}{8}$, $2\frac{3}{4}$, $3\frac{3}{8}$, 4, $4\frac{5}{8}$, $5\frac{1}{4}$, $5\frac{7}{8}$ Rule: add $\frac{5}{8}$

2. $1\frac{1}{2}$, 3, $4\frac{1}{2}$, 6, $7\frac{1}{2}$ Rule: _____

3. $3\frac{1}{3}$, $5\frac{2}{3}$, 8, $10\frac{1}{3}$, $12\frac{2}{3}$ Rule: _____

4. $2\frac{1}{5}$, 4, $5\frac{4}{5}$, $7\frac{3}{5}$, $9\frac{2}{5}$ Rule: _____

5. $\frac{7}{8}$, $4\frac{1}{8}$, $7\frac{3}{8}$, $10\frac{5}{8}$, $13\frac{7}{8}$ Rule: _____

6. $3\frac{5}{6}$, $4\frac{5}{6}$, $6\frac{5}{6}$, $9\frac{5}{6}$, $13\frac{5}{6}$ Rule: _____

7. $1\frac{1}{2}$, 4, $2\frac{3}{4}$, $5\frac{1}{4}$, 4 Rule: _____

8. $7\frac{1}{2}$, 8, $9\frac{1}{2}$, 12, $15\frac{1}{2}$ Rule: _____

9. $3\frac{7}{10}$, $4\frac{9}{10}$, $6\frac{3}{10}$, $7\frac{9}{10}$, $9\frac{7}{10}$ Rule: _____

10. 9, $8\frac{1}{3}$, $10\frac{1}{6}$, $9\frac{1}{2}$, $11\frac{1}{3}$ Rule: _____

Bonus Box: You're a maestro if you can figure out the next term in this pattern: $1\frac{1}{8}$, $3\frac{3}{8}$, $6\frac{3}{4}$, $11\frac{1}{4}$, $16\frac{7}{8}$, _____.

Race to 25!
Challenge a friend in this race to 25!

Object of the game: to get a final score closer to 25

How to play:

1. Player 1: Roll the die and write the number in the Start box. Roll the die again and find the matching fraction in the list below. Write that fraction in the Start box beside the whole number to make a mixed number.

$$1 = \frac{1}{8} \quad 2 = \frac{1}{4} \quad 3 = \frac{3}{8} \quad 4 = \frac{1}{2} \quad 5 = \frac{5}{8} \quad 6 = \frac{3}{4}$$

2. Player 2: Take a turn in the same manner.

3. Player 1: Repeat Step 1 and write the mixed number in the Round 1 blank. Then either add that number to or subtract it from the Start number. If you add, color an addition sign at the bottom of the page. If you subtract, color a subtraction sign.

4. Player 2: Check Player 1's work. If Player 1 is incorrect, rework the problem. Then take a turn in the same manner, with Player 1 checking your work.

5. Play continues for ten more rounds. Each player adds five times and subtracts five times, coloring a matching sign at the bottom of the page for each round. Each player keeps a running score by adding each round's mixed number to or subtracting it from the answer of the previous round.

   Bonus Box: At any time during the game, you may use the Bonus Box at the bottom of the page. During this round, you may either add *or* subtract. Then color the Bonus Box.

6. The winner is the player who has a final score closer to 25.

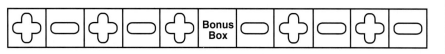

Start:
Round 1: _____
answer:
Round 2: _____
answer:
Round 3: _____
answer:
Round 4: _____
answer:
Round 5: _____
answer:
Round 6: _____
answer:
Round 7: _____
answer:
Round 8: _____
answer:
Round 9: _____
answer:
Round 10: _____
answer:
Round 11: _____
answer:
Final score:

Note to the teacher: Give each pair of students a die and two copies of this page. Read over the steps listed in the "How to play" section. Remind students that their final answers may be less than or greater than 25.

Measure by Measure

Tune up your measuring know-how with the following activities! Use a customary ruler to make each measure. Show all of your adding and subtracting on another sheet of paper. Then write your answers in the blanks provided. In Part 5, EFI is a triangle; AHED is a quadrilateral.

Part 1 Measure each segment.	**Part 2** Measure and add.	**Part 3** Measure and subtract.	**Part 4** Find the distance.	**Part 5** Find the perimeter.
1. AB = _____	7. AB + EC = ___	12. AD – AH = ___	17. H to B to C to E = _____	21. EFI = ___
2. BC = _____	8. EI + IF = ___	13. EI – IF = ___	18. F to I to E to D = ___	22. EHB = ___
3. HE = _____	9. BF + EC = ___	14. EB – EF = ___	19. G to F to E to H = _____	23. AHED = ___
4. GF = _____	10. HE + HB = ___	15. HE – AH = ___	20. A to B to F to I = _____	24. HBFI = ___
5. EF = _____	11. EC + HB = ___	16. IF – FB = ___		25. DEFG = ___
6. AG = _____				

Bonus Box: Which route is shorter from A to C: A–G–I–E–C or A–B–E–C? By how much?

Investigating Integers

Just when students thought they had learned everything there was to learn about numbers, the number of numbers suddenly doubles! Guide your junior detectives as they investigate integers with the following creative activities and games.

by Irving P. Crump, Contributing Editor

Opening the Files

Skill: Introducing integers

To introduce this new set of numbers to your students, program eight 9" x 12" sheets of white construction paper with the following letter and number pairs. Write the letter on one side of a sheet and the number on the opposite side: *G* and 0, *S* and ⁺20, *I* and ⁻32, *R* and ⁺8, *T* and ⁻6, *E* and ⁺5, *E* and ⁻1, N and ⁻10. Distribute the sheets to eight students.

Next, ask the class the riddles shown below one at a time. After students determine each answer (listed in italics), have the student holding that number stand at the front of the classroom with his paper turned so that the number shows. After all eight students are standing, ask the rest of the class if the numbers are in correct least-to-greatest order. If not, have the class arrange the students correctly. Then ask the eight standing students to turn over their sheets to reveal the name of the new set of numbers they'll be studying: *INTEGERS!*

Questions:
1. What integer is neither positive nor negative? *(0)*
2. If a quarterback is sacked for a ten-yard loss, how would that be shown? *(⁻10)*
3. If you had $8 in your bank account and deposited $12 more, how much do you now have in the account? *($20 or ⁺20)*
4. If the temperature is ⁻2°F and drops four degrees, what is the temperature now? *(⁻6°F or ⁻6)*
5. What number is the opposite of 32? *(⁻32)*
6. An ocean is one mile deep. The distance from the bottom of the ocean to the top of a mountain is six miles. How tall is the mountain? *(5 miles or ⁺5)*
7. If you shoot a round of 44 at a par 36 miniature golf course, how much are you over par? *(⁺8)*
8. If ⁺1 represents gaining a pound, what represents losing a pound? *(⁻1)*

Who Has...?

Skill: Understanding and ordering integers

Help students gain a deeper understanding of integers with this fun game. Program 25 large index cards with the integers ⁻12 through ⁺12. (If necessary, adjust the number of cards so that each student will have one.) Distribute the cards randomly to students. Then ask the questions listed on the right one at a time. Have the student who holds the card with a correct answer to a question come to the front of the classroom. If more than one student has an answer (such as in the question "Who has a positive integer?"), have all of those students stand in correct order from least to greatest. After discussing each question and its answer, have students return to their seats. Follow up the game with questions that involve adding and subtracting.

Who has...
- the only integer that is neither positive or negative?
- a positive integer?
- a negative integer?
- an even integer?
- an odd integer?
- the integer that is the opposite of ⁺5?
- the integer that is the opposite of ⁻10?
- the integer that is the opposite of 0? *(No one! 0 doesn't have an opposite.)*
- an integer greater than ⁻1 but less than ⁺5?
- an integer less than 0 but greater than ⁻6?
- the integer halfway between ⁺2 and ⁺12?
- the largest negative integer?
- the smallest positive integer?
- an integer between ⁻5 and ⁺5?

Life-Size Adding and Subtracting

Hand students some life-size problems that are big enough to help them remember how to add and subtract integers! Give half of the class 9" x 12" sheets of green construction paper and the other half red sheets. Tell students that each green sheet represents $^+1$ and each red sheet represents $^-1$. Then guide them through these steps:

1. Have a group of green students go to the front of the classroom and demonstrate $^+7 + {}^+3$. *($^+10$; Remind students that when two positive integers are added together, their sum is always positive.)*

2. Have a group of red students go to the front of the classroom and demonstrate $^-7 + {}^-5$. *($^-12$; Remind students that the sum of two negative integers is always negative.)*

3. Have four red students and nine green students demonstrate $^-4 + {}^+9$. *($^+5$; Review with students that each red represents $^-1$ and each green represents $^+1$. Since reds and greens are opposites, red + green = 0. To complete the addition, have students form pairs consisting of one green and one red. Then have those pairs sit down. Remaining are five greens or $^+5$.)*

4. Have ten reds go to the front of the room. Ask those students to demonstrate $^-10 - {}^-6$. *($^-4$; Six reds must sit down, or be subtracted from, the group of ten. That leaves four reds or $^-4$.)* Ask the same ten reds to return to the front of the room. Also have six greens join them. Ask this group to demonstrate $^-10 + {}^+6$. *($^-4$; Since each green represents $^+1$ and each red represents $^-1$, red + green = 0. Direct students to form pairs consisting of one green and one red. Then have those pairs sit down. Remaining are four reds or $^-4$. Remind students that subtracting a negative number is the same as adding its opposite.)*

5. Have nine reds go to the front of the class. Next, tell four greens to sit down. *(Since there are no greens standing, none can sit down.)* Challenge students to figure out how to demonstrate $^-9 - {}^+4$. *($^-13$; Since red + green = 0, have four green students and four more red students join the group. Ask the class to name the value of those students who joined the group [0; $^+4 + {}^-4 = 0$]. Now tell four greens to sit down, thus representing "subtract $^+4$." Remaining are 13 reds or $^-13$. Remind students again that subtracting $^+4$ is the same as adding $^-4$.)*

Hot on the Integer Trail!

Challenge students in this game of strategy; then send them off to complete their own investigations! First, provide each pair of students with a copy of page 44. Also make a transparency of the page. Read and discuss the directions with the class; then challenge the class to play against you as a way to become familiar with the game's rules. To begin, roll a die, find the matching integer in the code, and write that integer in the first box of a trail on the transparency. Next, add that integer to 0 or subtract it from 0 and write the answer in the first blank. Roll the die again and announce the roll to the class. Have each

pair find the matching integer in the code and write it in a box on their copy of the sheet. Continue play until you and every pair of students have completed all four trails.

To score, determine by how much each target was missed. Remind students that these numbers will be positive integers. For example, if the final answer of the first trail is $^-2$, then the target was missed by 12. If the answer is 5, then the target was missed by 5. Use an integers number line to help students determine their scores. Then provide each pair of students with two clean copies of page 44 to play on their own.

Hot on the Integer Trail!

Challenge a classmate to track down these hot targets!

Target

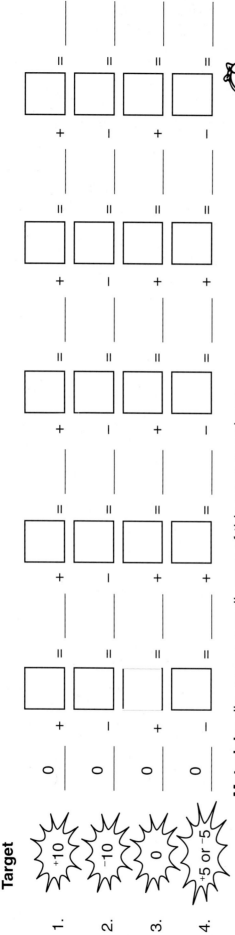

1. +10

2. -10

3. 0

4. +5 or -5

code

1 = 0
2 = ⁻1
3 = ⁻2
4 = ⁻3
5 = +2
6 = +5

Materials: die, paper, pencil, copy of this page per player

Objective: add and subtract integers to reach a target number

To play:

1. Roll the die to see who begins. The player with the higher roll is Player 1.
2. Player 1 rolls the die and finds the matching integer in the code.
3. Player 1 writes that integer in the first box of any trail 1–4. He then adds that value to 0 or subtracts it from 0 and writes the answer in the first blank.
4. Player 2 repeats Steps 2 and 3.
5. Player 1 takes another turn and writes his next integer in a box of any trail 1–4. Player 1 adds the box number to or subtracts it from the number in the blank on the left. The new sum or difference is written in the next blank. Play continues left to right on each trail. Boxes cannot be skipped.
6. Play continues until each player reaches the end of all four trails.
7. Continue play until each player completes the scoring box, then adds his 4 numbers to find his total. The *lower* total is the winner.
8. Each player completes the scoring box, then adds his 4 numbers to find his total. The *lower* total is the winner.

Scoring

I missed Target 1 by __ . __
I missed Target 2 by __ . __
I missed Target 3 by __ . __
I missed Target 4 by __ . __
                Total: __ . __

©The Education Center, Inc. • *The Best of The Mailbox® Math • Book 2* • TEC1492

Note to the teacher: Use with "Hot on the Integer Trail!" on page 43.

In "Purr-suit" of Percents

Use the following activities to help your students chase down a greater understanding of important concepts about percents.

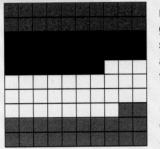

Somali (red): 20%
Bombay (black): 27%
Persian (yellow): 31%
Burmese (brown): 22%

"Purr-cent" Grids
Skills: Representing the percent of a number, problem solving

Start the chase for better percent skills with this activity on how to represent the percent of a number. First, display a transparency of a 10 x 10 grid. Ask students how many squares the grid contains *(100)*. Write the symbol for percent on the board. Explain that *percent* is a comparison of a number to 100. Also explain that a percent can be written as a ratio (47 to 100), a fraction ($^{47}/_{100}$), or a decimal (0.47).

Next, announce that a certain group of 100 domestic cats has 20 Somali, 27 Bombay, 31 Persian, and 22 Burmese. Using wipe-off markers, color any 20 of the grid's squares red to represent the Somali cats. Color any 27 squares black to represent the Bombay cats. Then color any 31 squares yellow to represent the Persian cats and any 22 squares brown to represent the Burmese cats. Ask students to identify the fractions and percents that represent the squares for each type of cat *(Somali: $^{20}/_{100}$ or ⅕, 20%; Bombay: $^{27}/_{100}$, 27%; Persian: $^{31}/_{100}$, 31%; Burmese: $^{22}/_{100}$ or $^{11}/_{50}$, 22%)*. Finally, ask students a question that can be answered using the grid, such as "If Al's Pet Emporium sells only Somali cats, what percent of these 100 cats cannot be purchased at this pet store?" *(100% – 20% = 80%)* To see how well students grasp the concept, give each child his own 10 x 10 grid and red, yellow, brown, and black markers. Then have each student write a similar problem for a partner to represent and solve on his grid.

Which Way'd They Go?
Skills: Finding the percent of a number, problem solving

Take the mystery out of finding the percent of a number with this problem-solving activity. Copy each problem shown (without its italicized answer) onto a different index card. Next, share the following problem with students: Seventy-five percent of the 24 mice who were running from Whiskers the cat darted into the mouse hole. How many mice got away from Whiskers by pulling this trick? *(18)* How many did something different? *(six)* To demonstrate how to solve the problem, write 75% as a decimal *(0.75)* or as a fraction *($^{75}/_{100}$)*. Reduce the fraction to simplest terms *(¾)*. Then multiply 0.75 x 24 (or ¾ x 24) to get 18, and subtract 18 from 24 to get 6.

Next, divide your class into six groups and give each group one of the cards programmed earlier. Allow each group up to five minutes to solve its problem. When time is up, have each group pass its card to another group. Continue having groups solve problems in this manner until every group has had a chance to solve each one. Then collect the cards and check the problems together.

- If 30% of 60 mice hid in the barn to get the cat off their trail, how many didn't? *(42)*
- If 30% of 40 mice doubled back on their tracks, 40% jumped into mouse holes, and the rest ran through water, how many mice pulled each trick? *(12 doubled back, 16 jumped into mouse holes, and 12 ran through water)*
- If 25% of 36 mice ran through water, 50% doubled back, and the rest jumped into mouse holes, how many jumped into mouse holes? *(nine)*
- If 20% of 90 mice doubled back on their tracks, 40% jumped into mouse holes, and the rest ran through water, how many ran through water? *(36)*
- If 25% of 44 mice doubled back on their tracks, how many didn't? *(33)*
- If 50% of 40 mice didn't run through water, how many did? *(20)*

The Great Mouse Escape
Skill: Using mental math to find percent

Use this fun-to-play game to teach students how to identify common percents that "mousequerade" as decimals and fractions. In advance, obtain a party horn for each student. Copy each fraction, decimal, and percent from the chart shown onto a different index card. Set the percent cards aside. Shuffle the remaining cards. Then give each student one or more decimal or fraction cards along with a party horn. (Have each student write her name on her horn so it can be used again.) Explain to students that their cards represent mice being chased by cats. Next, draw a percent card, announce the percent to the class, and place the card in the chalk tray. Have students study their cards. If a player thinks her card shows the equivalent decimal or fraction for that percent, she blows her horn. If correct, she places her card on the chalk tray next to the percent card, showing that her mouse is safe inside a mouse hole. If incorrect, she keeps her card. The correct decimal and fraction cards for each percent should be identified before announcing the next percent. Continue in this manner until all the mice have made it into holes.

Fractions	Decimals	Percents
½	0.50	50%
⅓	0.33	33⅓%
⅔	0.66	66⅔%
¼	0.25	25%
¾	0.75	75%
⅕	0.20	20%
⅗	0.60	60%
⅛	0.125	12½%
⅜	0.375	37½%
¹⁄₁₀	0.10	10%
³⁄₁₀	0.30	30%
²⁄₁	2.00	200%

Shortcut
To change a decimal to percent, move the decimal two places to the right.

0.48 = 0.48.% = 48%

0.09 = 0.09.% = 9%

1.52 = 1.52.% = 152%

Special Discount Sale!

Kitty's Cat Corner

Kitty Carrier		$95.00
Kitty Cape and Leash		$84.00
Kitty Climber Condo		$125.00
Super Soft Kitty Bed		$45.00
Feline Food Bowl		$29.00
Kitty Toy Collection		$38.00

Discount Code
Rolling a 1 = 50% off
Rolling a 2 = 40% off
Rolling a 3 = 30% off
Rolling a 4 = 25% off
Rolling a 5 = 15% off
Rolling a 6 = 10% off

Percent of Total Cost After Discount

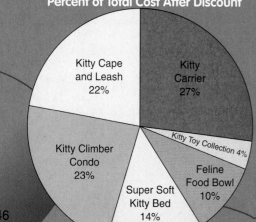

Kitty Cape and Leash 22%
Kitty Carrier 27%
Kitty Climber Condo 23%
Kitty Toy Collection 4%
Feline Food Bowl 10%
Super Soft Kitty Bed 14%

Shop Till You Drop!
Skills: Finding percent, making a circle graph

Help your students "purr-fect" their percent skills by sending them on a cat-friendly shopping spree. Copy on the board the list of pet store items and prices shown. Next to the list, copy the discount code. Next, give each pair of students a die. Explain that each student will be buying the six listed items at a discount. Direct each student to list each item on paper and then roll the die (once for each item) to determine the discount. Then have each shopper find the total cost of his purchases.

Follow up by guiding each child through the steps below to make a circle graph showing the percent of the final total each item cost. Provide students with calculators, compasses, and protractors.

1. Divide the discounted cost of each item by the total cost of all six items. Round the resulting decimal to the nearest hundredth.
2. Write the decimal as a percent.
3. Multiply each percent by 360° to find the number of degrees represented by each percent. Round each answer to the nearest whole number if necessary.
4. Draw a circle. Draw a radius. Measure, draw, and label each angle.
5. Title the graph.

Proverbial Percents Puzzle

Macauley Mouseworth, a clever ol' mouse, would like to share his favorite proverb with you. But first, he wants you to show him how to find percents! Write the answer to each problem on the path in the blank. Then write the bold words from the boxes on the kitty dish in least to greatest numerical order according to the answers.

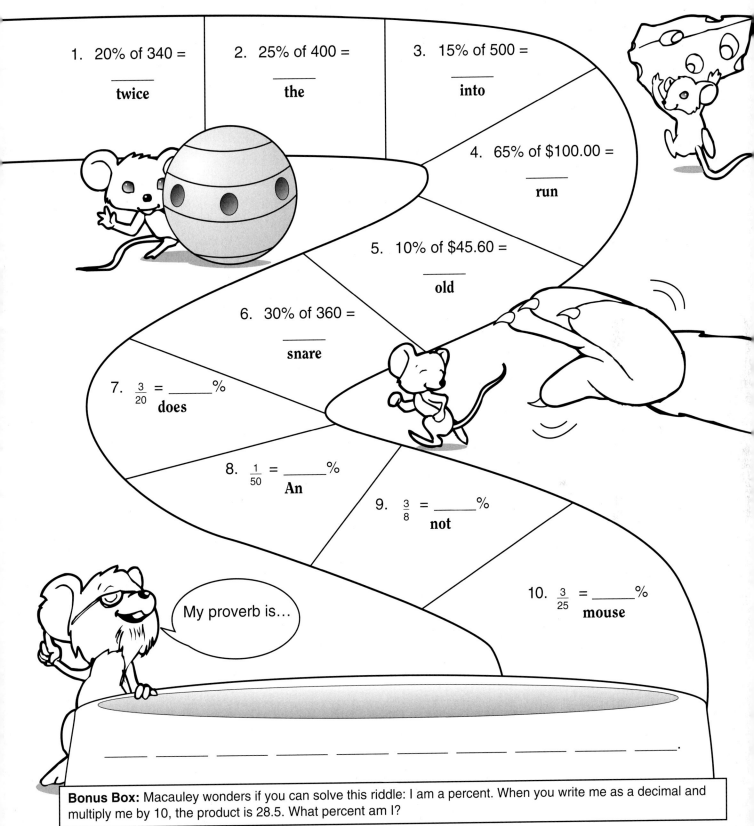

1. 20% of 340 =
_____
twice

2. 25% of 400 =
_____
the

3. 15% of 500 =
_____
into

4. 65% of $100.00 =
_____
run

5. 10% of $45.60 =
_____
old

6. 30% of 360 =
_____
snare

7. $\frac{3}{20}$ = _____%
does

8. $\frac{1}{50}$ = _____%
An

9. $\frac{3}{8}$ = _____%
not

10. $\frac{3}{25}$ = _____%
mouse

My proverb is...

Bonus Box: Macauley wonders if you can solve this riddle: I am a percent. When you write me as a decimal and multiply me by 10, the product is 28.5. What percent am I?

Taking a Bite out of Algebra!

Creative Teaching Suggestions for Introducing Algebra Concepts

Patterns, relations, and functions—oh my! Intermediate graders may not be familiar with these algebra terms, but they have already begun to think and talk algebraically. Help your students make the connection between arithmetic and algebra with the following creative teaching ideas and reproducibles.

by Irving P. Crump

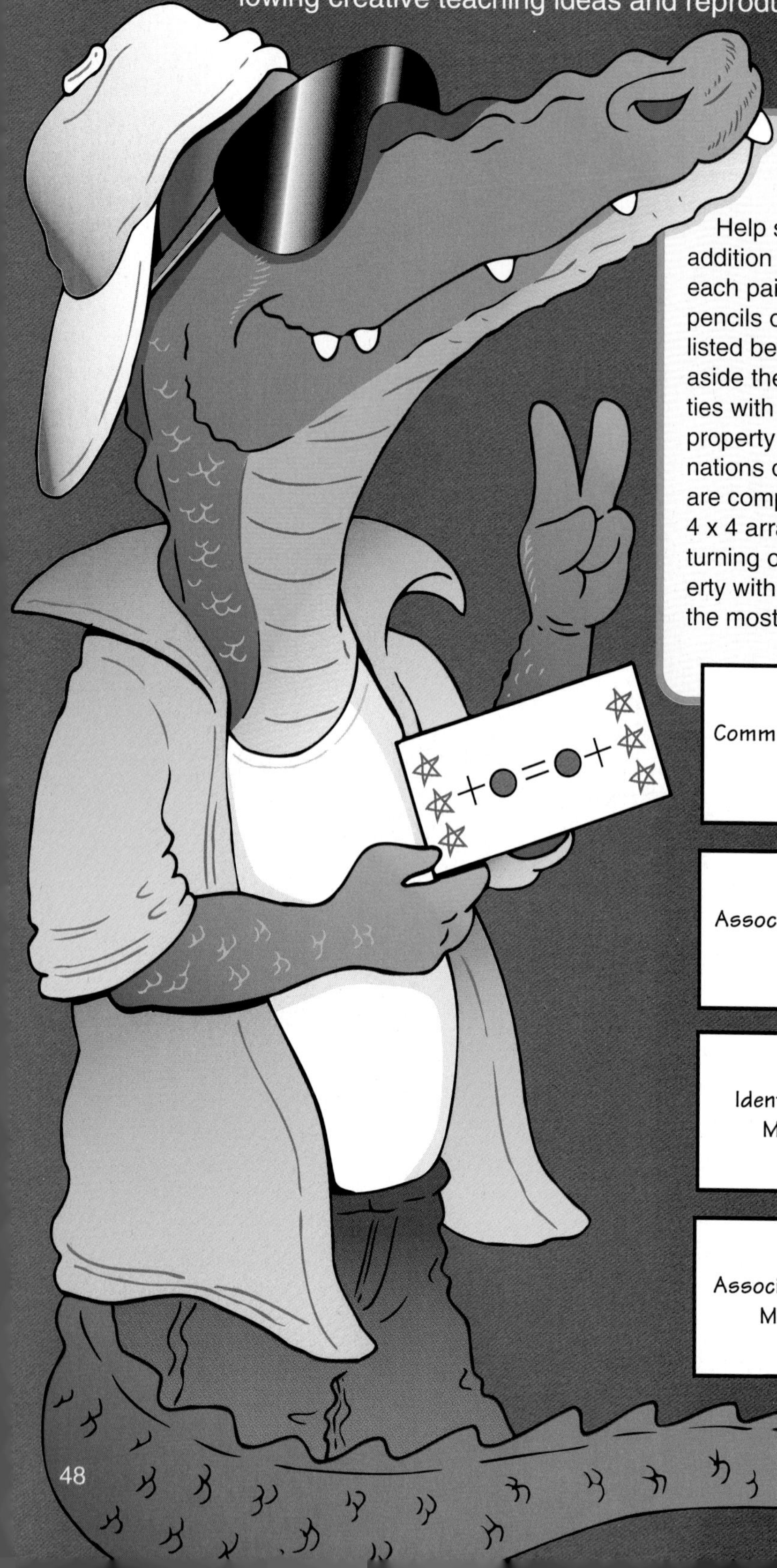

Property Matches

Skill: Understanding properties

Help students better understand the special properties of addition and multiplication with this matching activity. Provide each pair of students with 16 large index cards and colored pencils or crayons. Instruct each pair to write each property listed below on a separate index card. Have students set aside the remaining eight cards. After reviewing the properties with your students, direct each twosome to illustrate each property on one of the eight remaining cards, using combinations of pictures, numbers, and symbols. When all 16 cards are completed, have each pair lay its cards upside down in a 4 x 4 array. Direct each twosome to play a matching game by turning over one pair of cards at a time, trying to match a property with its illustration. The winner is the player who makes the most correct matches.

Commutative Property— Addition	Identity Property— Addition
Associative Property— Addition	Commutative Property— Multiplication
Identity Property— Multiplication	Property of Zero— Multiplication
Associative Property— Multiplication	Distributive Property

Input-Output Relay

Skills: Basic operations, completing input-output tables

Have students put on their algebraic thinking caps with this relay game! Begin by drawing on opposite ends of the chalkboard two input-output tables similar to the one shown. Next, divide the class into two teams and have the first player from each team go to one of the tables on the board. Call out five numbers—such as 15, 18, 22, 41, and 36—for each player to write in the input column of his table. Remind students that an *input number* is the number that an operation rule is applied to and that the *output number* is the result of that operation. Next, announce a rule, such as "add 13," for each player to write at the top of his table.

On a signal, the two players complete their tables by applying the rule to each number in the input column and writing the answer in the output column. When a student finishes, direct him to put down his chalk and turn around to face the class. With the class's assistance, check both players' tables. To score, award one point for each correct response, subtract a point for each incorrect response, and add a five-point bonus to the score of the student who correctly completed his table first. Continue play with other rules that are appropriate to use with the list of input numbers, such as "subtract 9" and "multiply by 2." Play additional rounds with new sets of input numbers and different rules.

rule:	
input	output

Thinking in Reverse

Skill: Inverse operations

Understanding inverse operations and their relationships will help students when solving algebraic equations. After every student has had an opportunity to participate in the input-output relay above, continue with additional rounds in which students must determine the input numbers for a table. To play, provide a list of numbers for each player to write in the output column of his table, such as 48, 36, 12, 54, and 30. Next, call out the rule for each player to write at the top of his table, such as "times 6." Instruct each player to work in reverse to determine the input number that, when the rule is applied, results in the output number. Lead students to discover that to find each input number, they should perform the inverse operation. For example, students should *divide* by 6 since the rule is *times* six. Play and score the relay game as described in "Input-Output Relay" above.

To further extend this activity, provide one or both numbers for each row of an input-output table like the sample shown. Then direct the two players to complete the table by first determining the rule and then filling in the missing input and output numbers.

rule:	
input	output
?	20
?	26
10	22
30	42
19	?

Taking a Look at Two Steps

Skills: Inverse operations, solving two-step problems

Do a little two-steppin' right in your classroom with this activity on inverse operations! Review with students that addition and subtraction, as well as multiplication and division, are inverse operations. Have students create addition-subtraction and multiplication-division fact families like the ones shown to help them see these relationships.

Next, draw and label Diagram 1 on the chalkboard. Ask students what the output number will be *(6 + 2 = 8; 8 x 3 = 24)*. Share several more examples in which you provide an input number and a pair of operations (one operation should be either addition or subtraction; the other either multiplication or division). Have students determine the output number for each example.

To extend this activity, draw Diagram 2 on the board. Tell students that this diagram has the output number and two operations, but the input number is not known. Have students work in reverse from the output number to the input number, one operation at a time. Have them note that inverse operations can be used to determine the input number. *(In the example, 12 − 3 = 9; 9 x 3 = 27. Thus, the input number is 27.)* Have students double-check by working left to right with 27 as the input number.

Fact Families

6 + 2 = 8	4 x 5 = 20
2 + 6 = 8	5 x 4 = 20
8 − 2 = 6	20 ÷ 5 = 4
8 − 6 = 2	20 ÷ 4 = 5

Diagram 1

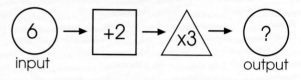

Diagram 2

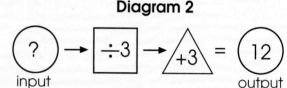

Mystery Numbers

Skills: Understanding variables, solving equations

Using variables helps students identify number relationships and solve equations. Divide students into pairs and have each twosome draw a circle and a square at the top of a sheet of paper. Assign each pair two different digits, instructing the pair not to reveal the digits to its classmates. Instruct the pair to write one digit in the circle and the other digit in the square.

Next, have each pair use its two digits to create five math sentences. The math sentences may include addition, multiplication, subtraction, and division. Invite each pair, in turn, to go to the chalkboard and write its first math sentence, using the corresponding circles and squares instead of the digits. (See the examples.) Call on a volunteer to see if she can determine the digits that the circle and square represent in the sentence. If she can't, have the pair write another math sentence on the board; then call on another volunteer. Continue with the pair writing its sentences and volunteers trying to identify the variables until a student discovers the two numbers that the circle and square represent. Extend this activity by having each pair of students add a triangle to the top of the sheet of paper; then assign each pair three digits to use in writing its math sentences.

○ x □ = 36

○ + □ = 13

○ + ○ + □ = 22

□ + □ = 8

○ − □ = 5

○ = 9   □ = 4

Crack the Codes!

Are you a crackerjack code cracker? Put your skills to the test by breaking the codes below.

Part I: There are ten different symbols below. Each one stands for a digit 0–9. Can you figure out the digit each symbol represents? When you decide on a digit, write it inside that symbol. If you get stumped, read the upside-down clues at the bottom of the page. Now get crackin'!

1. △ + △ = △

2. ○ + ○ = ⬡△

3. ○ × □ = ⬡○

4. ○ + □ = ♣

5. ○ − ☆ = ⬡

6. □ × ◇ = ♡

7. ⬭ − ♣ = ⬡

8. ☆ + □ = ◗

Part II: Now crack this code. The letters A–J in this code stand for the digits 0–9. When you decide on a digit, write it above its letter. (Sorry, no clues!)

1. J × F = J

2. F × F = F

3. C − A = F

4. F + F = J

5. J + J = I

6. E × D = D

7. I − F = G

8. G × H = FH

9. B − G = E

10. H − J = G

Clues for Part I

1. The triangle is 0. The only number that can be added to itself to get a sum that is the same number is 0.

2. Since the triangle is 0, the hexagon is 1. The hexagon can't be a larger digit. If the hexagon were 2, then circle plus circle would equal 20; that means the circle would equal 10, which isn't a digit 0–9. Since the hexagon and triangle make the numeral 10, each circle is 5.

3. Circle (5) × square = hexagon/circle (15). The square is 3.

4. Circle (5) + square (3) = shamrock. Shamrock is 8.

5. Circle (5) − star = hexagon (1). Star is 4.

6. Square (3) × diamond = heart. Heart is a single digit, so diamond could be 0 (3 × 0), 1 (3 × 1), 2 (3 × 2), or 3 (3 × 3). Since 0, 1, and 3 are already being used, 2 is the only one that works. 3 × 2 = heart. Diamond is 2 and heart is 6.

7. Oval − shamrock (8) = hexagon (1). Oval is 9.

8. Star (4) + square (3) = semicircle. Semicircle is 7.

Follow the Rules!

Can you complete each of the following input-output tables? First, decide on the rule that is being used in each table and write it where indicated. Apply that rule to each number in the input column; then write your answer in the output column. Or, if you have the output number, work backward to find the input number. Two tables have been done for you.

Part I: Each rule has one operation.

1. rule: − 3	
input	output
10	7
14	11
6	3
7	4
9	6
20	17

2. rule:	
input	output
3	10
4	11
5	
10	
	21
20	27

1. rule:	
input	output
0	0
1	4
	8
5	20
8	
11	44

2. rule:	
input	output
10	
15	3
20	
30	6
50	10
45	

Part II: Each rule has two operations. See the hint. (The operations in the hint may not be used in the order in which they are listed.)

1. rule: ✕ 2, + 1	
input	output
6	13
7	15
10	21
14	29
2	5
20	41

1. rule:	
input	output
	10
16	11
22	14
50	28
8	
30	18

1. rule:	
input	output
2	11
	20
	35
7	26
15	50
6	23

1. rule:	
input	output
10	12
15	22
21	
6	4
29	50
	2

(Hint: x and +)   (Hint: ÷ and +)   (Hint: + and x)   (Hint: − and x)

Part III: Each rule has two operations. No hints!

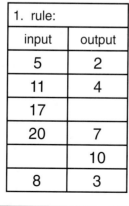

1. rule:	
input	output
5	2
11	4
17	
20	7
	10
8	3

1. rule:	
input	output
5	15
	19
10	25
1	7
20	
22	49

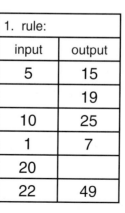

BONUS BOX: Make an input-output table that includes fractions or decimals. (Don't write your rule in the table.) List six input and six output numbers. Exchange tables with a partner and see if you can figure out each other's rule.

Home, Sweet Home

Where do some alligators go in the winter while they wait for springtime? They make homes with their bodies! To find out what these homes are called, follow the directions below.

Directions:
1. Match each phrase (1–16) with a math expression in the box.
2. Circle the expression; then write it in the blank.
3. You will not use nine expressions.
4. The first one has been done for you.

1. the quotient of four and another number ___$\frac{4}{z}$___

2. five times the difference of two numbers _____

3. six pounds less than Marty _____

4. Janis read three times as much _____

5. five more than the difference between 16 and another

    number _____

6. a number increased by five _____

7. sold four boxes of candy; half of my earnings was profit _____

8. scored field goals playing basketball, plus four free throws _____

9. ten more than a number _____

10. served some drinks from a 12-pack _____

11. the sum of six and another number, multiplied by five _____

12. the product of eight and another number _____

13. half of my baseball cards _____

14. six times the sum of two numbers _____

15. earned the same amount of pay for each of three hours

    of work; then spent five dollars _____

16. double the quotient of three and another number _____

$b + 5$
$a - 5$
$10 + j$
$m - 6$
$6 - e$
$12 - w$
$r - 12$
$8s$
$3f$
$5\left(\frac{o}{6}\right)$
$\left(\frac{4}{z}\right)$
$\frac{n}{2}$
$16 - y + 5$
$\frac{t}{3}$
$7o + 7$
$2k + 4$
$2(g + 4)$
$3p - 5$
$6(c + d)$
$5(p - q)$
$2\left(\frac{3}{x}\right)$
$2\left(\frac{h}{3}\right)$
$\frac{4v}{2}$
$4 \times l + 2$
$5(6 + u)$

List all of the letters in the expressions that you didn't use: _____. Arrange the letters in the blanks below to answer the question: What do you call an alligator's winter home?

__ __ __ __ __   __ __ __ __ __

SCOUTING OUT SPATIAL RELATIONSHIPS

Do your students think they need eagle-eye vision to improve their spatial-reasoning skills? The following hands-on explorations can change their thinking. Scout's honor!

Tessellating Triangles
Skills: Visualizing spatial relationships, creating a tessellation

To help students visualize spatial relationships, try this tessellation investigation! First, display pictures that illustrate repeating geometric patterns, such as checkerboards, honeycombs, bricks in a wall or sidewalk, floor or ceiling tiles, or mosaics. Have students describe how the shapes are positioned in a plane to form a pattern. *(They completely cover the area, fitting together exactly without overlapping or leaving gaps.)* Explain that *tessellations* are special geometric patterns made up of one or more shapes that can be extended indefinitely. Help students understand that the patterns in the pictures were formed by rotating a congruent shape through a series of slides, flips, or turns.

Next, give each student a sheet of white construction paper, a pencil, colored markers, and a triangle pattern (acute, obtuse, right, isosceles, equilateral, or scalene) cut from an index card. Direct the student to trace his cutout in a series of slides, flips, and turns to create a repeating pattern that completely covers his paper and fits together without overlapping or leaving gaps. (Allow partial tracings at the paper's edge.) Then have the student color the triangles and, if desired, add patterns of dots and lines. Extend the activity by having each student use his triangle cutout to create a different repeating pattern on another sheet of paper.

Toothpick Tricks
Skills: Spatial reasoning, problem solving

Develop students' spatial-reasoning skills by having them solve some tricky toothpick puzzles. Display 17 flat toothpicks on an overhead projector as shown. Give each student the same number of toothpicks and have her use them to duplicate the arrangement on her desktop. Challenge students to determine which five toothpicks should be removed so that only three squares remain. Let the first student who correctly solves the puzzle demonstrate the solution on the projector. Continue by having students solve the puzzles below.

	Puzzle	Solution
• Arrange 17 toothpicks as shown. Remove six toothpicks so that two similar squares remain.		
• Arrange 12 toothpicks as shown. Rearrange four toothpicks to form three same-size squares.		
• Arrange nine toothpicks to form four triangles within a larger triangle.		

Three Ways of Looking at It

Skills: Constructing a 3-D object and representing it with a 2-D drawing, understanding perspective

Sharpen spatial-reasoning skills by having students study objects from three different perspectives. First, use wooden or plastic cubes to construct a model of a building, such as the one shown. Next, demonstrate on a graph paper transparency how to shade boxes that represent the model's top, side, and front views. Then give each student a sheet of graph paper and a supply of wooden or plastic cubes. Have him use the cubes to construct a building similar to the one displayed. Then have the student draw on the graph paper blueprints of the building's front, side, and top views as shown. After he dismantles his building, have each builder trade blueprints and blocks with a classmate and try to construct his partner's building.

front   side   top

FORT SPATIAL

Netting 3-D Figures

Skills: Using 2-D drawings to represent 3-D figures, identifying polyhedrons

Use this two-part activity to have students investigate how 2-D drawings can represent 3-D figures. In advance, give each pair of students one of the following: a small empty cube-shaped or rectangular tissue box, a crayon box, a cereal box, a gift box, or a Toblerone candy box. Also give each pair a pencil, a sheet of paper, scissors, and tape. Instruct each pair to cut its box apart (keeping it in one piece) and trace its flattened shape on the paper, adding dashed lines to show the folds. Afterward, have each pair reconstruct its box by folding and taping it into its original shape. Explain to students that each tracing is a *net*, a 2-D drawing of a 3-D figure. Also explain that each box is a *polyhedron*, a solid figure made up of polygons. Point out that the shape of a prism's or pyramid's parallel bases determines its name. Ask each pair to label its net correctly. *(A tissue box is a cube or rectangular prism. A Toblerone candy box is a triangular prism. A cereal, crayon, or gift box is a rectangular prism.)* Have students compare nets for the same polyhedron to note that the faces can be in different positions.

Conclude by having each student complete a copy of page 56 as directed to explore the nets of other solid figures. To have students construct edible models of the solid figures pictured on page 56, see "Mmmm, Mmmm Models!" on this page.

Mmmm, Mmmm Models!

Skill: Constructing models of solid figures

Extend "Netting 3-D Figures" on this page with a yummy activity that invites students to build and *eat* their own space-figure models! Divide students into groups of four. Give each student an 18" x 24" sheet of construction paper to use as a desk mat. Also give each group a resealable plastic bag filled with 58 miniature marshmallows and 88 pretzel sticks. Refer each student to the pictures of the solid figures on his copy of page 56. Then have each group construct the eight figures (two for each student). Reward your hardworking students by allowing them to snack on their models!

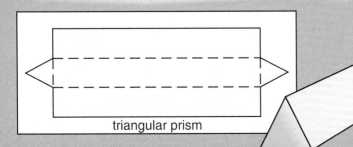

triangular prism

Scouting Out Nets

Scout D. V. Krockett needs your help scouting out some nets. He knows that *nets* are two-dimensional drawings and that *polyhedrons* are solid figures made up of polygons. But he can't figure out which net matches each polyhedron below. Help him by writing each net's letter in the blank next to its matching polyhedron. Then answer questions 9 and 10.

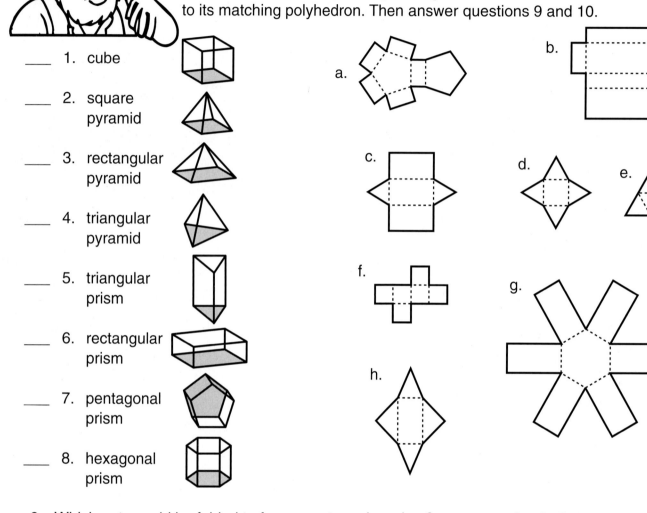

___ 1. cube

___ 2. square pyramid

___ 3. rectangular pyramid

___ 4. triangular pyramid

___ 5. triangular prism

___ 6. rectangular prism

___ 7. pentagonal prism

___ 8. hexagonal prism

9. Which nets could be folded to form a rectangular prism? _____ A cube? _____

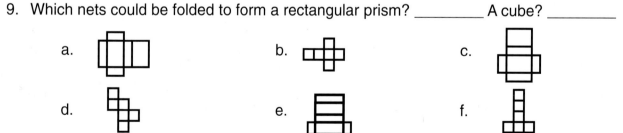

10. What polygon shapes make up the faces of the following solid figures? Write the name and how many of each shape.
    a. triangular prism

    b. square pyramid

    _____   _____

Bonus Box: The solid figures above all have flat surfaces. Name three solid figures that have curved surfaces.

Conquering Transformations and Symmetry

Equip students to master transformations and symmetry with the following tasks—all guaranteed to help them succeed in their worthy quest!

Task 1: Slip-Sliding Away!
Skill: Translations

Focus your students on translating figures with this fun manipulative activity. Display a transparency of a sword drawn on a grid (see the illustration). Have each student copy the drawing anywhere on a sheet of ¼-inch graph paper. Explain that a figure makes a *translation* when it slides up, down, right, or left. Then draw a second sword several squares northeast of the first one. Point out that the new drawing is the same size and shape as the first. Add an arrow to show the direction in which the figure moved. Next, have each student draw a simple knight (with one outstretched arm) anywhere on her grid. Then have the student draw at least five translations, moving the sword to different places before having it rest in the knight's hand. Remind students to include arrows so the sword's path can be easily traced.

Task 2: Acrobatic Reflections
Skill: Reflections

Make students flip over practicing reflections with this race-to-the-finish game! Explain to students that a figure makes a *reflection* (creates a mirror image of itself) when it flips over a line. Point out that the reflected image matches the original figure in size and shape. Display a transparency of a sheet of triangle grid paper (see the illustration). Explain that the shared sides between the triangles represent lines of reflection. Color one triangle with a wipe-off marker. Then cover that triangle with a green pattern block. Next, flip the pattern block over a line to cover its reflection. Remove the pattern block and color the triangle beneath it. Discuss how continuing the reflection process could make a path across the grid.

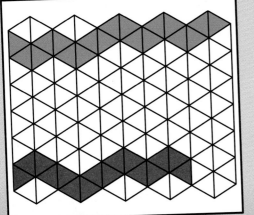

Next, give each pair of students a sheet of triangle grid paper, a green pattern block, a die, and two different-colored markers. Tell students that they are to simulate somersaulting acrobats. Direct each acrobat to use a different marker to color a triangle along one side of the grid. Then have the pair take turns rolling the die to determine the number of somersaults (times to flip the pattern block over a line) and coloring the corresponding number of triangles. Declare the first performer to reach the opposite side of the grid the faster acrobat!

Task 3: Making the Rounds With Rotations
Skill: Rotations

Pull up a chair at King Arthur's Round Table with this can't-be-beat activity on rotations! Label a circle transparency with the names shown. Also write each name on a slip of paper. Place the paper slips in a container. Display the circle, telling students that it represents King Arthur's legendary Round Table. Then explain that a figure makes a *rotation* when it turns around a point.

Next, divide students into two teams and assign each team a different color. Have a player from Team 1 draw a paper slip and then point a toothpick (Arthur's sword) from the center of the table to the knight whose name was drawn. Direct the same player to roll a die and turn the sword according to the directions in the box shown. This will determine which knight Arthur will dismiss. If the player turns the sword correctly, dismiss the knight by circling his name with that team's color. Then have a player from Team 2 take a turn. Watch the teams begin to strategize, anticipating the rolls that mean certain dismissal. After every knight has been dismissed (had his name circled), count each team's circled names; then dub the team with more names your Knights of Rotation!

Roll	Rotation
1	$\frac{1}{4}$ turn to the right
2	$\frac{1}{4}$ turn to the left
3	$\frac{1}{2}$ turn
4	your choice
5	$\frac{3}{4}$ turn to the right
6	$\frac{3}{4}$ turn to the left

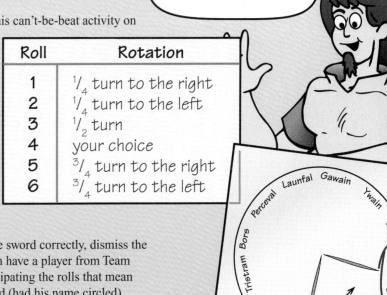

Bye, Palomides! You're a quarter turn to the right!

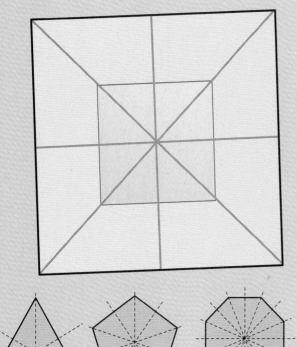

Task 4: Drawing the Line
Skill: Line symmetry in regular polygons

Use this activity to show students how to draw the line when it comes to line symmetry! Display a 12-inch paper square, telling students it represents a banner once carried by a knight. Explain that a figure has *line symmetry* if folding it in half creates two matching halves of the figure. Also point out that a figure can have more than one line of symmetry. Ask students to guess how many lines of symmetry the banner has. Then fold the paper in half once vertically and horizontally and twice diagonally (matching opposite corners). Unfold the paper and point out each fold line as a line of symmetry. Have a student identify the banner's shape *(a square, which is a regular polygon)* and compare its number of sides with its lines of symmetry *(four sides and four lines of symmetry)*.

Next, give each student a ruler, crayons, and three paper shapes: an equilateral triangle, a regular pentagon, and a regular octagon. Have the student draw each banner's lines of symmetry *(triangle, three; pentagon, five; octagon, eight)* and count the number of its sides. Help students conclude that the number of sides in a regular polygon equals the number of its lines of symmetry. Then invite students to decorate their banners.

A Message for King Arthur

An important message must be delivered to King Arthur, and time is of the essence! Follow the directions below to help you and a partner determine which knight—Galahad or Gawain—can deliver the message in a timelier way.

Directions:

1. Cut out the game pieces below (dotted lines only) and color both sides. Fold each game piece in half along the solid line and tape the sides together.
2. Place the game pieces on START. Player 1 is Galahad, and Player 2 is Gawain.
3. Take turns spinning a paper clip on the spinner. Move your game piece as directed by the spinner. Translate (slide), reflect (flip), or rotate (turn) from one square to another to reach King Arthur. Use tally marks to record the number of moves made.
4. Before reaching Arthur, each knight *must* land in the Face the Dragon! space and be turned facing the dragon.
5. The knight who reaches King Arthur in fewer moves is the winner.

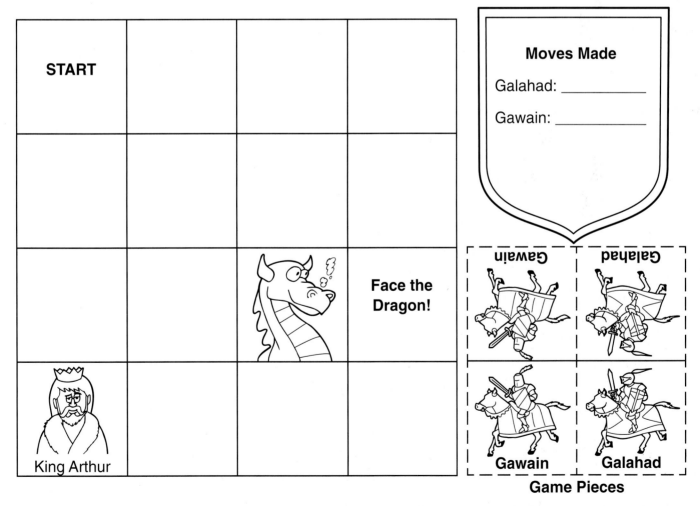

Moves Made

Galahad: _____

Gawain: _____

START

Face the Dragon!

King Arthur

Gawain   Galahad

Gawain   Galahad

Game Pieces

Note to the teacher: Each pair of students will need scissors, crayons or markers, a paper clip, tape, and a pencil to complete this page.

Serving Up Circles

Looking for ideas that deliver plenty of hands-on learning about circles?
Then serve up these "pizza-rific" activities and reproducibles!

by Lori Sammartino, Cranberry Township, PA

Any Way You Slice It

Skills: Circle parts and attributes

Introduce students to the basic parts and attributes of a circle with this pizza-slicing activity. First, ask students to identify a pizza's shape *(circle).* Next, give each child a four-inch white paper circle (or have him use a compass to construct his own), scissors, a ruler, and crayons in the following colors: red, black, green, blue, orange, and purple. Guide students through the steps below in order. Then conclude by having students brainstorm real-life objects—other than pizzas!—that are circular or contain circular shapes. List students' responses on chart paper to use with "Concentric Pizzas" on page 63. Challenge students to add items to this list throughout the unit.

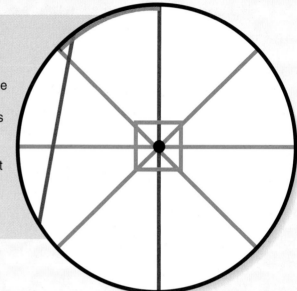

Steps:

1. **Circumference (the distance around the outside of a circle):** Use the black crayon to trace the outer edge of the circle.

2. **Diameter (any straight line that passes through the center of a circle):** Fold the circle in half. Unfold it. Use the red crayon to trace the fold line. Measure the diameter *(four inches).*

3. **Center of circle (the point in the exact middle of the circle):** Refold the circle in half and fold it in half again to make fourths. Unfold it. Use the black crayon to mark the point where the fold lines intersect.

4. **Radius (the distance from the center of the circle to any point on the circumference of the circle):** Use the green crayon to trace the new fold line outward in each direction from the center. Measure each radius *(two inches).* Identify the angles formed *(four right angles)* by marking them as shown. Calculate the total degrees in a circle *(4 x 90° = 360°)* and in a half circle *(180°).* Fold the circle in fourths and then in half again to make eighths. Use the blue crayon to trace the new fold lines. Find the degrees in $\frac{1}{8}$ circle *(45°).*

5. **Arc (any section of the circumference):** Use the orange crayon to trace $\frac{1}{8}$ of the circle. Determine if tracing $\frac{1}{4}$, $\frac{3}{8}$, $\frac{1}{2}$, $\frac{5}{8}$, $\frac{3}{4}$, or $\frac{7}{8}$ of the circle each represents an arc. *(yes)*

6. **Chord (a straight line that connects any two points on the circle):** Use the purple crayon to trace a line from one point on the circle to another without passing through the center.

If desired, extend the activity by having students use protractors to help them create two circles, one having six equal pieces *(60° angles)* and another with nine equal pieces *(40° angles).*

Circular Stories

Skills: Connecting math and literature, writing a review

Connect reading and writing to your circles study with this well-rounded activity! Have your media specialist gather circle-related books, such as those suggested below. Encourage students to read as many of the books as they can. If desired, read several selections aloud to the class. Explain that some of the selections are written in a circular pattern in which events flow from one to the next, with the main character always ending up where he or she started. Point out that others feature circle-shaped characters or teach younger readers about circles. Then challenge each student to write a review about one of the following to share with the class: (1) a circular story, (2) a story that has a circle-shaped character, or (3) a story that teaches a concept about circles.

Circular stories:

What Comes Around Goes Around
   by Richard McGuire
Where the Wild Things Are by Maurice Sendak
If You Give a Mouse a Cookie
   by Laura Joffe Numeroff
Circle Song by Diana Engel
The Missing Piece by Shel Silverstein
Rosie's Walk by Pat Hutchins

Books with circle characters:

Circle Dogs by Kevin Henkes
Rolie Polie Olie by William Joyce

Books that teach circle concepts:

*Sir Cumference and the First Round Table: A Math
   Adventure* by Cindy Neuschwander
So Many Circles, So Many Squares by Tana Hoban
What Is Round? by Rebecca Kai Dotlich
Ed Emberley's Picture Pie: A Circle Drawing Book

Discovering Pizza "Pi"

Skill: Diameter and circumference

Use this activity to help students discover that a circle's circumference is a little more than three times its diameter. Give each student a 12-inch length of string, a ruler, a calculator, and a copy of page 64 to complete as directed. When students have completed the sheet and its Bonus Box, check the answers together. Help students conclude that the numbers in the table's last column are all close to three. On the board, write "pi = 3.14." Explain that *pi* represents the relationship between a circle's circumference and its diameter (found by dividing the circumference by the diameter). Have students prove this by first using their string to measure the circumference of any circle on page 64 and then calculating the number of diameters needed to equal that length *(three)*. If desired, extend the activity by having students write an equation for finding circumference when only the diameter is known $(C = d \times 3.14)$. Afterward, have each student use the formula to calculate the answers on page 64 and explain why the answers differ *(3.14 is a more exact number than 3)*.

Pizza Estimations

Skills: Estimating the area of a circle, constructing circles

Practice estimating the area of circles with this nifty activity. Begin by drawing a circle on the board and asking students how they could determine its area. If no one suggests drawing square units, start drawing intersecting horizontal and vertical lines inside the circle. Guide students to conclude that they can count the square units to estimate the circle's area. Point out that some squares are partial units. Together, discuss strategies for simplifying the counting process (*adding whole units first and then partial units, or dividing the circle into four equal parts and multiplying the whole units in one quadrant by four*). Then give each student a compass, several sheets of graph paper, and a copy of page 65 to complete as directed.

For more practice on finding circumference and diameter, give students a ruler and a length of string with which to measure the circles on page 65. For an extra challenge, have students use the formula $A = 3.14 \times r^2$ to calculate the actual area of each circle; then have them explain why the estimated and exact areas differ.

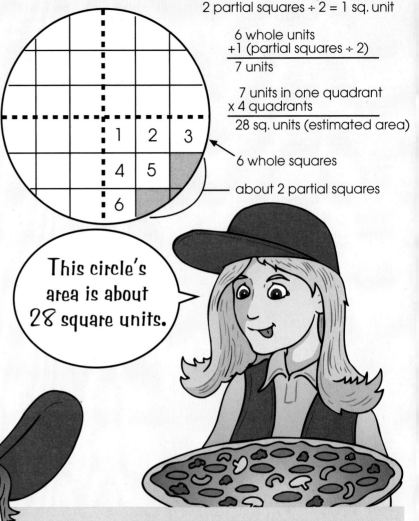

2 partial squares ÷ 2 = 1 sq. unit

$$\begin{array}{l} 6 \text{ whole units} \\ +1 \text{ (partial squares} \div 2) \\ \hline 7 \text{ units} \end{array}$$

$$\begin{array}{l} 7 \text{ units in one quadrant} \\ \times\ 4 \text{ quadrants} \\ \hline 28 \text{ sq. units (estimated area)} \end{array}$$

6 whole squares

about 2 partial squares

This circle's area is about 28 square units.

Pizza Topping Preferences

Students	Topping
40%	pepperoni
35%	mushrooms
10%	green peppers
10%	black olives
5%	Canadian bacon

Making a Pizza Pie Graph

Skills: Calculating percent, using a compass and protractor

Show students that constructing circle graphs can be as easy as pizza pie! In advance, copy the table shown onto the board or a transparency. Review with students that there are 360 degrees in a circle, 180 degrees in a half circle, and 90 degrees in a quarter circle. Have student volunteers illustrate these amounts on the board by drawing circles that are 100 percent shaded, 50 percent shaded, and 25 percent shaded. Afterward, model how to calculate the degrees represented in a circle that is 20 percent shaded: 0.20 (the decimal equivalent of 20 percent) x 360° = 72°. Then construct a circle on the board. Use a protractor to measure a 72 degree angle in the circle and shade it in. Next, give each student a sheet of white paper, a compass, a protractor, and crayons or markers. Have each child construct on his paper a circle with a two-inch radius. Display the table; then challenge each student to follow the procedure you modeled to convert each percent in the table to degrees. After checking students' calculations (*pepperoni = 144°, mushrooms = 126°, green peppers = 36°, black olives = 36°, and Canadian bacon = 18°*), have each child construct and color a circle graph that represents the data.

Overlapping Pizzas
Skill: Using overlapping circles to make comparisons

Serve up a lesson on overlapping circles with the following hard-to-beat activity! Cut three circles from cellophane: one red, one yellow, and one blue. Overlap the blue and yellow circles and display them on an overhead projector. Point out the new color produced in the overlapping area *(green)*. Tell students it represents a combination of the two colors. Next, overlap the red and yellow circles (creating an orange area) and the blue and red circles (making a purple area). Finally, overlap all three circles, as shown, to create areas of orange, green, purple, and black. Then give each student a copy of page 66. Have students complete and check Part 1 together before completing Part 2 independently.

Concentric Pizzas
Skill: Constructing concentric circles

Build your own concentric-circle pizzas with this circle-within-a-circle activity. On the board, draw a lollipop made of concentric circles as shown. Together, brainstorm other real-world items that suggest (or have) the shape of one circle within another, such as a bull's-eye, a bagel, or a CD. Have students also refer to the chart made in "Any Way You Slice It" on page 60 for other items that might represent concentric circles. Next, give each student a sheet of paper and a compass. Have her construct a circle with a three-inch radius. Inside that circle, have her construct a smaller circle with a two-inch radius; then have her create a circle with a one-inch radius inside the two-inch circle. After this practice, give each child scissors, glue, and three 9" x 12" sheets of construction paper (one tan, one red, and one yellow). Have her make an eight-inch tan circle, a seven-inch red circle, and a six-inch yellow circle. Then have her stack and glue the circles together to form the crust, sauce, and cheese layers of a pizza. From her scraps, have her cut out six different toppings and glue them on top of the cheese before delivering her concentric pizza to you to display!

A Circular Celebration
Skill: Identifying circular shapes

Conclude your unit by having students create a colossal class mural of circular shapes! Have students cut out magazine pictures that represent different types of circles. Then have one small group of students at a time mount the cutouts on a bulletin board until it is filled with different-size, overlapping, and concentric circles. Celebrate the project's completion by letting students munch on a variety of round snacks. What a circular celebration!

63

How Big Is Your Pizza "Pi"?

Discover a special relationship between a circle's circumference and its diameter by following the directions below.

Directions:

1. Use string to measure the distance around each pizza shown.
2. Place the string atop a ruler. Measure the string to the nearest half inch. Record the measurement in the "Circumference" column of the table.
3. Use a ruler to measure the diameter of each pizza. Record the measurement in the table.
4. Use a calculator to divide the circumference by the diameter. Record your answer in the table. (*Hint:* ¹/₂ *inch = 0.50*)

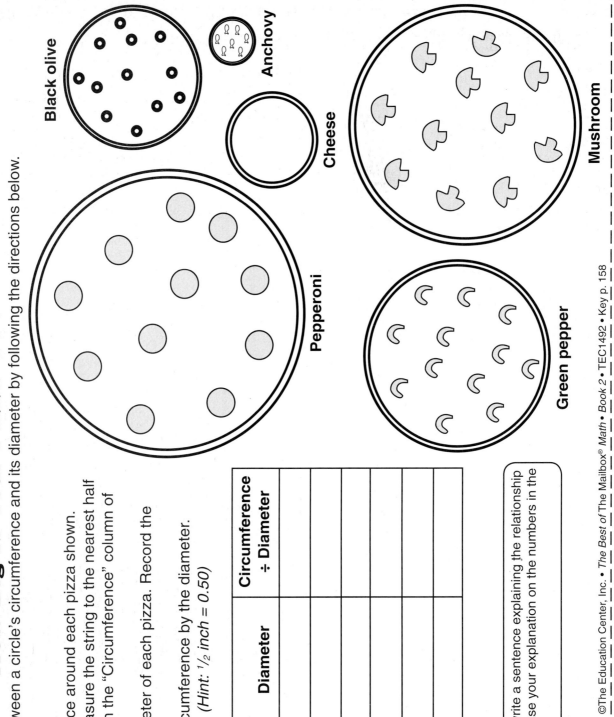

Pizza	Circumference	Diameter	Circumference ÷ Diameter
Pepperoni			
Black olive			
Cheese			
Anchovy			
Green pepper			
Mushroom			

Bonus Box: On the back of this page, write a sentence explaining the relationship between circumference and diameter. Base your explanation on the numbers in the last column above.

©The Education Center, Inc. • *The Best of The Mailbox*® *Math • Book 2* • TEC1492 • Key p. 158

Note to the teacher: Use with "Discovering Pizza 'Pi'" on page 61.

Name _____

Peppi's Pizza Predicament

The pizza chefs at Peppi's Pizza Parlor are in a dilemma. They don't know how to estimate the area of the pizzas they've made! Help them out by following the directions below.

Part 1: For each circle, count all of the whole squares and all of the partial squares in the shaded area. Next, divide the number of partial squares by 2. If necessary, round the quotient to the nearest whole number. Then add the whole squares and the answer to *b* together. Finally, multiply the answer in *c* by 4 to find the estimated area of the circle.

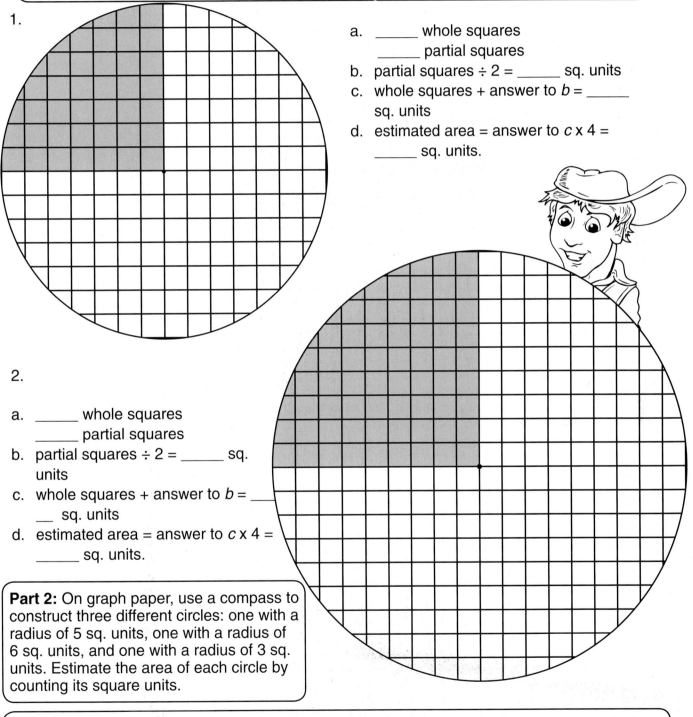

1.

a. _____ whole squares
   _____ partial squares
b. partial squares ÷ 2 = _____ sq. units
c. whole squares + answer to *b* = _____ sq. units
d. estimated area = answer to *c* x 4 = _____ sq. units.

2.

a. _____ whole squares
   _____ partial squares
b. partial squares ÷ 2 = _____ sq. units
c. whole squares + answer to *b* = _____ sq. units
d. estimated area = answer to *c* x 4 = _____ sq. units.

Part 2: On graph paper, use a compass to construct three different circles: one with a radius of 5 sq. units, one with a radius of 6 sq. units, and one with a radius of 3 sq. units. Estimate the area of each circle by counting its square units.

BONUS BOX: What method did you use to find the area of the circles you drew in Part 2? Explain your method on the back of this page.

Note to the teacher: Use with "Pizza Estimations" on page 62.

Name _____

Overlapping Pizzas

Peppi

A marketing team for Peppi's Pizza Parlor has come up with a new concept. They want Peppi to create overlapping pizzas to start a new combination-pizza craze. So Peppi made the test samples below.

Part 1: Look carefully at the overlapping pizzas. Then answer the questions.

1. What toppings are in the overlapped section of these two pizzas? _____

_____

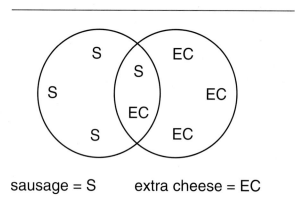

sausage = S   extra cheese = EC

2. How many different topping combinations are possible in these three overlapping pizzas? _____ List them. _____

_____

_____

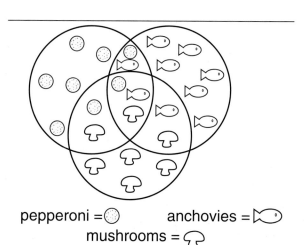

pepperoni = ⊙   anchovies = ⋈
mushrooms = ⌒

Part 2: Now it's time to create overlapping pizzas of your own! Complete a key for each pizza. Include a symbol for each topping.

3. Use two different toppings to make this overlapping pizza. Cover one pizza with one topping and the second pizza with the second topping. What toppings are in the overlapped section? _____

_____

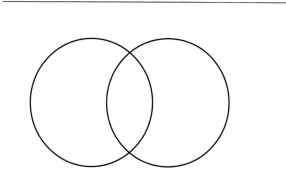

4. Use three different toppings to make this overlapping pizza. Cover one pizza with one topping, the second pizza with the second topping, and the third pizza with the third topping. How many different toppings are possible? _____ List them on the back of this page.

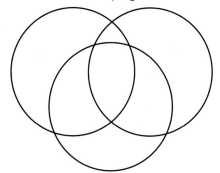

Note to the teacher: Use with "Overlapping Pizzas" on page 63. Each student will need a compass and crayons or colored pencils to complete the page.

Take a "Geo-Journey"!

Helping Students Discover Geometry in Their World

Why do intermediate students love geometry so much? Because there's lots of *doing*—classifying, putting shapes together, expanding patterns, and making three-dimensional shapes. Watch the beauty and logic of geometry come alive for your students with the following creative, hands-on activities and reproducibles.

ideas by Irving P. Crump and Gail Peckumn

Staying Organized With Geo-Folders

Skill: Building geometry vocabulary

Our world is filled with patterns and shapes—in other words, geometry! Help students become more comfortable with the language of geometry by making geo-folders. Provide each student with a folder and a copy of page 70. Instruct the student to color and decorate the cover art and then cut it out and glue it to the front of his folder. Next, have each student cut out the word list and glue it to the left side of his opened folder.

As you introduce geometry vocabulary, have each student list two or three words on each side of a sheet of notebook paper. After adding brief definitions and illustrations, students store their sheets in their folders. The list covers a wide range of geometry concepts; include only those that you teach at your level.

Understanding Horizontal and Vertical

Skill: Describing location

Help students better understand the concepts of *horizontal* and *vertical* with this simple demonstration. Fill a clear, clean, plastic two-liter soft-drink bottle about half full of water. Cap the bottle and set it upright on a tabletop. Ask a volunteer to describe the surface of the water. *(The surface of the water in the bottle is horizontal.)* Next, hold the bottle by its top and tilt it about 45°. Ask someone to describe the surface of the water. *(It remains horizontal.)* Finally, lay the bottle completely on its side, and ask a student to describe the surface of the water. *(It remains horizontal.)*

Tie a small stone or other weight to a piece of string and suspend it from the ceiling. Explain to the class that the string is vertical. Hold the bottle of water as still as possible behind the string. Ask students how vertical and horizontal relate to each other. *(They are at right angles to each other.)* Brainstorm with students different objects in the classroom, as well as outside the classroom, that are vertical and horizontal. Have students identify the objects in the list that have right angles. Ask the class, "Why are right angles so important?" *(Right angles are common in the environment. Walls are built at right angles to the ground. If they weren't, they would tend to fall over.)*

vertical

horizontal

- Find three examples of congruent objects.
- Find an object that has a vertical line of symmetry.
- Find an object that is a perfect square.
- Find five different rectangles.
- List five different sets of car parts that are congruent.
- Find an object that has an acute angle.
- Find an object that has parallel line segments.
- Find a semicircle.
- Find two examples of spheres.
- Find an example of an octagon.

Schoolyard Geometry
Skill: Recognizing geometric concepts
Head to the great outdoors and take your students on a schoolyard geometry scavenger hunt! Duplicate a list (similar to the one shown) of various geometric concepts that are evident in your school environment. Is a water tower on your campus or nearby? Students should be able to identify different types of angles and shapes within its framework. Sidewalks, buildings, signs, playground equipment, fences, and vehicles all have distinct patterns and shapes that students will recognize. Give each student a copy of the list. Have students take their geo-folders with them and describe other examples of geometry concepts that they find.

Household Symmetry
Skill: Recognizing symmetrical shapes
Symmetry is everywhere—even in the mattress pads at home! To show students just how commonplace symmetrical designs are, bring in a mattress pad (or a copy of its pattern on a sheet of paper) and point out the symmetry in its pattern. Then, as a class, brainstorm other items found around the home that exhibit symmetry. For example: the pattern in a rug, a sofa, or the family china; the front panel of a boom box; or the design in a tiled kitchen floor.

For homework, instruct each student to draw examples of five objects that have symmetry—one object per side of a sheet of paper—that he finds at home. The next day, have each student share his examples with the class. Challenge class members to guess each design as it's presented. Afterward, have each student reveal the identity of each design and use a marker to draw all the lines of symmetry. Display students' work on a bulletin board titled "Around-The-House Symmetry!"

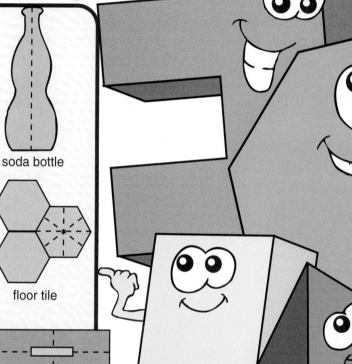

soda bottle

floor tile

drawer

What to Include on Your Map
- three streets that are parallel to each other
- two avenues that are perpendicular to the three parallel streets
- one boulevard that intersects three streets, but is not perpendicular to them
- five rectangular buildings, four square buildings, and six pentagon-shaped buildings
- a park with two triangular sandboxes and two circular swimming pools
- a name for your town

Linking Geometry and Maps
Skill: Recognizing geometric concepts
Connect basic geometric concepts to real-life situations with this creative map activity for pairs. Give each pair of students a copy of the same city map. Ask each pair to look at the map's key, name the geometric shapes shown in it, and tell what each shape represents. Next, have each pair use its map to answer questions—aloud or on paper—such as "Which street is parallel to Pentagon Street?" or "Which street intersects Octagon Avenue at an acute angle?"

Extend the activity by giving each student colored pencils, a ruler, and a sheet of drawing paper. Have him use the materials to design a city map that meets predetermined criteria that include geometric concepts (see the suggestions in the chart on the left). Encourage students to be creative in naming the items on their maps. Display the completed maps on a bulletin board titled "We're Mapping Our Way Through Geometry!"

Slide, Flip, Turn!
Skill: Creating transformations

Geometry deals with movement, as well as patterns and shapes. Review the concepts of *slide, flip,* and *turn* with your students, copying the diagrams at the right onto a chalkboard if desired. Then have one student go to the chalkboard. Draw a simple design in one corner of the board. Direct the student to "move" the design across the board as you direct him to "slide," "flip," or "turn." Repeat this activity several times with other students and different designs.

Next, divide students into groups of four. Give each group one copy of page 71, a die, scissors, and four different-colored crayons. Instruct students to follow the directions on the page to play the game. What a fun workout as the game pieces slide, flip, and turn on their way to the finish line!

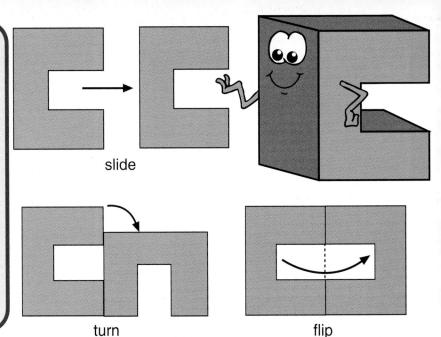

slide

turn

flip

Follow the Leader
Skill: Applying geometric concepts

Focus on following directions, listening skills, and geometry concepts with this fun drawing activity. Draw a simple picture, like the one shown below, on a transparency, without revealing it to your students. Instruct students to draw the picture on their own papers, as you give one geometric clue at a time. (See the list.) After students have finished their drawings, turn on the overhead so they can compare their pictures to yours. After completing two or three drawings with the entire class, divide students into pairs. Have each student make a geometric drawing without revealing it to his partner. Then have partners take turns describing and drawing each other's designs.

1. Draw a circle.
2. Draw a vertical diameter through the circle.
3. Draw a radius that is horizontal in the right semicircle.
4. Draw a square in the left semicircle.
5. Draw a chord that crosses the horizontal radius.

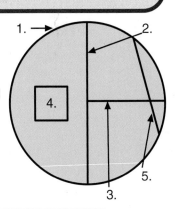

A Different Kind of Grid
Skill: Using visualization

Encourage your young mathematicians to be copycats with this nifty idea! Provide each student with a copy of page 72. Ask students how the grid on this page is different from other grids they've used. *(The distances between any two successive horizontal dots, as well as any two successive diagonal dots, are the same.)* Make a transparency of the page and display it on an overhead. Ask students to describe the different kinds of shapes that can be drawn on the grid, such as right, equilateral, and isosceles triangles; rectangles; hexagons; trapezoids; rhombuses; and parallelograms. Draw each shape with a wipe-off marker as a student describes it. Next, have students follow the directions on the bottom half of the page to complete the designs on the reproducible.

Hint: Make additional copies of the grid by gluing two copies of the top half of page 72 onto one sheet of paper. Then duplicate that sheet for each student.

Folder Cover Art

GEO-Folder

_____
(name)

Geometry Word List

Geo-Words

- three-dimensional
- space figure
- plane figure
- plane
- point
- line
- line segment
- ray
- angle
- right angle
- acute angle
- obtuse angle

- straight angle
- line of symmetry
- symmetric figure
- congruent figures
- perimeter
- area
- volume
- horizontal
- edge
- face
- vertex (corner)
- vertical

- diagonal
- intersecting lines
- perpendicular lines
- parallel lines
- polygon
- quadrilateral
- square
- rectangle
- trapezoid
- parallelogram
- rhombus
- triangle

- right triangle
- scalene triangle
- isosceles triangle
- equilateral triangle
- acute triangle
- obtuse triangle
- circle
- radius
- diameter
- circumference
- arc
- chord

- pentagon
- hexagon
- octagon
- cube
- prism
- pyramid
- cone
- cylinder
- sphere
- slide
- turn
- flip

©The Education Center, Inc. • *The Best of* The Mailbox® *Math* • *Book 2* • TEC1492

Note to the teacher: Use with "Staying Organized With Geo-Folders" on page 67.

Geometric Aerobics

Ready for a real workout? Use your game pieces below to practice slides, flips, and turns—and try to be the first player to reach the finish line!

Directions for four players:

1. Cut out the four game pieces at the bottom of this sheet. Give one piece to each player. Each player chooses a crayon and colors both sides of his or her game piece.
2. Roll the die to see who goes first.
3. On your first turn, place your piece on START. Roll the die. Then follow the directions in the box at the right to find out how to move your game piece. The arrows indicate the direction in which you are to move. (Two or more game pieces can occupy a space on the gameboard at the same time.)
4. The first player to reach FINISH wins!

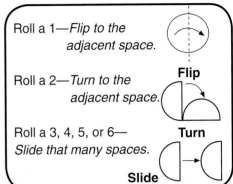

Roll a 1—*Flip to the adjacent space.*

Flip

Roll a 2—*Turn to the adjacent space.*

Turn

Roll a 3, 4, 5, or 6—*Slide that many spaces.*

Slide

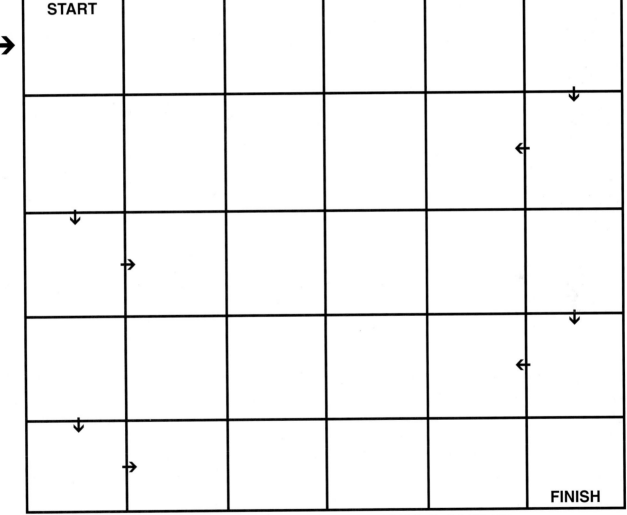

START

FINISH

©The Education Center, Inc. • *The Best of* The Mailbox® *Math* • *Book 2* • TEC1492

Note to the teacher: Use with "Slide, Flip, Turn!" on page 69. Give each group of four students one die, scissors, four different-colored crayons, and one copy of this sheet.

Be a Copycat!

Copy each of the following designs on the grid below. Use colored pencils to decorate your designs.

©The Education Center, Inc. • *The Best of* The Mailbox® *Math • Book 2 •* TEC1492

72   **Note to the teacher:** Use with "A Different Kind of Grid" on page 69.

GEO-TREK...
A Journey Into Real-World Geometry

Show students that geometry isn't just *out* of this world, but also smack-dab *in* it with the following ideas on geometric concepts in the real world!

by Irving P. Crump

They're Golden!

Skills: Identifying rectangles, using ratio

Are some rectangles more pleasing to look at than others? The ancient Greeks thought so! To find out what your students think, draw on a chalkboard four rectangles with these dimensions: 2" x 10", 10" x 16", 5" x 6", and 1" x 12". Ask students to vote on which rectangle they think is most pleasing to the eye. It will likely be the 10" x 16" one. Share with students that *golden rectangles* (ones with a length to width ratio of about 1.6 to 1) are more pleasing to the eye than other rectangles. Why? No one really knows.

Next, provide each student with a copy of the top half of page 75, which tells how to construct a golden rectangle. After students complete the activity, have them brainstorm examples of real-world rectangles as you list them on the board. (See the suggestions below.) Assign each pair of students one rectangle and ask whether it is similar to the one on the reproducible. Then instruct the pair to measure the length and width of its assigned rectangle and use a calculator to determine whether it is "golden." (Example: If the ratio of length to width is 30/16, divide both terms by 16 to get 1.9/1 or 1.9 to 1.) If the ratio of the rectangle's length to its width is approximately 1.6 to 1, then the rectangle is golden.

Examples: construction paper (different sizes), index card, notecard, credit card, driver's license, door, television, flag, desktop, sheet of notebook paper, sticky note, calculator face, wallet-size photo, textbook, mouse pad, computer screen, magazine, newspaper page, dollar bill, postage stamp, envelope, business card, classroom poster, framed picture or photo, greeting card, license plate, brochure, postcard

Flyin' High!

Skill: Identifying geometry concepts

The flag of the United States illustrates several geometric concepts. (See the illustration.) Share with students that the flag, however, is *not* a golden rectangle as described in "They're Golden!" The ratio of its length to its width is 1.9 to 1.

Many state flags and flags of other nations incorporate geometric concepts too. Assign each student a state or country from the list shown. Have the student research, draw, and color that state's or country's flag. Then have her list on an index card all of the geometric concepts that she can identify in the flag's design. After she shares her flag and geometry terms, instruct the student to attach the index card to the bottom of her drawing. Display the flags on a bulletin board titled "Flyin' High!"

translation   congruency

obtuse angle   decagon

plane

right angle

rectangle

parallel lines

acute angle

similar rectangles

Alabama, Arizona, New Mexico, Colorado, Ohio, Georgia, Hawaii, Tennessee, Texas, Maryland, Mississippi, Puerto Rico, Grenada, Congo, Liberia, Tanzania, Canada, South Africa, Guyana, St. Lucia, Kuwait, Philippines, Denmark, Greece, United Kingdom, Israel, Jordan, Jamaica, Cuba

73

Welcome to Geo-Village!

Skills: Identifying geometry terms, making three-dimensional models

Nowhere is geometry more evident in our world than in construction and architecture. Provide each student with a copy of page 77. Discuss the terms at the bottom of the page; then direct students to complete the activity as directed. Share with students that many of the terms listed are represented multiple times in the village.

After discussing page 77, divide students into six groups. Provide each group with a white sheet of poster board. Instruct each group to measure and draw a two-inch border around three sides of its poster board as shown below; then have the group color this border gray. Tell students that the border represents streets that surround three sides of a city block. Next, direct each group to use a variety of materials to create a three-dimensional model of a city block, with each structure facing the street. Students may also include items in the center of a block, such as a park, playground, or parking lot. Have students gather a variety of materials ahead of time (see below). As they work, have group members make a list identifying the geometric terms illustrated in its model.

When all six city blocks are completed, display them by laying the pieces of poster board together as shown. Have each group share its project by pointing out all of the examples of geometric terms.

Materials: clean, empty milk cartons (pint and ½-pint sizes); game pieces; cube tissue boxes; checkers; dominoes; construction paper; scissors; tape; dice; glue; different sizes of aluminum cans; straws; bottle caps; craft sticks; small paper cups; cardboard; small boxes

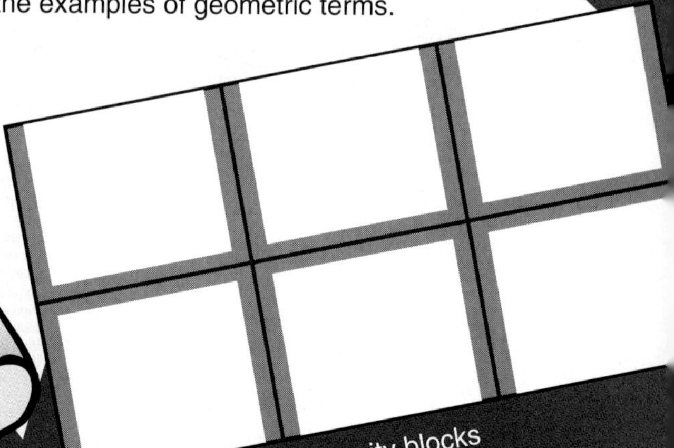

six city blocks

Geo-Scavenger Hunt

Skills: Finding examples of geometry terms, making an octahedron

As a homework extension, send your students out in the world on a geo-scavenger hunt! Have each student find examples of items that illustrate eight geometry terms. (Choose from the list at the bottom of page 77 and these three-dimensional shapes: *cone, disk, cylinder, cube, rectangular prism, triangular prism,* and *sphere.*) Encourage students to look in their neighborhoods, homes, or yards. Have each student sketch and label his examples and bring the drawings to school the next day for discussion.

After the discussion, provide each student with a copy of page 76. Have him draw and label each item from his list on a triangle in the pattern. Make sure that the student turns the pattern so that the label (1–8) is at the top of the triangle that he is working on. After decorating his completed pattern, have each child follow the directions on the page to make an *octahedron*—an eight-sided geometric shape. For an eye-catching display, have each student place his completed octahedron on top of an empty plastic soda or water bottle.

Looking for Gold!

Can you make a golden rectangle? Just follow the steps on the right very carefully. You only need a pencil and a ruler.

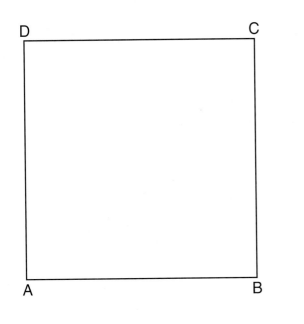

Steps:

1. Find the midpoint of $\overline{AB}$. Label it M.
2. Find the midpoint of $\overline{DC}$. Label it N.
3. Draw a straight line to connect M and C.
4. Measure $\overline{MC}$ and record the length. ___
5. Lay your ruler along $\overline{AB}$ with its end at point M.
6. Measure the length that you recorded in #4, making $\overline{MB}$ longer. Label the new endpoint E.
7. Lay your ruler along $\overline{DC}$ with its end at point N.
8. Measure the length that you recorded in #4, making $\overline{NC}$ longer. Label the new endpoint F.
9. Draw a straight line to connect E and F.
10. You did it! AEFD is a golden rectangle.

©The Education Center, Inc. • *The Best of* The Mailbox® Math • *Book 2* • TEC1492 • Key p. 158

A Puzzling Pair

Puzzle 1

How many squares do you see on the checkerboard? 64? 65? Not even close! (Hint: Be sure to count squares that are made up of smaller ones. For example, count all of the squares that are two small squares long and two small squares wide.)

My answer: _____ squares

Puzzle 2

How many triangles do you see? Six? Seven? You got it—not even close! (Hint: Label each of the six small triangles with a letter. Then list each different triangle with a combination of letters.)

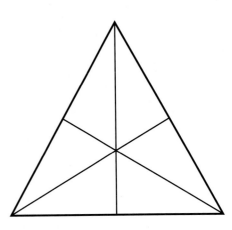

My answer: _____ triangles

©The Education Center, Inc. • *The Best of* The Mailbox® Math • *Book 2* • TEC1492 • Key p. 158

- -

Note to the teacher: Use the top half of this reproducible with "They're Golden!" on page 73. Provide each student with a ruler. Use the bottom half ("A Puzzling Pair") as a free-time challenge.

Geo-Scavenger Hunt

Draw each scavenger hunt item on a triangle in the pattern. Each number is at the top of a triangle; be sure to turn the pattern so that the number is at the top when you draw. Then follow the steps below to make an octahedron.

1. Carefully cut out the pattern.
2. Turn the pattern over and fold up each tab (A–E).
3. Next, fold at each remaining dashed line, keeping the drawing to the outside.
4. Glue tab B under triangle 1. Hold the tab and triangle together until the glue dries.

5. Glue tab E under triangle 7. Hold the tab and triangle together until the glue dries.
6. Glue tab D to triangle 2, tab A to triangle 7, and tab C to triangle 6.
7. You've done it! You've made an *octahedron*—an eight-sided geometric shape.

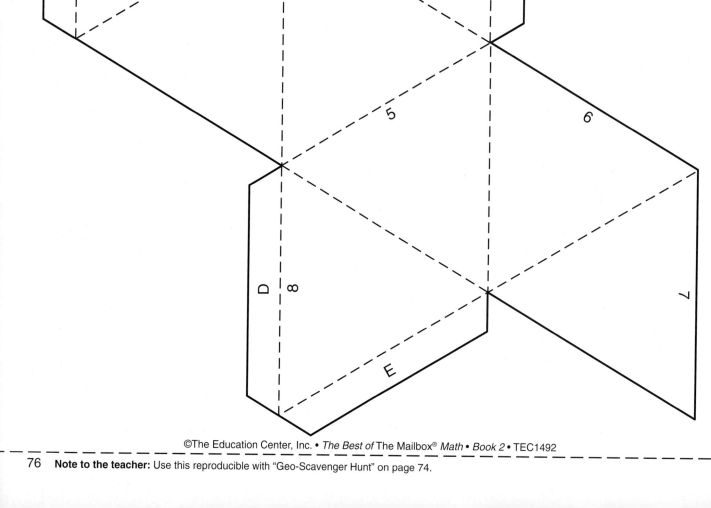

Note to the teacher: Use this reproducible with "Geo-Scavenger Hunt" on page 74.

Name _____

Welcome to Geo-Village!

How many of the following geometry terms can you find illustrated in Geo-Village? Find at least one example of each term. Write the number in a circle; then draw an arrow to the part of the village where that word is illustrated. Two examples (1 and 13) have been done for you.

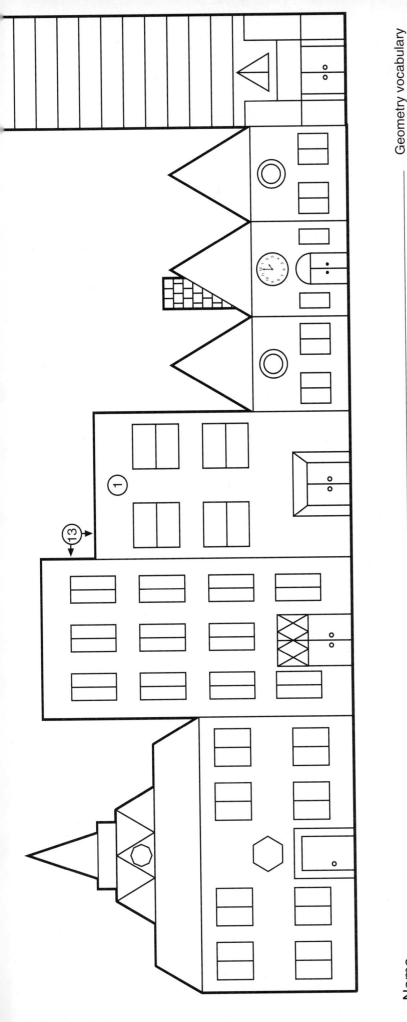

1.	plane	7.	line of symmetry	13.	perpendicular lines

1. plane
2. point
3. line segment
4. right angle
5. acute angle
6. obtuse angle

7. line of symmetry
8. symmetric figure
9. congruent figures
10. vertex
11. diagonal
12. intersecting lines

13. perpendicular lines
14. parallel lines
15. square
16. rectangle

17. trapezoid
18. parallelogram
19. rhombus
20. scalene triangle

21. isosceles triangle
22. equilateral triangle
23. acute triangle
24. right triangle
25. circle
26. semicircle

27. pentagon
28. hexagon
29. octagon
30. translation (slide)
31. rotation (turn)
32. reflection (flip)

BONUS BOX: *Congruent figures* have the same size and shape. *Similar figures* have the same shape. If two shapes are congruent, they are also similar. But two similar shapes may not be congruent. Find three pairs of similar shapes in Geo-Village. Label the pairs A, B, and C.

Note to the teacher: Use this reproducible with "Welcome to Geo-Village!" on page 74.

Measurement Magic
Hands-On Activities for Teaching Linear Measurement

There's no trick to it! If you want students' linear measurement skills to magically improve, just try the following hands-on learning activities.

by Irving Crump, Contributing Editor

Ready, Set, Review
Skill: Reviewing customary and metric units of measure

Introduce students to the magic of linear measurement by having them make measuring tapes to use with the activities in this unit. Give each student a copy of page 81, scissors, and glue. After each student makes a measuring tape as directed, point out that the tape represents one *meter.* Guide students to see that a meter is equivalent to 100 *centimeters,* and that each centimeter is divided into 10 *millimeters.* Ask students how many millimeters are in a meter *(1,000).* Also share that a *decimeter* (10 centimeters) is another metric unit that is not used as often as meter, centimeter, and millimeter. Ask students to name the metric unit they'd most likely use to measure each of the following:

length of the classroom *(m)*   thickness of a slice of bread *(mm)*

width of camera film *(mm)*   length of a swimming pool *(m)*

height of a door *(m or cm)*   width of a sheet of paper *(cm)*

length of a basketball court *(m)*   perimeter of a calculator *(cm)*

Also review with students the customary units that are on the opposite edge of the tape. Have students note that the tape is nearly 40 *inches* long and that each inch is divided into halves, fourths, and eighths. Point out that one *foot* (12 inches), two feet (24 inches), and three feet (36 inches) are marked, and that a *yard* is equivalent to three feet, or 36 inches. Then have students use their tapes with the following measuring activities.

Body Facts
Skill: Measuring in customary and metric units

There's a bit of magic in some of our body's measurements! To discover it, divide students into pairs. Direct one student in each pair to use the metric edge of his measuring tape and the other student to use the customary edge. Then have students in each twosome take turns measuring each other and recording their measurements using these directions:

1. Have your partner hold out his arms to the side. Measure him fingertip to fingertip to find his arm span. Next, measure your partner's height. *(The length of a student's arm span is about the same as his height.)*

2. Measure the circumference of your partner's thumb by wrapping the tape around the base of the thumb. Then multiply that measurement by two. Next, measure your partner's wrist. *(The measurement of a student's wrist is about twice the measurement of his thumb.)*

3. Measure the circumference of your partner's neck. Multiply the measurement of your partner's wrist (see Step 2) by two. *(The measurement of a student's neck is about twice the measurement of his wrist.)*

4. Measure your partner's forearm from elbow to wrist. Then measure his foot from heel to toe. *(The length of a student's forearm is about the same as the length of his foot.)*

The Great 2,500-Millimeter Race
Skill: Measuring in metric units

1 = cm
2 = mm
3 = cm
4 = mm
5 = cm
6 = dm

We're going to race *how* far? After their initial shock subsides, show students that a 2,500-millimeter race is actually very short (the same as $2\frac{1}{2}$ meters). Call on three students to demonstrate the distance with their measuring tapes. Then divide students into pairs. Give each pair a $2\frac{1}{2}$-meter-long strip of paper. List on the chalkboard the information shown; then direct each twosome to write the numbers 0–9 on a sheet of paper. Each pair will also need a measuring tape. The object of the game is to see which pair can get closest to 2,500 millimeters without going over. To play:

1. Roll a die and announce the number showing.
2. Each pair notes the matching unit of measure for that roll. For example, if 5 is rolled, then the matching unit is centimeters.
3. Each pair chooses a number from its list (0–9) to use with that measure. For example, if 5 is rolled (centimeters), the pair could choose 7 to equal seven centimeters. After the pair chooses a number, it is marked through and cannot be used again. The pair then measures and marks that distance at one end of the paper strip. (In the example, the pair would measure seven centimeters and make a mark.)
4. Repeat Steps 1–3 nine more times. For each roll, each pair continues measuring from the previous mark.
5. Declare the pair whose line is closest to 2,500 millimeters (without going over) the winner.

If desired, run the race a second time. Have pairs turn over their paper strips and use the reverse side.

Measurement Hunt
Skill: Measuring to the nearest inch, half inch, and quarter inch

Use this fun activity to hunt down better measurement skills using customary units. First, remind students that measurements in the real world are always approximate. Discuss the factors that can affect the precision of measurements that they make: the measurement tool used and its scale, how they read the scale on the tool, and how accurate students think a measurement needs to be. Then send pairs of students on the following measurement scavenger hunt.

Number and label about 12 classroom objects for students to measure. (See the suggestions.) Provide each pair of students with an index card and a measuring tape. Direct each twosome to visit each of the 12 objects and measure it to the nearest inch. After recording the object's number and measurement, the pair moves on to another item. Have the twosomes circulate about the classroom until they have measured each object. Then discuss with the class their measurements. Ask why some measures may have varied and what factors came into play. Then repeat the activity by having students measure each object to the nearest half and then quarter inch.

1. length of a sheet of art paper
2. length of a piece of chalk
3. width of a calendar date box
4. height of a lunchbox
5. width of a TV or computer monitor screen
6. diameter of a clock face
7. height of a file cabinet
8. width of a window
9. length of a shoe
10. circumference of a plant pot
11. diameter of a doorknob
12. perimeter of a tabletop or desktop

Measurement Hunt 2
Skills: Estimating, measuring to the nearest centimeter

Send students off on another measurement hunt—but this time, with a little bit of a twist! First, copy the list of measurements shown on a chalkboard or transparency. Provide each pair of students with an index card on which to copy the list. Next, send each pair to search for an item in or near the classroom that students estimate would equal each measure listed. For example, a pair might estimate that the circumference of a pencil is about ten millimeters or that the height of a file cabinet is 1½ meters. Have each twosome jot down the item beside its corresponding measure. Remind students to estimate only—not to measure.

After every pair has written an item beside each measure, send the twosomes back to the items they selected—this time with a measuring tape. Direct each pair to measure each object to the nearest centimeter to see how close the actual measure is to the estimate.

10 mm	3 mm
1½ m	2 m
15 cm	3 dm
6 m	½ m
40 cm	65 cm

Steps 1–2

Step 3

Step 4

Step 5

Step 6

How Tall Is That Flagpole?
Skills: Estimating, measuring a tall object

Show students a neat trick for measuring tall objects with this outdoor activity. Point out to your class a tall object on your school grounds, such as a flagpole, large tree, water tower, or utility pole. Ask students to describe all the methods they could use to go about measuring such an object. Then take the class outside. (Take a pencil with you.) Have students offer their estimates on the height of the object; then measure it! Follow these steps:

1. Stand at a distance from the object and hold the pencil in a vertical position and out in front of you.
2. Move toward or away from the tall object until the pencil seems to extend from its top to its base. See the illustration.
3. Direct a student to stand at the base of the object.
4. Turn the pencil to the left or right so that it is aligned with the ground.
5. Tell the student at the object to start walking along the "path of the pencil" until he reaches the end of the pencil. Then tell him to stop and stay at that position.
6. Have two pairs of students use their measuring tapes to measure from the base of the object to where the student is standing. This measurement will equal the approximate height of the object.

The measurement should be fairly accurate. Identify other tall objects on your campus. Then have pairs of students work together to measure the heights of those objects.

Metric or Customary? Both!

Follow the directions below to make your own metric and customary measuring tape:

1. Carefully cut out the 5 sections.
2. Glue the sections to each other in the correct order.
3. Write your name on the back of the tape.

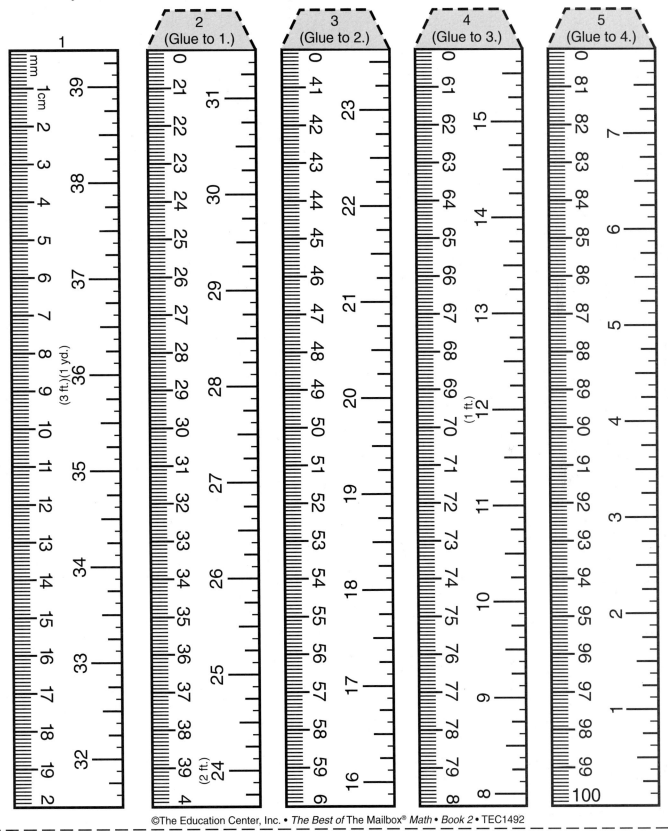

Note to the teacher: Use with the activities on pages 78–80 and 83.

Name_____

Masters of Magic

Part 1: He was an *illusionist,* a magician who performed large-scale tricks. One of his most amazing tricks was the "fantastic suitcase." He pulled birds, cages, hats, and pans from a thin suitcase. Then he ended the trick by lifting out his young son!

Who was this magician? To find out, read each letter and its measurement. Find that measurement on the ruler and write its letter above the arrow. The first one is done for you.

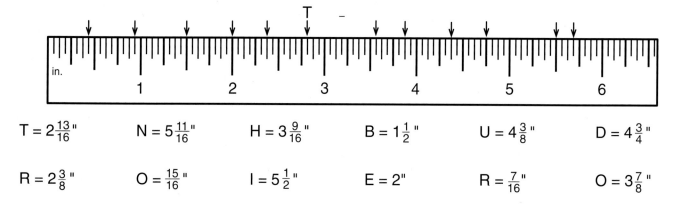

$T = 2\frac{13}{16}"$ $N = 5\frac{11}{16}"$ $H = 3\frac{9}{16}"$ $B = 1\frac{1}{2}"$ $U = 4\frac{3}{8}"$ $D = 4\frac{3}{4}"$

$R = 2\frac{3}{8}"$ $O = \frac{15}{16}"$ $I = 5\frac{1}{2}"$ $E = 2"$ $R = \frac{7}{16}"$ $O = 3\frac{7}{8}"$

Part 2: He was one of the world's most famous escape artists. He could quickly free himself from leg irons, handcuffs, jail cells, and nailed crates. One of his most amazing tricks was escaping from an airtight tank that was filled with water!

Who was this magician? To find out, read each measurement marked with an arrow. Then write the letter at that arrow in the blank above its matching measurement. The first one is done for you.

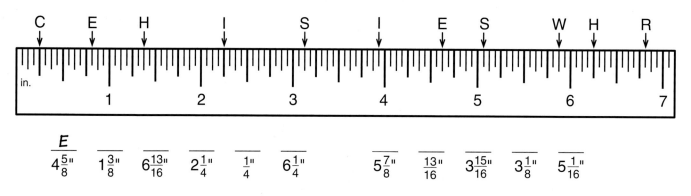

$\dfrac{E}{4\frac{5}{8}"}$ $\dfrac{}{1\frac{3}{8}"}$ $\dfrac{}{6\frac{13}{16}"}$ $\dfrac{}{2\frac{1}{4}"}$ $\dfrac{}{\frac{1}{4}"}$ $\dfrac{}{6\frac{1}{4}"}$ $\dfrac{}{5\frac{7}{8}"}$ $\dfrac{}{\frac{13}{16}"}$ $\dfrac{}{3\frac{15}{16}"}$ $\dfrac{}{3\frac{1}{8}"}$ $\dfrac{}{5\frac{1}{16}"}$

Part 3: The magician in Part 2 was born in Hungary. When he was a child, his family moved to Wisconsin. He took a new stage name when he began performing.

What was this magician's stage name? To find out, read each measurement below. Find the measurement on each of the two rulers above. Then write the letter that is closest to that measurement. One has been done for you.

$1\frac{5}{16}" =$ _____ $1" =$ _____ $4\frac{1}{4}" =$ _____ $4\frac{13}{16}" =$ _____ $5\frac{7}{16}" =$ _____ $5\frac{3}{4}" =$ _____ $2\frac{3}{16}" =$ _____

Bonus Box: In the first puzzle, what is the distance between the first and last letters of the magician's name?

Now You See It...Now You Don't!

Sleight of hand is one of the most common kinds of magic. It includes tricks that depend on the skillful use of the hands. Sleight-of-hand tricks are often performed with a deck of cards. One of the oldest sleight-of-hand routines was performed in ancient Egypt!

Complete the puzzle below to learn another name for sleight of hand. Use a metric ruler to measure each segment. Write the segment name in the blank with its matching measurement.

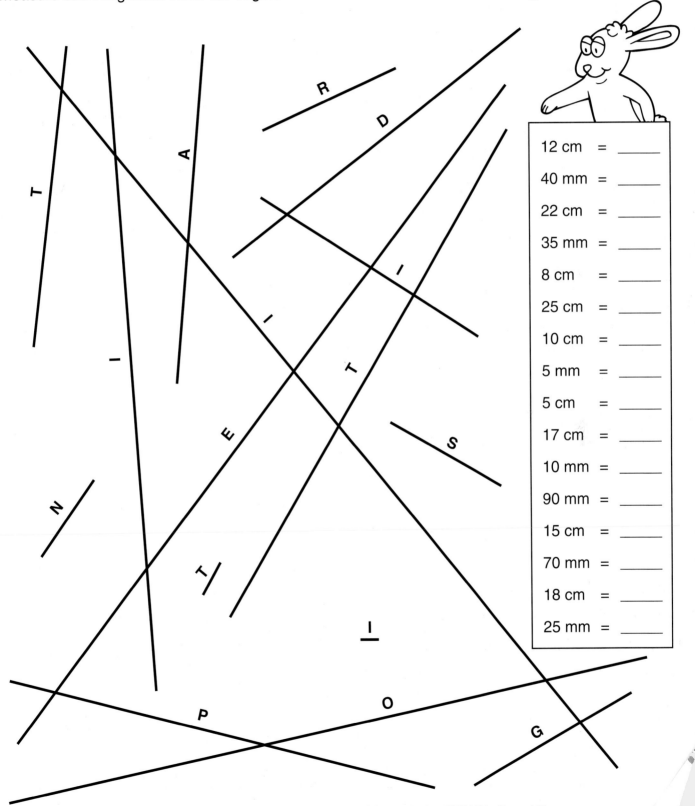

12 cm = _____
40 mm = _____
22 cm = _____
35 mm = _____
8 cm   = _____
25 cm = _____
10 cm = _____
5 mm   = _____
5 cm   = _____
17 cm = _____
10 mm = _____
90 mm = _____
15 cm = _____
70 mm = _____
18 cm = _____
25 mm = _____

Taking the Mystery out of Measurement

Hands-On Activities for Teaching Perimeter, Area, and Volume

Investigating perimeter, area, and volume has never been easier—especially with the following creative activities and reproducibles!

by Irving P. Crump

A Card Mystery

Skill: Comparing perimeter and area

Do shapes with the same area also have equal perimeters? Have your junior detectives find out with this simple hands-on activity. Have each student label three 3" x 5" index cards with one card's dimensions. Then lead students in the following activities:

1. Review the formula for finding the perimeter of a rectangle: $P = 2(L + W)$. Then direct each student to lay his cards on his desk end to end as shown. Have the child compute the perimeter of the shape. *(36 in.)* After reviewing how to find the area of a rectangle ($A = L \times W$), have each student determine the shape's area. *(45 sq. in.)*

2. Have each student lay his cards on his desk as shown. Ask the class to determine the area of this shape. *(45 sq. in.)* Help students see that the total area of the three cards, regardless of how they're arranged, remains 45 square inches. Ask volunteers to predict whether the perimeter of the shape will be the same as when the cards were placed end to end. Then have each student compute this shape's perimeter. *(28 in.)*

3. Have each student lay his cards on his desk as shown. Ask students the area of this shape. *(45 sq. in.)* Then ask if the shape's perimeter will be 36 or 28 inches. Remind students that they must add the measures of all the sides of this shape to find its perimeter. Finally, have students compute the shape's perimeter, which is 32 inches!

Point out to students that although two or more shapes have the same area, they may not have the same perimeter.

The Mystery Continues

Skill: Comparing perimeter and area

Do shapes with the same perimeter have the same area? To find out, give each student a copy of page 86. In Part 1, direct the student to draw a 4-cm square and three rectangles with the following dimensions: 1 cm x 7 cm, 2 cm x 6 cm, and 3 cm x 5 cm. Next, have students determine each shape's perimeter. *(16 cm)* Ask which shape is the largest. After students have shared their predictions, have them compute the area of each shape. *(The areas are 4 cm x 4 cm = 16 sq. cm, 1 cm x 7 cm = 7 sq. cm, 2 cm x 6 cm = 12 sq. cm, and 3 cm x 5 cm = 15 sq. cm. The largest shape is the square.)*

Extend this activity by having students complete Part 2 on the page. After students have drawn their shapes, have each child color the one he thinks has the greatest area. Then have students find the area of each shape. Help students see that although two or more shapes have the same perimeter, they may not have the same area.

More Card Mysteries
Skill: Computing area

Square: Have each student fold down a corner of a 3" x 5" index card to the bottom edge and then cut along the intersection as shown. Then have him unfold this shape and identify it and its dimensions *(a 3-in. square).* Review the formula for finding the area of a square (L x W or s^2); then have students find the shape's area *(9 sq. in.).*

Right triangle: Have each student cut along the fold of her square to form two right triangles. Have her compare one triangle to the whole square. *(It's one-half of the square.)* Then ask students to predict the area of each triangle. *(Since each right triangle is one-half of the square, its area is one-half of the square's area, or $4\frac{1}{2}$ sq. in.)* Help students see why the formula for finding this triangle's area is A = $\frac{1}{2}$ bh, or $\frac{1}{2}$ x base x height.

Any triangle: Have each student fold a second index card in half, cut along a diagonal through both sides as shown, and then unfold the folded section to create three triangles. Have the student place the three pieces back together. Ask students to compare the area of the large triangle to the combined area of the two smaller triangles. *(The areas are equal.)* Ask students to compare the area of the large triangle to the area of the entire card. *(The area of the large triangle is half the area of the card.)* Have students determine the large triangle's height and base *(h = 3 in.; b = 5 in.).* Then ask them how they can find the area of the large triangle. Lead students to see that to find the area of a triangle, one must multiply the base by the height and then halve it. By applying the formula A = $\frac{1}{2}$bh to the large triangle, the students will get $7\frac{1}{2}$ sq. in. *($\frac{1}{2}$ x 5 x 3).* Point out to students that the height and base of a triangle must be known in order to determine the triangle's area. The height and base of a triangle must be perpendicular to each other—they must form a right angle.

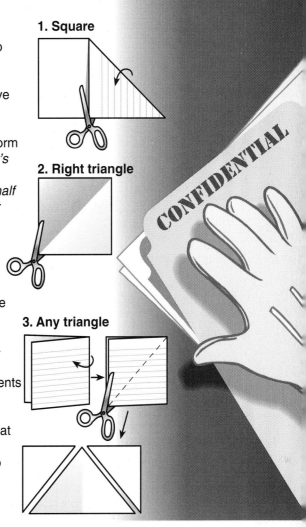

1. Square

2. Right triangle

3. Any triangle

4. Parallelogram

Parallelogram: Have each student flip one of the smaller triangles and then lay the two triangles side by side, as shown, to form a rectangle. Ask students whether they can determine the dimensions of this rectangle *(3 in. x $2\frac{1}{2}$ in. Remind students that one-half of 5 is $2\frac{1}{2}$.).* Then have them compute the area of this rectangle *($7\frac{1}{2}$ sq. in.).* Next, have students place the two shapes together as shown to form a parallelogram. Ask students to predict the area of this parallelogram. *(It's the same as the rectangle: $7\frac{1}{2}$ sq. in.)* Ask if students can determine a formula for finding the area of a parallelogram. Help them discover that the area of a parallelogram is found by multiplying its base by its height *($2\frac{1}{2}$ in. x 3 in.).* Remind students that, like triangles, the height is needed to find the area of a parallelogram. And, like triangles, the base and height must be perpendicular to each other.

Have students move the two small triangles to form a different parallelogram (see the illustration). Ask students to determine the area of this parallelogram. *(Since it's the same size as the original rectangle and the first parallelogram formed above, its area is $7\frac{1}{2}$ sq. in.)* Have students determine the base and height of this parallelogram; then apply the formula A = bh to find the area. *(b = 3 in. and h = $2\frac{1}{2}$ in., so the same area results: $7\frac{1}{2}$ sq. in.)*

The Case of Perimeter vs. Area

Part 1: Draw 1 square and 3 rectangles according to your teacher's directions.

Part 2: Draw 1 square and 3 rectangles. Each shape must have a perimeter of 24 cm.

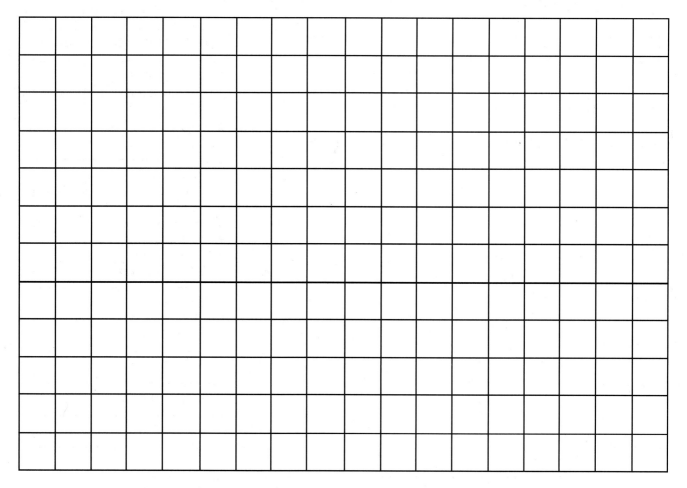

Note to the teacher: Use with "The Mystery Continues" on page 84.

The Scene of the Crime

It's a crime that happens nearly every day. But it won't make the headlines of your local newspaper. The diagram below shows the floor plan of the crime scene. Follow the directions below to identify the crime.

Directions:

The dimensions of some rooms in the diagram are not given. Use the number clues provided to help you determine the missing lengths and widths. Write them on the diagram. Then complete the following steps:

1. Find the perimeter and area of each room. Show all of your work on another sheet of paper.
2. Match each room's letter to that room's perimeter and area listed in the chart.
3. When you're finished, you will identify the crime. Case closed!

The crime:

perimeter/area	letter
84 ft./216 ft.^{2}	
40 ft./96 ft.^{2}	
60 ft./216 ft.^{2}	
108 ft./288 ft.^{2}	
48 ft./108 ft.^{2}	
36 ft./72 ft.^{2}	
84 ft./432 ft.^{2}	
84 ft./96 ft.^{2}	
72 ft./180 ft.^{2}	
72 ft./324 ft.^{2}	
96 ft./252 ft.^{2}	
44 ft./120 ft.^{2}	

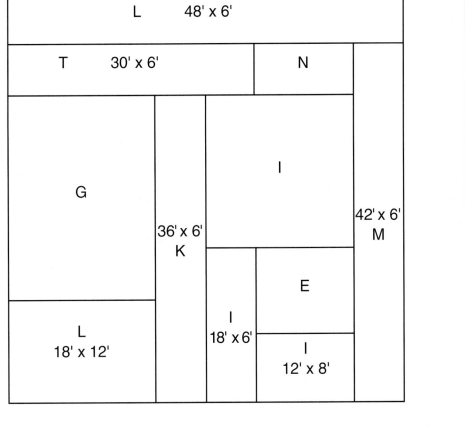

(Floor plan rooms: L 48' x 6'; T 30' x 6'; N; G; K 36' x 6'; I; M 42' x 6'; L 18' x 12'; I 18' x 6'; E; I 12' x 8')

Bonus Box: Compute the perimeter and area of the entire building above.

A Backlog of Cases

There's a backlog of cases that need to be investigated! Below are eight cases for you to solve. Are you up for the challenge? Use your knowledge of area and perimeter—and a little logical detective work—to solve each one. Write each answer on the file folder.

1. _____ This unusual rug is made up of five square sections, each the same size. The area of the entire rug is 80 square feet. What is the perimeter of the rug?

2. _____ This box of fencing will be used to enclose a rose garden. What is the area of the largest possible garden that the fence will go around? Sketch the garden in the space provided. Show its length and width.

Garden Depot
36 1-ft. Sections

3. _____ How many 4" x 6" cards can be cut from the sheet of poster board?

36 in.

48 in.

4. _____ A square sheet of drawing paper has an area of 400 square inches. It was cut in half to make two equal rectangles. What is the perimeter of each rectangle?

5. _____ The sidewalk around the pool is five feet wide. What is the total area of the sidewalk?

80 ft.

50 ft.

6. _____ A farmer divided her square garden into six equal rectangular sections. The area of the garden is 144 square yards. What is the perimeter of each section?

7. _____ The walkways that cut through and surround this garden are three feet wide. What is the area of the garden? (Hint: Cut out the garden.)

← 10 ft. →

3 ft.

8. _____
   _____ Cut out the square, two triangles, and parallelogram. Put them together to make a rectangle. What is the perimeter of the rectangle? What is its area?

6 ft.

Bonus Box: On the back of this sheet, draw a square whose area and perimeter are the same.

Edible Explorations

Activities for Teaching Two- and Three-Dimensional Measurement

Investigate *area, perimeter, volume,* and more with unique exercises that have kids measuring with standard and nonstandard units. Just solicit snack donations from parents; then measure away with activities that are packed with edible fun!

by Peggy W. Hambright

Positively Perimeter

Skill: Measuring perimeter

Captivate students with a fun activity that develops the concept of *perimeter* as the distance around the outside of a closed figure. Give students the listed materials; then guide them through the steps below, pausing to answer questions and give assistance as needed.

Materials for each student:
box of raisins (1$\frac{1}{2}$-ounce size)
color-segmented gummy worm
six to eight pretzel sticks
sheet of duplicating paper
centimeter ruler
desk mat (12" x 18" sheet of construction paper)
copy of the top half of page 94

Directions:
1. Look at the size of your raisin box. Then study your gummy worm, noting the length of its colored segments. Estimate how many segments are needed to make one trip around the outside of your raisin box. Record this number on your sheet.
2. Trace the raisin box on the recording sheet; then label the box's sides 1, 2, 3, and 4.
3. Using the candy worm, measure how many segments long—to the nearest whole segment—each side of the box is. Then write each length on your recording sheet.
4. Add the four measurements together to find the perimeter of the box in gummy worm segments.
5. Repeat this procedure using pretzel sticks.
6. Next, estimate the length of each of the raisin box's sides to the nearest centimeter; then record the estimate for each side in the chart on your sheet.
7. Use a centimeter ruler to measure each of the four labeled sides to the nearest centimeter. Record the measurements for each side in the chart.
8. Find the perimeter of the raisin box in centimeters by adding the four lengths together.
9. Now enjoy your gummy worm, pretzel sticks, and raisins as you write your own definition of *perimeter* in the blanks!

89

Making Circumference Make Sense

Skill: Measuring circumference

Introduce *circumference* as simply circular perimeter with another snackin'-good activity. Give each student the listed materials; then guide him through the steps below to discover that circumference is the distance around a circle.

Materials for each student:
chocolate chip cookie
rice (or popcorn) cake
York Peppermint Pattie, unwrapped
Ritz cracker
length of Twizzlers Pull-N-Peel candy
desk mat (12" x 18" sheet of construction paper)
centimeter ruler
straight pin
copy of the bottom half of page 94

Directions:
1. Arrange the circular snacks on your desk mat. Estimate the distance around each one in centimeters; then record the estimates on your sheet.
2. Using your length of Twizzlers candy, measure the distance around each snack. To help in marking each measurement, stick the straight pin into the candy length at the end of the measured distance.
3. Measure the marked length of Twizzlers candy with your centimeter ruler; then record the measurement on your sheet. Remove the pin from the candy.
4. Next estimate the length of each snack's *diameter* (the line segment which passes from one side of a circle to the other through its center). Record each estimate.
5. After estimating, use a centimeter ruler to measure each snack's diameter. Then record each diameter on your sheet.
6. Compare the measured diameter and circumference of each snack. For example, if the cookie's diameter is 6 cm and its circumference is 18 cm, how are these numbers related? If the numbers are related, what is the rule? Is one number a multiple (or close to being a multiple) of the other?
7. Enjoy your snacks while you write a definition of *circumference*. Also explain the relationship between diameter and circumference. *Note: Circumference ≃ (is approximately equal to) three times the diameter.*

Nothing but Perimeter?

Skills: Estimating and measuring perimeter

Incorporate critical thinking with linear measurement by having students first investigate which rectangular candy bars are the best buys—based on perimeter. Give a different candy bar to each student. Have each student estimate what he thinks the candy bar's perimeter is in centimeters. Then instruct him to measure the four sides of the candy bar with a ruler and determine its actual perimeter. List the name of each candy bar on the board or on chart paper next to the perimeters supplied by students. Have students assume that the cost of each candy bar is the same. Then invite each student to enjoy his candy bar while he writes a paragraph giving reasons why he thinks a particular candy bar is the best buy. Encourage the student to also consider the candy bar's *mass* when stating his reasons. (For more information, see the answer key on page 159.)

Zooming In on Volume

Skill: Estimating and measuring volume

Involve students in an activity that zeros in on the concept of volume. Distribute the listed materials to student groups. Then lead the groups through the steps below to help them understand that volume is the amount of space enclosed by a space figure.

Materials for each student:
box of raisins (1½-ounce size)
desk mat (12" x 18" sheet of construction paper)
copy of the top half of page 95
scissors
transparent tape
calculator
80 cubic centimeters (per group)
Note: If cubic centimeter models are not available, have students construct them using centimeter grid paper. Instruct students to cut six-unit shapes like the one shown below; then have them tape the sides together to make cubes. Cubes can be taped together to make the rows needed for Step 5 below.

Directions:
1. Remove one raisin from your box. Based on its size, estimate how many raisins are inside the box. Record this number on your sheet. Also record estimates from other group members. Then use a calculator to find the group's average estimate of raisins per box, rounding the quotient to the nearest whole number.
2. Empty your box of raisins onto the desk mat. Count and record the exact number of raisins. How close was your estimate to the exact count? Record the exact count from other group members' boxes; then find the average number of raisins per box for your group.
3. Pick up one cm³ (cubic centimeter) and study it. Estimate the total number of cm³ it will take to fill your raisin box if you place them side by side in neat rows. Record your estimate and each of your group members' estimates.
4. Find the average number of cm³ that your group thinks it would take to fill the box as described. Record the group's average estimate.
5. As a group, work together to construct the rows of connected cm³ needed to fill just one raisin box. Then count the total number of cm³ and record it on your sheet as the box's volume.
6. Compare the actual number of cm³ it took to fill the box with the number you estimated. How close was your estimate to the exact number?
7. Now enjoy eating your raisins as you write your own definition of volume!
   Note: Collect the empty raisin boxes and save them for the surface-area activity that follows on page 92.

Pam Crane

Squaring Off With Area

Skills: Estimating and measuring area

Let students come face-to-face with *area* by disassembling a raisin box and following a few simple directions. First, demonstrate how to open the raisin box saved from the "Zooming In on Volume" activity on page 91 so that it does not tear and lies flat. Next, give each student the materials listed below. Then guide students through the steps that follow to help them understand that area is the number of square units inside a closed area.

Materials for each student:
empty raisin box ($1\frac{1}{2}$-ounce size—saved from "Zooming In on Volume" on page 91)
9" x 12" sheet of colored paper
transparent tape
small plastic bag filled with Corn Chex cereal
piece of centimeter grid paper
copy of the bottom half of page 95
pencil

Directions:

1. Open the raisin box's flaps and sides so that it lies flat. Place the box on the colored paper. Tape down the edges of the box so that they lie flat. Notice the box's irregular shape.

2. Hold a piece of Corn Chex cereal in your hand. Estimate how many of these pieces it would take to cover the box's flattened surface. Record this number on your sheet.

3. Cover all but the irregular edges of the box's surface with cereal squares, placing them side by side in neat rows.

4. Estimate how many more cereal pieces are needed to cover the area that's still showing (the irregular parts of the box's shape). Add this estimate to the number of cereal pieces that already cover the box. Then record the total on your sheet.

5. Carefully remove the taped box from the colored paper. Place the box on the centimeter paper and trace around it.

6. Remove the box from the centimeter paper. Count the whole centimeter squares and record this number on your sheet.

7. To estimate how many whole squares are represented by the remaining p artial ones, count and record the number of partial squares. Find out what half of that number is by dividing it by two and rounding the quotient to the nearest whole number. Add this number to the number of whole squares; then record the total on your sheet as the box's estimated surface area.

8. Now write your own definition of area on your sheet as you enjoy your Corn Chex cereal!

The Right Combination

Skills: Area and perimeter, problem solving

Challenge students to combine measurement concepts and problem solving with this critical-thinking activity. Give each student a supply of pretzel sticks, a desk mat (a sheet of 12" x 18" construction paper), and several sheets of centimeter-spaced dot paper (see the illustration). Tell the student that he is to construct, with you, a rectangle on his desk mat that has a perimeter of 10 units and an area of 6 square units. Make Figure 1 on the overhead with toothpicks while class members make the same shape with pretzel sticks on their mats. Verify and discuss with students that the constructed shape indeed has the same perimeter and area that you designated. Discuss with students whether this figure could be turned another way and still have the same perimeter and area (Figure 2). Repeat this same procedure by constructing a nonrectangular figure with a perimeter of 10 units and an area of 4 square units (Figure 3).

Next, write the measurements from the list shown below on the overhead. Explain to students that the letters P and A stand for perimeter and area. Instruct the students to copy the list onto their own papers. Have them construct the figures with pretzels and then draw each one on dot paper. When students have finished building and sketching their figures, ask volunteers to come to the overhead and reconstruct each one on a dot-paper transparency. (See the answer key on page 159.)

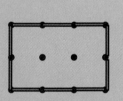

Figure 1   **Figure 2**   **Figure 3**

Construct the following rectangles:
1. P: 12 units; A: 8 sq. units
2. P: 12 units; A: 9 sq. units
3. P: 14 units; A: 12 sq. units
4. P: 6 units; A: 2 sq. units
5. P: 10 units; A: 9 sq. units
6. P: 20 units; A: 9 sq. units
7. P: 18 units; A: 20 sq. units
8. P: 22 units; A: 18 sq. units

Construct the following nonrectangular figures:
9. P: 10 units; A: 5 sq. units
10. P: 12 units; A: 6 sq. units

93

Positively Perimeter

Measuring With Nonstandard Units

1. Estimated perimeter in gummy worm segments: _____
2. Actual length in gummy worm segments:

   Side 1: _____   Side 2: _____

   Side 3: _____   Side 4: _____

3. Perimeter of raisin box in gummy worm segments: _____
4. Estimated perimeter in pretzel-stick units: _____
5. Actual length in pretzel sticks:

   Side 1: _____   Side 2: _____

   Side 3: _____   Side 4: _____

6. Perimeter of raisin box in pretzel-stick units: _____

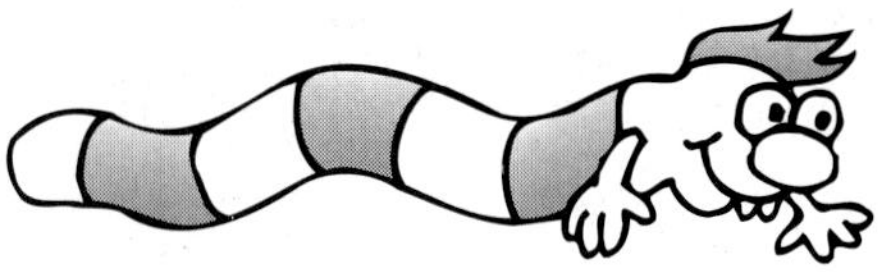

(Trace around the raisin box inside this space.)

Perimeter is _____

_____

_____

Measuring With Standard Units

	Estimated	Actual
Side 1		
Side 2		
Side 3		
Side 4		

Perimeter of raisin box: _____ cm

Bonus Box: Trace an item from your desk on the back of this sheet. Use your centimeter ruler to find its perimeter.

©The Education Center, Inc. • *The Best of* The Mailbox® Math • *Book 2* • TEC1492 • Key p. 159

Making Circumference Make Sense

Circular Snack	Estimated Circumference in cm	Measured Circumference in cm	Estimated Diameter in cm	Actual Diameter in cm

1. Circumference is _____

_____

2. Explain how diameter and circumference are related: _____

_____

_____

Bonus Box: List the circumference of the snacks from largest to smallest on the back of this sheet.

©The Education Center, Inc. • *The Best of* The Mailbox® Math • *Book 2* • TEC1492 • Key p. 159

Note to the teacher: Use the top reproducible with "Positively Perimeter" on page 89. Use the bottom reproducible with "Making Circumference Make Sense" on page 90.

Name _____

Zooming In on Volume

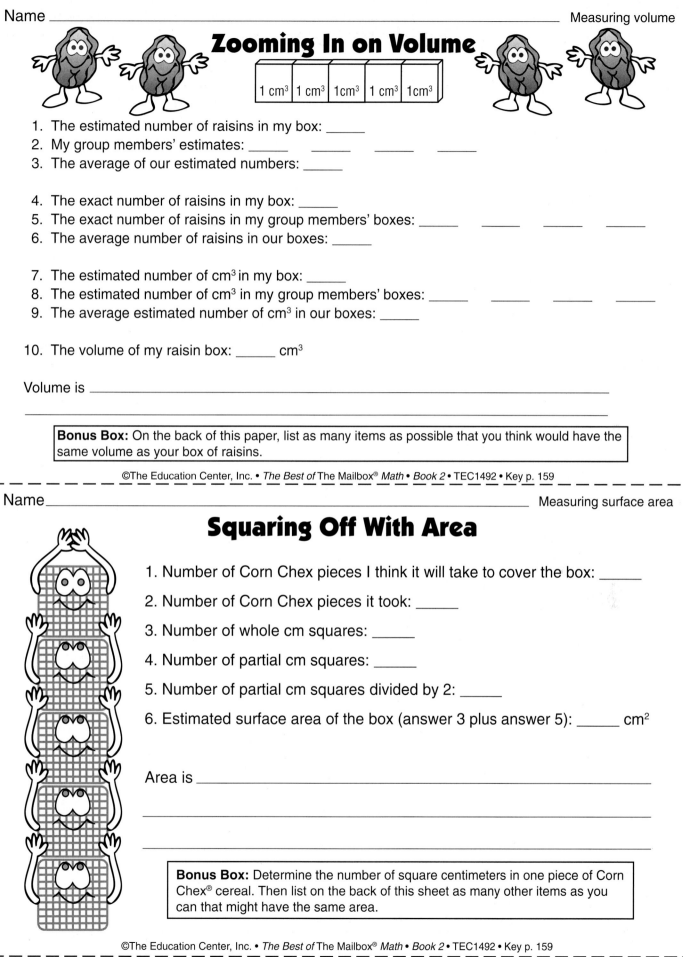

| 1 cm³ | 1 cm³ | 1cm³ | 1 cm³ | 1cm³ |

1. The estimated number of raisins in my box: _____
2. My group members' estimates: _____   _____   _____   _____
3. The average of our estimated numbers: _____

4. The exact number of raisins in my box: _____
5. The exact number of raisins in my group members' boxes: _____   _____   _____   _____
6. The average number of raisins in our boxes: _____

7. The estimated number of cm³ in my box: _____
8. The estimated number of cm³ in my group members' boxes: _____   _____   _____   _____
9. The average estimated number of cm³ in our boxes: _____

10. The volume of my raisin box: _____ cm³

Volume is _____

_____

> **Bonus Box:** On the back of this paper, list as many items as possible that you think would have the same volume as your box of raisins.

Name _____

Squaring Off With Area

1. Number of Corn Chex pieces I think it will take to cover the box: _____

2. Number of Corn Chex pieces it took: _____

3. Number of whole cm squares: _____

4. Number of partial cm squares: _____

5. Number of partial cm squares divided by 2: _____

6. Estimated surface area of the box (answer 3 plus answer 5): _____ cm²

Area is _____

_____

_____

> **Bonus Box:** Determine the number of square centimeters in one piece of Corn Chex® cereal. Then list on the back of this sheet as many other items as you can that might have the same area.

Note to the teacher: Use the top reproducible with "Zooming In on Volume" on page 91. Use the bottom reproducible with "Squaring Off With Area" on page 92.

Graphing Activities That Hit the Spot!

Looking for ideas that will help students collect, organize, display, and interpret data? Then check out the following creative teaching activities and reproducibles. They're sure to hit the spot!

Graph SPOTS
Skill: Interpreting graphs

Information in our world is growing at an astounding rate, and a lot of it is often presented in graphs. Help students better understand the graphs they encounter with this evaluative activity. Collect graphs from a variety of sources, such as newspapers, magazines, advertisements, and food products. Glue the graphs onto 12" x 18" sheets of poster board, including many graphs of the same type (or a variety) on each sheet. Laminate the sheets; then give them to individual students, pairs, or small groups. Also provide each student with a copy of "Graph SPOTS" on page 99. Have the student choose one graph, read and interpret the information on it, and complete the reproducible. Post the students' evaluations and the graph posters on a bulletin board titled "Graphs We've Spotted!" *Lisa Groenendyk—Gr. 4, Pella Christian Grade School, Pella, IA*

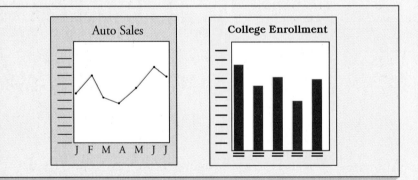

"Para-graphs"
Skill: Making bar and double-bar graphs

Challenge students to take a closer look at the words they read with this data-collecting activity! First, have each student bring to class a magazine or newspaper article. Instruct each student to read the first eight sentences in the article and count the number of words in each sentence. Then have students create bar graphs to display their data.

Next, discuss with students the vocabulary and the lengths of sentences they encounter in different types of reading material. Ask students how a paragraph in a newspaper article compares to one in a class novel. Then have each student choose a paragraph from each of three different types of reading materials, such as a novel, a magazine, a newspaper, an encyclopedia, a primary-level library book, etc. Have the student read the first five sentences in each selection and count the number of words and syllables in each sentence. Then instruct her to make a double-bar graph that compares the numbers of words and syllables in the three paragraphs chosen. To complete the activity, have each student share her conclusions in a brief paragraph. *adapted from an idea by Libby Latham-Davis—Gr. 4, Wateree Elementary, Lugoff, SC*

	total years working	total years teaching	years teaching at our school
1.	12	10	10
2.	17	16	14
3.	9	9	9
4.			

We Love Our Teachers!
Skill: Making a histogram

Students will learn more about the teachers in your school with this data-collecting activity! First, copy the following questions on the chalkboard.

- Including jobs in high school and college, how many total years have you been working?
- How many total years have you been teaching?
- How many years have you been teaching in our school?

Next, divide students into pairs. Instruct each twosome to copy the questions on a large index card. Then send one student pair to interview each teacher in your school.

When all data has been collected, draw on the board a chart similar to the one shown; then have each pair write its information in the chart. To complete the activity, divide the class into three groups. Assign one set of data—work years, teaching years, or years teaching in your school—to each group. Then have each student work independently to make a histogram that displays his group's assigned set of data.

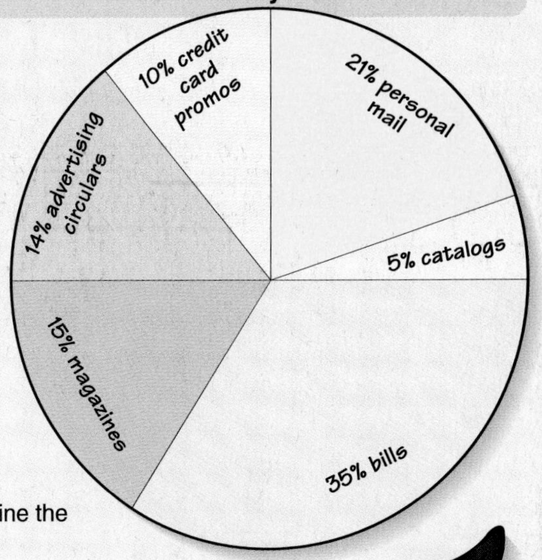

It's in the Mail!
Skill: Making a circle graph

How much mail does the average family receive each week? Find out with this data-collecting activity! Brainstorm with students the different types of mail their families receive, such as bills, personal letters, magazines, advertising circulars, catalogs, credit card promotionals, and postcards. Next, have each student keep a tally of each piece of mail his family receives during a six-day period (Monday through Saturday), collecting his data in a frequency table. After the data has been collected, give each student a copy of the pattern on page 99. Then direct him to follow these steps:

1. Add to find the total pieces of mail.
2. Count the total pieces of mail in each category.
3. Find the percentage of the total pieces of mail that each category represents.
4. Multiply each percentage times 360 (the number of degrees in a circle) to determine the section size for each category.
5. Draw, label, and color each section of the circle.
6. Give the graph a title.

Family Mail

(Circle graph)
- 10% credit card promos
- 21% Personal mail
- 14% advertising circulars
- 5% catalogs
- 15% magazines
- 35% bills

In the News
Skill: Making a line graph

There's more to a newspaper than just news, as students will find out with this line-graphing activity. Each day for a week, bring to class a local daily newspaper (including Saturday and Sunday editions). Ask students to donate their copies too. Next, divide students into groups of three. Assign each group one of the topics shown. Then have the group determine its data for each day and display it in a line graph. Remind students that a line graph shows change over a period of time, so they'll be graphing data from seven days' worth of newspapers. Have each trio glue its final graph on a 12" x 18" sheet of poster board. Display the graphs on a bulletin board backed with newspapers and titled "Line Graphs in the News!"

Topics:
- the number of pages in each edition
- the number of photographs in each edition
- the number of column inches devoted to the major front-page news story
- the daily high or low local temperatures listed in the newspapers
- the number of column inches devoted to advertising in one section
- the number of people whose photographs are featured in a particular section
- the number of different cities listed in the datelines of a particular section
- the number of games reported on in the sports section

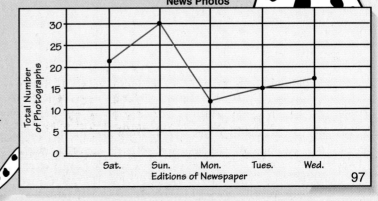

News Photos

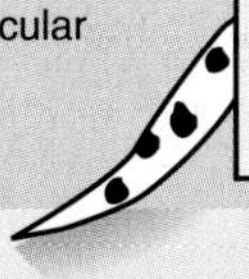

(Line graph: Total Number of Photographs vs. Editions of Newspaper)
Y-axis: 0, 5, 10, 15, 20, 25, 30
X-axis: Sat., Sun., Mon., Tues., Wed.

My Very Own Graphing Project

Skill: Planning a data-collecting and graphing project

After you've completed a unit on statistics and graphing, challenge each student to complete his own investigative graphing project! First, explain that each student will decide on a question (one that includes a comparison between two or more sample populations) that can be answered by conducting a survey and collecting data. Then the student will organize, display, and analyze that data. Give each student or student pair a copy of the planner on page 100. Then have students follow along on their planners as you share the sample project with them.

- The *problem statement* states the question. (For example: Does a person's age affect his or her music preference?)
- The *hypothesis* states what you believe to be true. (For example: People under 21 years of age are more likely to enjoy rock music than people over 21.)
- The *materials* list includes anything that you need to complete the project.
- The *procedure* is a detailed plan explaining how you will carry out the research. You must identify your population groups and describe the sample you will survey, making sure it is representative of the population. You'll also explain how you will conduct your survey, describe how you will organize the data, and determine which graph to use for displaying the data. For example:
  1. The population samples are adults over 21 and people under 21.
  2. Survey 25 people in each group.
  3. Offer limited responses with these choices: rock, classical, folk, jazz, and easy listening.
  4. Use a frequency table to collect and organize the data.
  5. Display the data using a double-bar graph. The x-axis will list the music choices; the y-axis will represent the number of respondents.
  6. One bar will represent people over 21, the other bar people under 21. The title will be "Musical Preferences."
- The *conclusion* analyzes and interprets your results, deciding if your hypothesis was correct. Use the data collected to draw conclusions. Then prepare a report that shares your project with the rest of the class.

Post the list of topics below for students to choose from. Remind students that you must sign off on their completed planner sheets before they begin to collect data. *Terry Castoria—Gr. 5, Frank Defino Central School, Marlboro, NJ*

Ideas for Graphing Project

- types of transportation that students in different grade levels use to travel to school
- sleeping needs of different age groups
- exercise habits of different age groups
- how different age groups spend their leisure time
- types of television shows that different age groups watch
- amount of television-viewing time of different age groups
- automobile preferences of different age groups
- food preferences of different age groups
- types of reading materials that different age groups prefer
- whether or not kids of different ages wear appropriate safety equipment when riding bikes, scooters, and/or skateboards
- time spent on the computer by different age groups
- types of snack food preferred by different age groups
- how different age groups prefer to get the news: TV, radio, newspaper, magazine, etc.
- most popular form of entertainment of different age groups

Name______________________________ Evaluating a graph

Graph SPOTS

Can you spot the following information on the graph that you're evaluating? After examining the graph, answer the following questions.

Source: Who or what organization created the graph?

____

What date is on the graph? ______________________________

Is the information current? __________ Explain. ______________

____

Purpose: What does the graph communicate to us?

____

____

____

Organization: What type of graph is it? ______________

Title: What is the title of the graph? ______________

____

Scale and/or symbols: What number scales are used in the graph? What symbols are used, and what do they represent? ______________

____

____

____

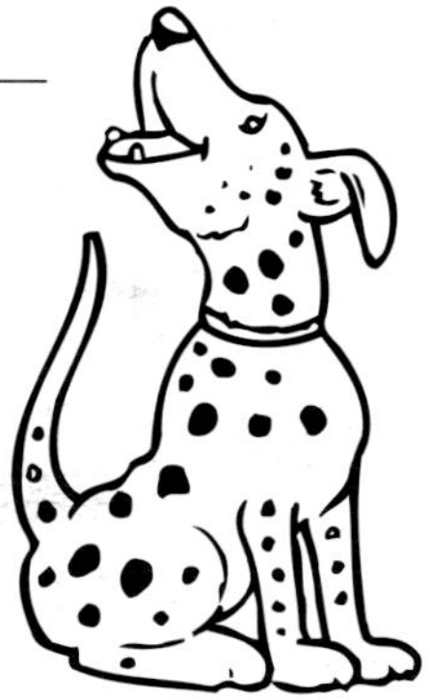

Circle Graph Pattern

____

(title)

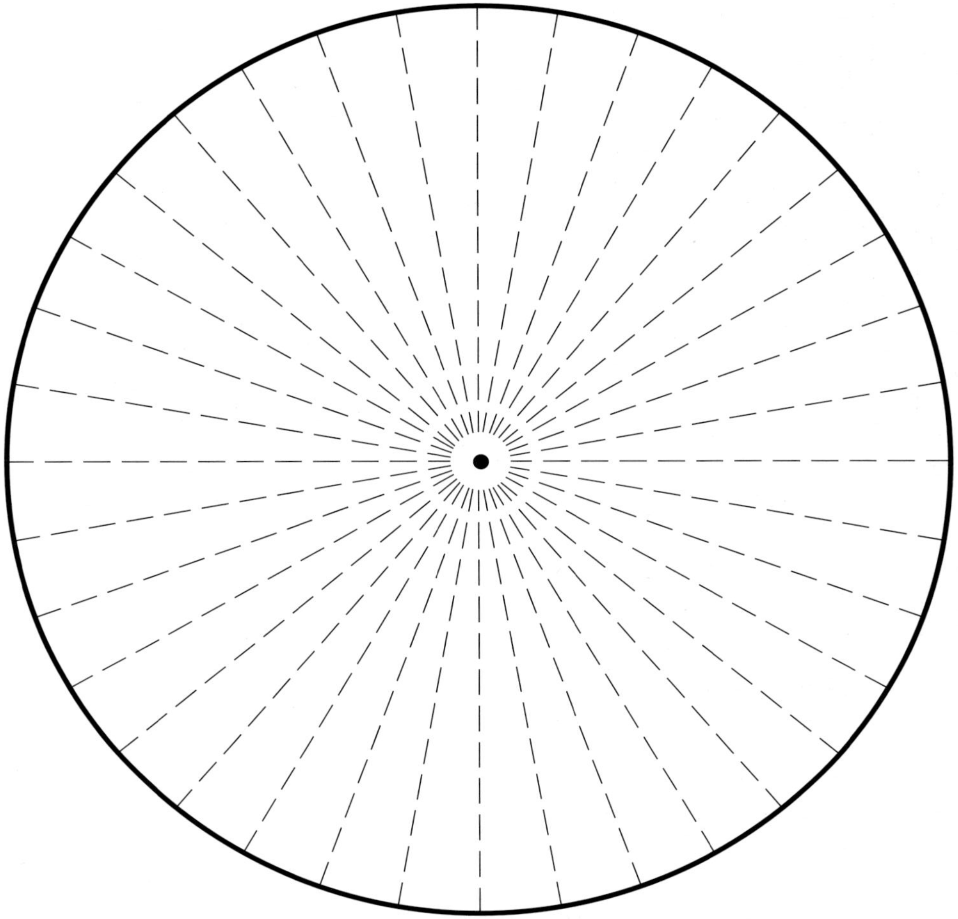

Note: Each section of the circle represents 10°.

Note to the teacher: Use the graph evaluation form with "Graph SPOTS" on page 96. Use the circle graph pattern with "It's in the Mail!" on page 97.

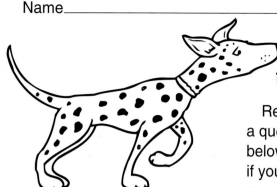

Pointing the Way
to a Great Graphing Project!

Ready to tackle a great graphing project? First, decide on a question you want to answer. Then complete the sections below. Staple additional sheets of paper to the back of this page if you need more space. Finally, ask your teacher and a parent/guardian to sign the blanks at the bottom of the page.

Project Planner

Problem Statement: Write the question you want to answer. _____

_____

Hypothesis: What do you believe to be true? _____

_____

Materials: List any materials that you need.

_____   _____   _____

_____   _____   _____

Procedure: Explain how you will carry out your research.

1. Identify your population groups. _____

   _____

2. Describe the sample you will survey, making sure it is representative of the population.

   _____

3. Explain how you will conduct your survey. _____

   _____

4. Explain how you will organize the data you collect. _____

   _____

5. What kind of graph will you use to display your data? _____

6. How will you set up your graph? _____

   _____

   _____

Conclusion: Analyze and interpret your results. Was your hypothesis accurate? Use the data to draw conclusions. Then prepare a report about your project to share with the rest of the class.

Teacher: _____   Parent/guardian: _____

©The Education Center, Inc. • *The Best of* The Mailbox® *Math* • *Book 2* • TEC1492

100   **Note to the teacher:** Use with "My Very Own Graphing Project" on page 98.

Making a stem-and-leaf plot

Spots and More Spots!

How many spots do 101 dalmatians have all together? Well, what about 23 dalmatians? Look at the doghouses below that show the number of spots on each dalmatian. Then follow the steps below to make a stem-and-leaf plot to organize and display the data. In a stem-and-leaf plot, the ones digits appear in rows as leaves. Tens (and larger) digits appear in a column as stems. The plot has been started for you.

Bo: 20
Bob: 38
Bib: 9
Bub: 27
Spot: 12
Brock: 27
Bear: 24

Al: 22
Hal: 33
Sal: 15
Kyle: 14
Cal: 23

Ed: 41
Jed: 45
Ned: 17
Fred: 43
Ted: 31
Red: 39

Timmy: 7
Sammy: 18
Pammie: 5
Jimmy: 27
Tammy: 12

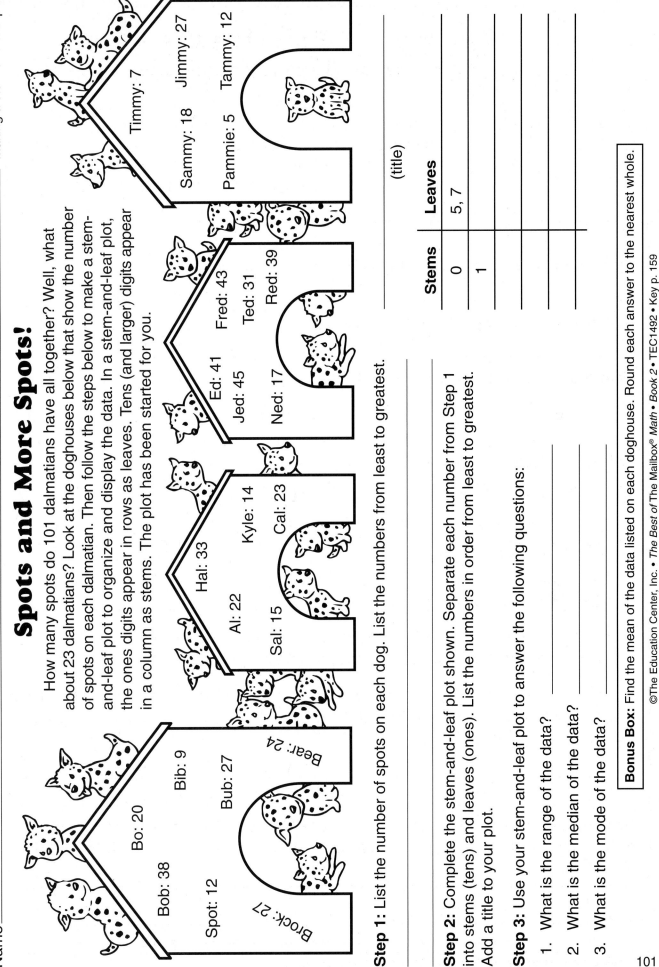

Stems	Leaves
0	5, 7
1	

(title)

Step 1: List the number of spots on each dog. List the numbers from least to greatest.

_____

Step 2: Complete the stem-and-leaf plot shown. Separate each number from Step 1 into stems (tens) and leaves (ones). List the numbers in order from least to greatest. Add a title to your plot.

Step 3: Use your stem-and-leaf plot to answer the following questions:

1. What is the range of the data? _____

2. What is the median of the data? _____

3. What is the mode of the data? _____

Bonus Box: Find the mean of the data listed on each doghouse. Round each answer to the nearest whole.

GRAPHS UNDER CONSTRUCTION

Creative, Hands-on Activities for Building Graphing Success

Collecting data—then graphing that data—is one way students can make sense of the tons of information in their lives. Include the following creative teaching suggestions and learning experiences to help your students build graphing skills.

by Irving P. Crump

Keeping It All Together
Skill: Building vocabulary

One key for successfully collecting and displaying data is organizing. Help students with this skill throughout your graphing activities by providing them each with a copy of the miniposter on page 105 and a blank folder. Have each student color and decorate his miniposter and then open his folder and paste the miniposter on the left side. On the side adjacent to the miniposter, have each student copy the math terms shown, allowing plenty of space for definitions and examples. Have students refer to their folders often, adding definitions and other terms as needed. Encourage students to store all related work and reproducibles in the folder as well.

- statistics
- tally sheet
- frequency table
- bar graph
- pictograph
- number scale
- interval
- vertical axis
- horizontal axis
- histogram
- line graph
- circle graph

Graphs in the News
Skill: Recognizing differences in data displays

Introduce the term *statistics* to your students, asking what it means to them. Then share that statistics is "the branch of math that deals with collecting, organizing, displaying, and analyzing data." Discuss with your students the different types of graphs they've seen. Then ask them to cut out and bring to class some of those graphs. Newspapers and newsmagazines—especially *USA Today, Time, Newsweek,* and *U.S. News & World Report*—regularly include bright, colorful graphs that display a variety of trends, information, and current events. Title a bulletin board "Picture This!" and post the graphs on it. Invite students to view the graphs and discuss them with each other.

On a sheet of chart paper, list the different types of data that are shown in the graphs. Ask students, "Why is a graph a useful way to display data?" *(A graph is concise and easy to read and provides a pictorial display of information.)* Continue having students add graphs to the display throughout your unit.

Introducing the Histogram
Skill: Making a histogram

A *histogram* is a special bar graph that shows the number of times data occurs within a certain range. While the bars in a bar graph and in a histogram are of the same width, the bars in a histogram are connected with no space between them. Another difference between the two is that a bar graph shows specific information and a histogram's information is much more general.

To collect data for students to use in a histogram, tape two yardsticks end-to-end on a wall so that each student can measure her height. Then divide students into pairs. Have the students in each pair measure each other's height to the nearest inch. When all heights are determined, have each student write her initials and her height on the chalkboard. Ask students to study the data and think about what intervals (ranges) should be included in a histogram to display the data (examples: 50–54 in., 55–59 in., 60–64 in., etc.). Stress that the intervals must all be equal. Next, provide each student with a copy of page 107 on which to make a histogram of the class data.

Clevell Harris

hour	number of visitors
8:00 – 9:00	
9:00 – 10:00	
10:00 – 11:00	
11:00 – 12:00	
12:00 – 1:00	
1:00 – 2:00	
2:00 – 3:00	

On the Line
Skill: Making a Line Graph

A *line graph* shows changes and variations over a period of time. To make a line graph, students follow the same guidelines as those for making a bar graph—except that lines are drawn instead of bars.

Early one morning before your instructional day begins, direct each student to label a sheet of paper as shown. Then tell students that they are going to keep a record of the number of visitors to your class during the day—both adults and children. Beginning with the 8:00 to 9:00 interval, have each student make a tally mark for each individual who comes to the classroom door during that hour. Even if the visitor does not enter the classroom, have students make a tally mark for him or her. Then, near the end of the day, instruct each student to make a line graph displaying the collected data for homework. Have each student draw his graph on a copy of the reproducible on page 107. Have student groups compare their graphs the next day.

A Piece of the Pie
Skill: Making a circle graph

A *circle graph* (also called a pie chart) shows the parts of a whole and the relationships among those parts. Model a circle graph by sharing with students a typical Saturday in your life! Since a day has 24 hours, such a graph should be divided into 24 equal parts. Approximate the time you spend on each activity to the nearest hour; then list the data on the board. To get—and keep—your students' attention, embellish your day somewhat. For example, list the following data on the board: 7 hours—sleeping, 1 hour—schoolwork, 2 hours—meals, 3 hours—skateboarding, 4 hours—skydiving lessons, 5 hours—mountain climbing, and 2 hours—training your pet boa constrictor.

Next, draw on the chalkboard the 24-section circle graph shown (or make a transparency of the one on page 106). Have students assist you as you complete your graph. As a follow-up, give each student a copy of page 106. Instruct each student to complete the 24-section circle graph to show a typical Saturday in his life—or perhaps one he would like to experience!

103

Tally Sheet

number of letters in name	number of students
2	
3				
4	‡‡
5			
6	‡‡ |||
7			
8					

Tally Up!
Skill: Collecting Data

Using a *tally sheet* is a simple way to collect data. Ask students, "Who in our class has the longest first name? How many students have names with that many letters?" Call on several volunteers to suggest how they would organize the data you're asking for. Their responses will likely include:

- List students' names. Then count the letters in each one. Write that number beside the name.
- Make columns with number headings (2 letters, 3 letters, etc.). Write each name in the matching column.
- List numbers (2 letters, 3 letters, etc.) in a column. Write each name beside the matching number.

Next, make a tally sheet, like the one shown, on a transparency or the chalkboard, adding more numbers if necessary. In turn, have each child state his name and the number of letters it has. As each number is given, make a tally mark beside the corresponding number on the transparency. When finished, ask students whether your original questions have now been answered. Also ask whether this method was an efficient way to answer the questions. Then continue with the next activity to show a simple way to display this information.

Using a Frequency Table
Skill: Making a frequency table

Beside the tally sheet (from the preceding activity), make a *frequency table* like the one shown. Then ask, "Which number of letters on the tally sheet has the most matching names? How many names?" Write this information in the first line of the table. Continue with the number of letters that has the second-most matching names. Add this information in the second line of the table. Continue filling the table until every student is represented. Then ask, "Which display is easier to read: the tally sheet or the frequency table?" *(The frequency table is easier to read because the information is listed in an orderly fashion. Also there are no tally marks to count, and facts can be found more readily.)*

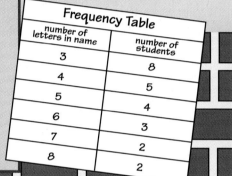

Frequency Table

number of letters in name	number of students
3	8
4	5
5	4
6	3
7	2
8	2

---

1. Let A be the *year* in which you were born.
   A = 1994
2. Let B be the *day of the year* on which you were born.
   January: 31 days
   February: 28 days (unless it is a leap year)
   March: 31 days
   April: 12 days
   B = 102nd day of the year (31+ 28+ 31+12 = 102)
   B = 102
3. Find C: C= (A − 1) ÷ 4. Ignore the remainder.
   C = (1994 − 1) ÷ 4 = 1993 ÷ 4 = 498 R1
   C = 498
4. Find D: D = A + B + C
   D = 1994 + 102 + 498
   D = 2,594
5. Divide D by 7.
   2,594 ÷ 7= 370 R4. Note the remainder: **4**

Use the table below to see which day of the week matches the remainder of the division problem in Step 5.

(The student born on April 12, 1994, was born on a Tuesday.)

Remainder:	Birthday:
0	Friday
1	Saturday
2	Sunday
3	Monday
4	Tuesday
5	Wednesday
6	Thursday

Bar Graphs and Pictographs
Skill: Making bar graphs and pictographs

Ask students what kinds of graphs they see most often in magazines and textbooks, and they'll likely say *bar graphs* and *pictographs*. Share with students that these graphs show comparisons of data. And although a pictograph is usually colorful and eye-catching, it doesn't show specific data as well as a bar graph does. Have students collect data to display in a bar graph or pictograph by asking, "On which day of the week were you born?" Share the steps for determining one's day of birth shown in the chart at the left. Then, as you guide students, have them complete each step. (The chart includes a completed sample birthdate, April 12, 1994.) When everyone has finished, draw a tally chart and frequency table on the chalkboard. Ask each student to state his day of birth as you complete the tally sheet. Then organize the tally sheet results in the frequency table, beginning with the day of the week with the most tally marks.

To complete the activity, give each student a copy of page 107. Direct half of the class to make bar graphs and the other half to make pictographs of the information listed in the frequency table. Suggest that students review the information on their miniposters to help them.

_____
(architect's name)

Tally Sheet

Best Building Materials*	
straw	IIII
sticks	ℍℍ II
bricks	ℍℍ ℍℍ II

*according to P.B.A. (Pig Builders Assoc.)

Frequency Table

Material	Number of Votes
bricks	12
sticks	7
straw	3

TIPS FOR BUILDING A GREAT GRAPH

1. Give your graph a title.
2. Label the *vertical axis*—from the base to the top.
3. Label the *horizontal axis*—from left to right at the bottom.
4. If you're making a *pictograph,* show the symbol and its value in a key.
5. If you're making a *bar graph,* make sure the bars are the same width. Also use equal space between the bars.
6. If you're making a *histogram,* all of the bars should be side by side.
7. Use the correct number scale. Make sure the intervals are equal (1–5, 6–10, 11–15, 16–20, etc.).

Circle Graph
A Wolf's Day

12 hours exercising (to build up lungs!)

8 hours sleeping

4 hours eating

Pictograph
Wolf Exercises

aerobics weights running

♥ = 2 wolves

Histogram

Time It Takes P.B.A. Members To Build Houses

number of builders

0–6 7–12 13–18 19–24

hours

Bar Graph
Wolf Puffs Blown at Each House

number of puffs

straw sticks bricks*

materials

*gave up after 16 puffs!

Line Graph
Pigs' Home Insurance Costs

hundreds of dollars

May June July

Note to the teacher: Use with "Keeping It All Together" on page 102.

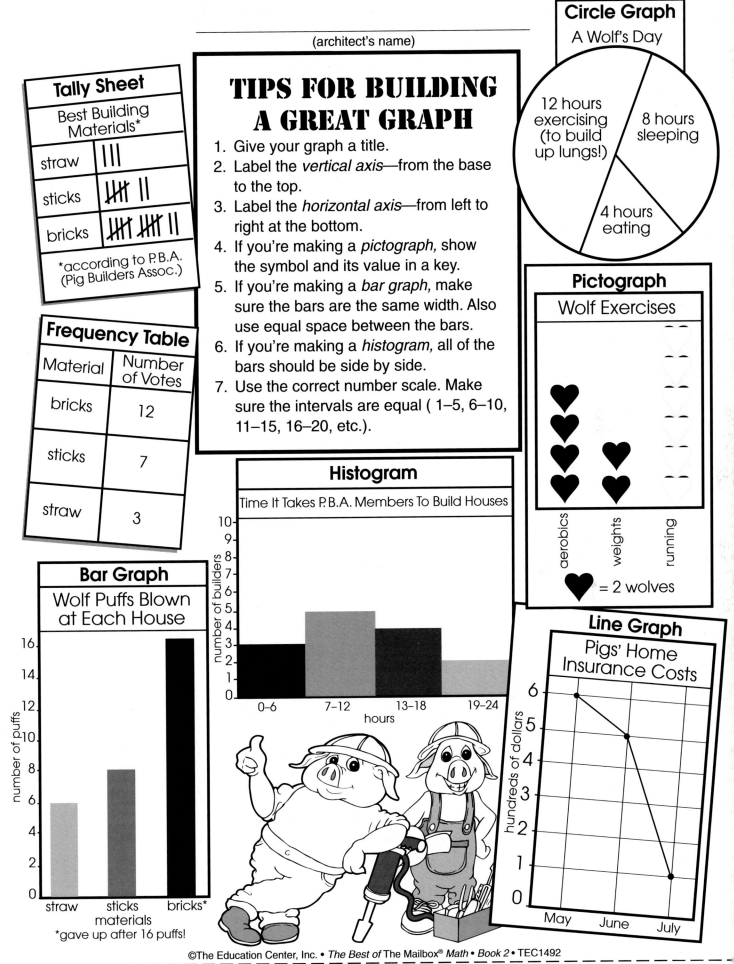

Name

106

BUILDING CIRCLE GRAPHS

A circle graph divided into 24 equal sections can be used to show a variety of data:

- Use the graph to display data about a 24-hour day.
- Divide the graph into 3, 4, 6, 8, or 12 (all factors of 24) equal sections to display other data. For example: 1 of 12 equal sections equals 5 minutes of an hour.

A circle graph divided into 100 equal sections can be used to show a variety of data:

- Use the graph to display percentages, which are based on 100.
- Use the graph to show parts of a dollar. For example: 10 of 100 equal sections equals $0.10.
- Divide the graph into 5, 10, 20, 25, or 50 (all factors of 100) equal sections to display other data. For example: 8 of 50 equal sections equals 8 U.S. states.

0

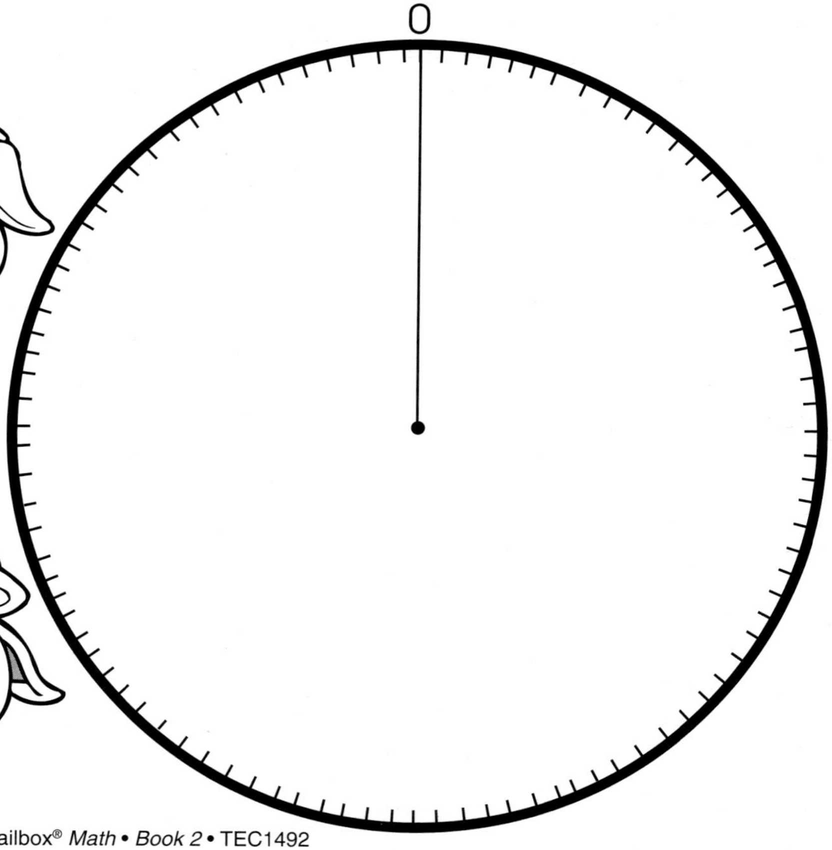

0

©The Education Center, Inc. • *The Best of The Mailbox® Math • Book 2 • TEC1492*

Note to the teacher: Use with "A Piece of the Pie" on page 103.

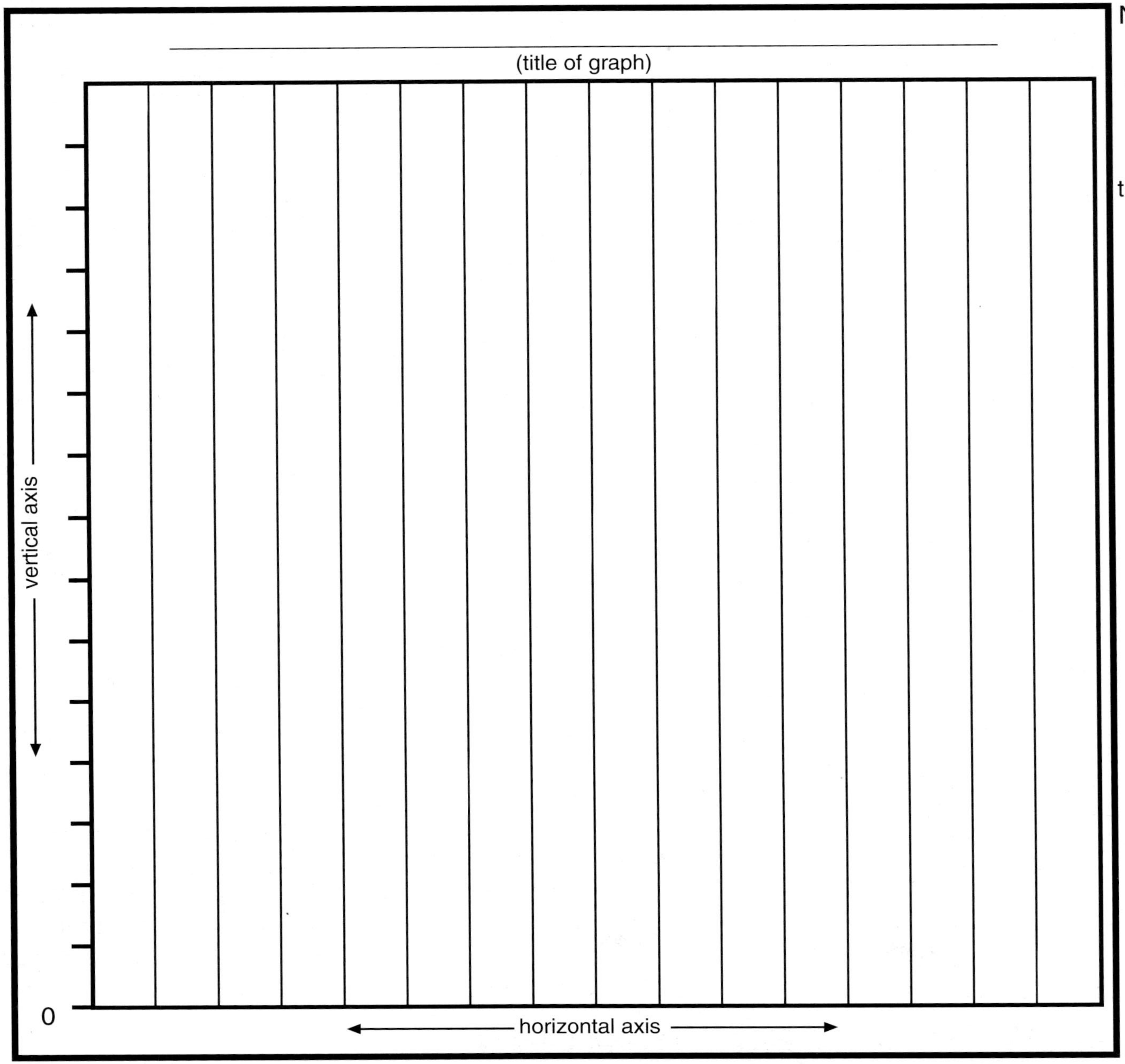

A BLUEPRINT FOR BUILDING GRAPHS

Follow this plan to create graphs that are the envy of the neighborhood!

1. Title the graph.
2. Label the vertical axis: base to top.
3. Label the horizontal axis: left to right at the bottom.
4. *Bar Graph:*
   a. Bars should be of equal width.
   b. Use equal space between bars.
   c. Use a number scale with equal intervals (ranges).
   d. Use a ruler to make sure the bars are the right heights.
5. *Pictograph:*
   a. Use a key to show the symbol and its value.
   b. Label only one axis.
6. *Histogram:*
   a. Bars should be of equal width.
   b. Bars are connected. There is no space between them.
   c. A histogram gives general information (for example: the number of runners who finish a race between 50 and 60 minutes).
7. *Line Graph:*
   a. Make a bar graph, but leave off the bars!
   b. Mark points on a line graph.
   c. Connect the points with straight lines.

(title of graph)

← horizontal axis →

← vertical axis →

0

Note to the teacher: Use with "Introducing the Histogram" and "On the Line" on page 103 and "Bar Graphs and Pictographs" on page 104.

DEALING WITH DATA

Hands-on Lessons for Teaching Range, Mean, Median, and Mode

Guide your students to gather, organize, and study data—and better understand *range, mean, median,* and *mode*—with the following creative teaching ideas.

with contributions by Sandy Spaulding—Gr. 5, Sacramento, CA

Presenting the Most Popular Letter
Skill: Using range, mean, median and mode to analyze data

Which letter appears most often in your students' names? This whole-group, warm-up activity is a fun way to introduce your class to the terms *range, mean, median,* and *mode.* First, write the letters of the alphabet in four or five columns on one half of a chalkboard. Spread out the columns to provide plenty of space for tally marks. In turn, have each student come to the board and make a tally mark beside each letter of his first name. If a letter appears more than once, it should be tallied that number of times.

After everyone has tallied his letters, have students assist you in listing the letters and numbers on the other half of the board—beginning with the letter(s) that occur(s) least often to the one(s) with the most tally marks. Have students study this list; then ask them:

- What is the greatest number of tally marks? The least? What's the difference between those two totals? *The difference between the greatest number and least number in a set of data is the* **range.**

- What is the sum of all tally marks? *(Allow students time to add the totals for all 26 letters.)* Find the average. *Students should divide the total by 26 and round the quotient to the nearest whole number. The* **mean** *is the average of a group of numbers.* Do any letters have numbers of tally marks that equal the *mean?*

- Which number in the list is exactly in the middle of the list? *Since there are 26 numbers, none can be exactly in the middle.* Which *two* numbers are in the middle? Find the average of those two numbers. *The 13th and 14th numbers are in the middle, so students must find the average of those two numbers. For example: If the 13th and 14th numbers are 12 and 18, then the average is 15. This middle number or average of the two middle numbers is called the* **median.**

- Which number(s) appear(s) most often? *There can be more than one answer—or maybe none. In this activity, there likely will be more than one. The number(s) that occur(s) most often in a group of numbers is called the* **mode.**

Announcing the Number One Number
Skill: Using range, mean, median, and mode to analyze data

Follow up the above activity with a similar exercise based on your students' telephone numbers. First, list the digits 0–9 in a column on a chalkboard. Have each student, in turn, come to the board and make tally marks for the *last four digits* of his phone number. When everyone has taken a turn, ask students to help you list the ten digits again, in order from the least number of tally marks to the greatest. Follow the same line of questioning from the above idea based on the new data that you now have. Guide students to independently determine the range, mean, median, and mode.

Data Days: A Week's Worth of Lessons on Range, Mean, Median, and Mode

Getting Ready

The following activities incorporate information that students can relate to and easily gather. First have each student store a copy of page 112 and 113 in a folder. Then make only one copy each of pages 110 and 111. Ask volunteers to color these pages for you. Cut the four signs apart; then laminate them for durability.

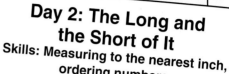

Day 1: Glued to the Tube?
Skills: Telling time to the nearest half-hour, ordering numbers

Post the first sign from page 110 (television) in the middle of a bulletin board or chalkboard. Discuss the sign; then give the homework assignment for that night. Have each student keep an accurate record of the amount of time she watches television—from right after school until bedtime. Instruct each student to note the time to the nearest half hour (0.5) in large numerals on her response sheet (page 112).

The next day, have each student cut out her response from page 112 and attach it to the board. Help students arrange their totals in a horizontal row in ascending order. Display duplicate responses in columns. Then assign Part 1 on page 113 as classwork or homework.

Day 2: The Long and the Short of It
Skills: Measuring to the nearest inch, ordering numbers

Discuss and check Day 1's assignment. Next, post the height sign (page 110). Divide students into pairs. Provide each pair with a 12-foot-long piece of string and scissors. Have each student cut a piece of string that matches his partner's height. After each student measures his own string to the nearest inch, he notes his height on his response sheet (the ball of string on page 112). Have each student cut out his response and tape the end of his string to it at the bullet. Help students arrange their responses in ascending order on the board. If there are duplicate responses, arrange them side by side. When everyone has posted his response, assign Part 2 on page 113 for classwork or homework.

Day 3: School Stats
Skill: Ordering numbers

After checking and discussing Day 2's assignment, post the class-size sign (page 111). Have volunteers visit each homeroom class in your school to find out its enrollment. Instruct each volunteer to note the total on his response sheet. Next, have each helper cut out the response and attach it to the board, arranging the numbers in a horizontal row in ascending order. If there are duplicate answers, place them in columns. When every response has been posted, assign Part 3 on page 113.

Day 4: In Search of Bigfoot
Skills: Measuring to the nearest half-inch, ordering numbers

Discuss and check Day 3's assignment. Next, post the foot sign (page 111). Divide students into pairs. Have each pair use the ruler on page 112 to measure each other's right foot (with the shoe on) to the nearest one-half inch. Have each student note the length of his foot on his response page and cut it out. Next, help students arrange their responses on the board in ascending order, placing duplicate responses in columns. After everyone has responded, assign Part 4 on page 113 for classwork or homework. Check students' responses based on the data that was collected.

How many hours of TV do you usually watch each day?

Write the number (to the nearest half hour) in the TV set on your response sheet. Cut out your response and attach it to the board with your classmates' responses in order from least to greatest.

©The Education Center, Inc. • *The Best of The Mailbox*® *Math* • *Book 2* • TEC1492

How tall are you?

Cut a piece of string the same length as your partner's height. Give your partner the piece of string. Now measure your piece of string (to the nearest inch) and write your height on your response sheet. Cut out the response and attach it to the board with your classmates' responses in order from least to greatest.

©The Education Center, Inc. • *The Best of The Mailbox*® *Math* • *Book 2* • TEC1492

Note to the teacher: Use with "Glued to the Tube?" and "The Long and the Short of It" on page 109.

How many students are in each class in our school?

Find out how many students are in one class at our school. Write the number on the response sheet. Cut out your response and attach it to the board with your classmates' responses in order from least to greatest.

©The Education Center, Inc. • *The Best of The Mailbox® Math • Book 2* • TEC1492

How long is your right foot?

Use the ruler on the response sheet to measure your partner's foot (with his or her shoe on) to the nearest 1/2 inch. Write your foot's length on the response sheet. Cut out your response and attach it to the board with your classmates' responses in order from least to greatest.

©The Education Center, Inc. • *The Best of The Mailbox® Math • Book 2* • TEC1492

Note to the teacher: Use with "School Stats" and "In Search of Bigfoot" on page 109.

Name _____

Day 1
Write your name and the number of hours of TV that you watched.

_____
(name)

watched

_____

hours of television.

©2003 The Education Center, Inc.

Day 2
Write your name and your height to the nearest inch. Then cut out the form and tape your string to it.

_____
(name)

is

_____

inches tall.
Tape the end of your string here: •

©2003 The Education Center, Inc.

Day 3
Write the teacher's name and the number of students in his or her class.

's

_____
(teacher's name)

class has

_____

students.

©2003 The Education Center, Inc.

Day 4
Write your name and your right foot's length to the nearest one-half inch (0.5).

's

_____
(name)

right foot is

_____

inches long.

©2003 The Education Center, Inc.

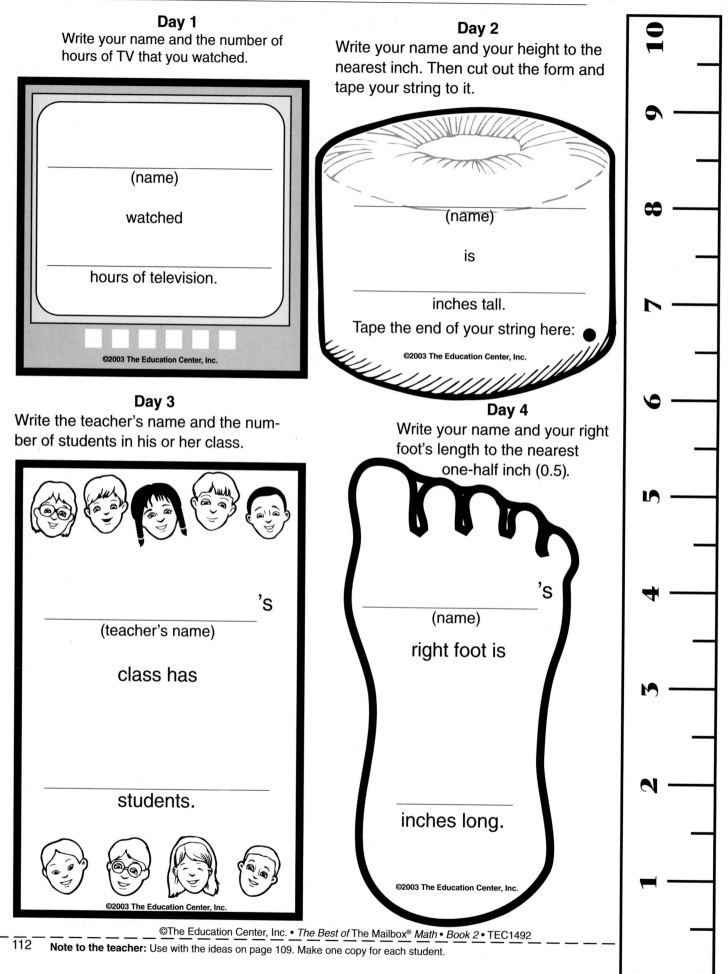

©The Education Center, Inc. • *The Best of* The Mailbox® *Math • Book 2 •* TEC1492

Note to the teacher: Use with the ideas on page 109. Make one copy for each student.

Staking Out Statistics

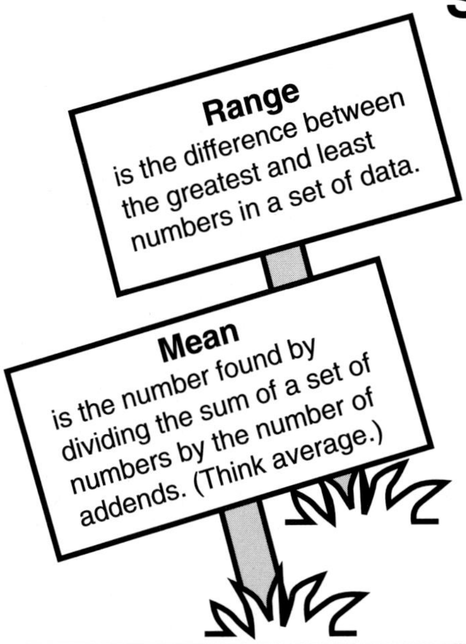

Range
is the difference between the greatest and least numbers in a set of data.

Mean
is the number found by dividing the sum of a set of numbers by the number of addends. (Think average.)

Fill in the chart with the data you and your class-mates gathered. Then com-plete the boxes at the right of each set of data. Find the *range, mean, median,* and *mode* of each set. Refer to the signs for review.

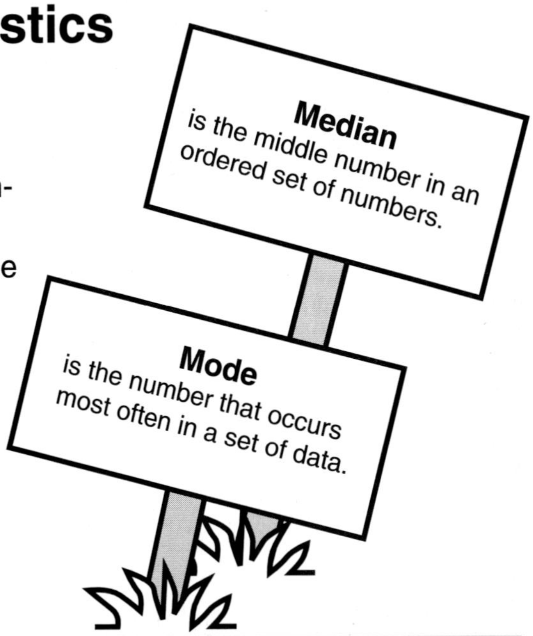

Median
is the middle number in an ordered set of numbers.

Mode
is the number that occurs most often in a set of data.

data	range	mean	median	mode
 1				
 2				
 3				
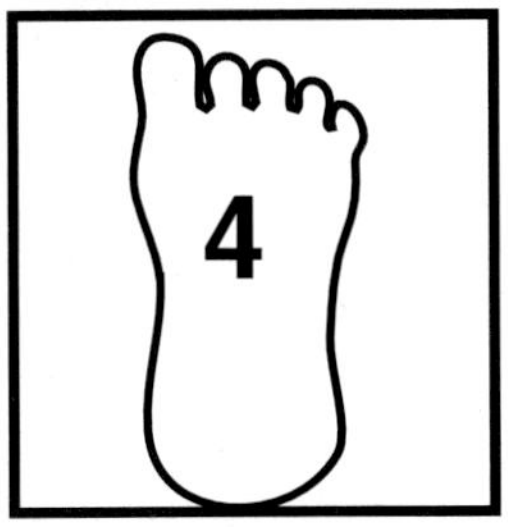 4				

Note to the teacher: Use with the ideas on page 109. Make one copy of this page for each student.

Chances Are...

Activities for Investigating Probability

Increase your students' chances of mastering probability with the following investigations!

Certain, Impossible, or Somewhere in Between?

Skill: Determining the likelihood of an event

What's the likelihood that students will love this activity? You can bet on it! Begin by briefly reviewing with the class the meanings of the following terms: *certain* (always happens), *likely* (could happen), *impossible* (could not happen). Next, have each student number a sheet of paper from 1 to 8. Then read aloud one statement at a time from the list shown. Have each student record whether he thinks that event's occurrence is certain, likely, or impossible. When students have responded to all of the statements, discuss the answers together. For more practice, challenge each student to write five similar statements of his own. Then have him trade with a classmate and check his partner's responses.

1. The clock will say six o'clock twice today unless it stops working. *(certain)*
2. You will grow nine feet today. *(impossible)*
3. I will eat a meat, a vegetable, a fruit, or bread today. *(likely)*
4. If you throw a paper airplane up into the air, it will come down unless something or someone interferes with it. *(certain)*
5. If I roll a die ten times, I will roll a five at least once. *(likely)*
6. The baby will take an afternoon nap. *(likely)*
7. I will sharpen my pencil today. *(likely)*
8. The girl walked 30 miles in just two hours. *(impossible)*

Smiley Probabilities

Skill: Representing the likelihood of an event with a number

Here's an easy-to-do probability activity that's sure to put a big :-) on every-one's face! Display the chart shown. Explain to students that the combinations of letters and symbols are called *smileys,* small pictures of faces (turned sideways) used to express different emotions. Ask, "If these 12 smileys are shown on cards, what is the likelihood of drawing a card that contains an exclamation point?" *(impossible)* Explain that this impossible event can be represented with the number 0. Ask, "What is the likelihood of drawing a card that does not contain the letter *S?*" *(certain)* Explain that this certain event can be represented with the number 1. Then ask, "What is the likelihood of drawing a card containing an asterisk?" *(2 of 12: kiss, hug and kiss)* Explain that this likelihood can be represented with the fraction $^2/_{12}$, which can be reduced to $^1/_6$. Finally, divide the class into pairs. Challenge each twosome to create three questions based on the chart: one to represent with a 0, one to represent with a 1, and one to represent with a fraction. Follow up by having each student complete a copy of "Odds Are…" on page 116 as directed.

:-)	Smile
:-(	Sad
:-D	Laugh
:'(	Cry
:-O	Shout
;-)	Wink
:-*	Kiss
{*}	Hug and kiss
:-&	Tongue-tied
:-()	Can't stop talking
%-(	Confused, unhappy
:-#	I wear braces.

Take a Spin!

Skills: Predicting the outcome of an event, testing predictions

Use this "spinner-ific" activity to help students learn more about predicting the outcome of events and testing their predictions. Pair students; then give each pair a sheet of unlined paper and two paper clips. Direct the pair to draw two spinners on its paper as shown. Next, display on a chalkboard or transparency the questions shown. Have each pair answer both sets of questions on another sheet of paper. Then have each twosome follow these steps to test its predictions:

1. Practice using the spinner with a paper clip and pencil as shown.
2. Copy the charts shown on another sheet of paper.
3. Spin each spinner 20 times and record the results in the appropriate chart.

Check students' results together.

TEST 1		TEST 2	
Results for A		**Results for A and B**	
Spin	**Result**	**Spin**	**Result**
1		1	
2		2	
3		3	
4		4	
5		5	
6		6	
7		7	
8		8	
9		9	
10		10	
11		11	
12		12	
13		13	
14		14	
15		15	
16		16	
17		17	
18		18	
19		19	
20		20	

TEST 1 Questions

If you spin Spinner A:
1. What is the probability of getting a 1? *($^1/_6$)*
2. What is the probability of getting an even number? *($^6/_6$ or 1)*
3. What is the probability of getting a number greater than 2? *($^4/_6$ or $^2/_3$)*
4. What is the probability of getting a 12? *($^0/_6$)*
5. What is the probability of getting a 2 or a 4? *($^2/_6$ or $^1/_3$)*

TEST 2 Questions

If you spin Spinners A and B:
1. What is the probability of getting two 3s? *($^0/_{36}$)*
2. What is the probability of getting a sum of 7? *($^4/_{36}$ or $^1/_9$)*
3. What is the probability of getting a sum of 10 or higher? *($^{21}/_{36}$ or $^7/_{12}$)*
4. What is the probability of getting a sum of 11? *($^6/_{36}$ or $^1/_6$)*
5. What is the probability of getting a sum of 3? *($^2/_{36}$ or $^1/_{18}$)*

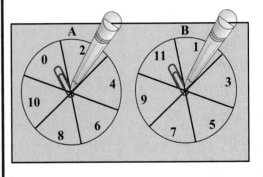

Fair and Square?

Skills: Determining the fairness of a game, identifying square numbers

Challenge students to predict a game's outcome before it's played with this nifty activity! Pair students; then give each twosome one die and six $^1/_2$-inch round removable labels. Have each pair program the labels with the numbers 49, 32, 86, 64, 144, and 16 and then affix them to the die. Explain that a *square number* is the product of a whole number multiplied by itself (for example, nine is the product of 3 x 3). Ask students whether they are more likely to roll a square number or a nonsquare number using the die *(square, because four of the six sides have square numbers)*. Then ask which type of number is less likely to be rolled *(nonsquare, because only two of the six sides have nonsquare numbers)*.

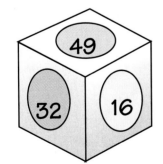

Next, display the game rules shown. Ask students which player they think will win the game *(the player assigned to the square numbers, since there are more square numbers on the die than nonsquare ones)*. Finally, have each pair play the game to see whether it is fair to both players *(no, because Player 1 has a greater chance to win than Player 2)*.

Rules for the game:
- Player 1 has the square numbers. Player 2 has the numbers that are not square.
- Each player takes turns rolling the die and recording the result of each roll in a frequency table for a total of 20 rolls.
- A player earns two points each time he or she rolls one of his or her assigned numbers.
- The winner is the player with more points after 20 rolls.

Number	Tally	Frequency
49		
32		
86		
64		
144		
16		

115

Name ———————————————————

Odds Are...

Is a giraffe likely to outlive a kangaroo? What are the chances of drawing a particular card from a deck? Find out for yourself by following the directions below!

Part 1: Study the chart of average animal life spans on the right. Use the words *likely* or *unlikely* to record the likelihood of each event below happening.

1. a giraffe outliving a kangaroo _____

2. a lobster outliving a polar bear _____

3. a gorilla living 15 years _____

4. a pig living 11 years _____

5. a mouse or a squirrel outliving _____ a lion

6. an Asian elephant living 70 _____ years

7. a Bactrian camel's life span _____ being triple that of a kangaroo

8. a chipmunk's life span being _____ half that of a cat

Animal	Average Life Span (in years)	Animal	Average Life Span (in years)
Box turtle	100	Cat (domestic)	12
Asian elephant	40	Dog (domestic)	12
Grizzly bear	25	Leopard	12
Horse	20	Giraffe	10
Gorilla	20	Pig	10
Polar bear	20	Squirrel	10
Rhinoceros (white)	20	Red fox	7
Black bear	18	Kangaroo	7
Lion	15	Chipmunk	6
Lobster	15	Rabbit	5
Rhesus monkey	15	Guinea pig	4
Rhinoceros (black)	15	Mouse	3
Bactrian camel	12	Opossum	1

(Source: *The World Almanac for Kids 1998*, K-111 Reference Corporation)

Part 2: Study the chart of Roman numerals on the left. Suppose that each number and its corresponding symbol is written on a different card. Use the code shown to represent the likelihood of each event below.

Number	Symbol	Number	Symbol
1	I	20	XX
2	II	30	XXX
3	III	40	XL
4	IV	50	L
5	V	60	LX
6	VI	70	LXX
7	VII	80	LXXX
8	VIII	90	XC
9	IX	100	C
10	X	200	CC
11	XI	300	CCC
12	XII	400	CD
13	XIII	500	D
14	XIV	600	DC
15	XV	700	DCC
16	XVI	800	DCCC
17	XVII	900	CM
18	XVIII	1,000	M
19	XIX		

Code

0 = impossible   1 = certain
fraction between 0 and 1 = possible

What is the likelihood of drawing a Roman numeral...

9. containing an *I, V, X, L, C, D, or M*? _____

10. having both an *X* and a *V*? _____

11. not containing four of any letter? _____

12. having two *V*s? _____

13. that is a multiple of 10 and has an *X*? _____

14. having two *L*s? _____

15. that is a multiple of 3? _____

16. from 400 to 900 and having three *C*s? _____

©The Education Center, Inc. • *The Best of* The Mailbox® *Math • Book 2* • TEC1492 • Key p. 159

116   **Note to the teacher:** Use with "Smiley Probabilities" on page 114.

LASSOING LISTS

Creative Ideas for Teaching Organized Listing

It's a student's worst math nightmare: a problem has more than one possible answer! What to do? A complete and organized list can help show all of the choices. Include the following creative ideas on *your* list of activities when you teach this useful problem-solving strategy.

by Irving P. Crump

Put It There, Pardner!

Skills: Using the act-it-out strategy, making an organized list

Introduce organized listing with this fun demonstration. Have two students come to the front of the classroom and shake hands with each other. Ask the class, "Is there any other possible combination of handshakes when two people shake hands with each other?" *(no)* Write the data shown on a chalkboard, replacing the letters with students' names.

> **A-B**
> **1 handshake**

- Invite a third student to join the pair. Then ask, "If *three* students shake hands with each other, how many different handshakes are possible?" Next, have Student A shake hands with Students B and C. List these two combinations on the board as shown. Have Student B shake hands with Student C. Write this combination on the board. Ask, "Should Student B shake hands with Student A? Should Student C shake hands with either Student A or B?" *(No, these combinations have already been made.)* With three students, three different handshakes are possible.

> **A-B   B-C**
> **A-C**
> **3 handshakes**

- Next, have a *fourth* student join the three at the front of the class. Ask, "If *four* students shake hands with each other, how many different handshakes are possible?" Then have Student A shake hands with Students B, C, and D. Write these combinations on the board. Next, have Student B shake hands with Students C and D, and write these combinations on the board. Ask why Student B shouldn't shake hands with Student A. *(They have already shaken hands with each other.)* Lastly, have Student C shake hands with Student D and write that combination on the board. Ask, "Should Student D shake hands with any of the other three students?" *(No, students A, B, and C have already shaken hands with student D.)* Six different handshakes are possible with four students.

> **A-B   B-C   C-D**
> **A-C   B-D**
> **A-D**
> **   6 handshakes**

- Repeat the activity on page 117 with *five* students shaking hands and then with *six*. List each combination (as shown) as students shake hands. Have students compare the number of students to the number of handshakes and look for a pattern. (See the table below.) Have students determine how many different handshakes are possible if *ten* people shake hands with each other.

- Remind students that a list needs to be *ordered* or *organized* in some way. Writing down all possible combinations in random order can be confusing: a combination may be left out or repeated. But most importantly, it takes more time, even if the answer is correct! See the ideas below and the reproducible on page 119 for more listing activities.

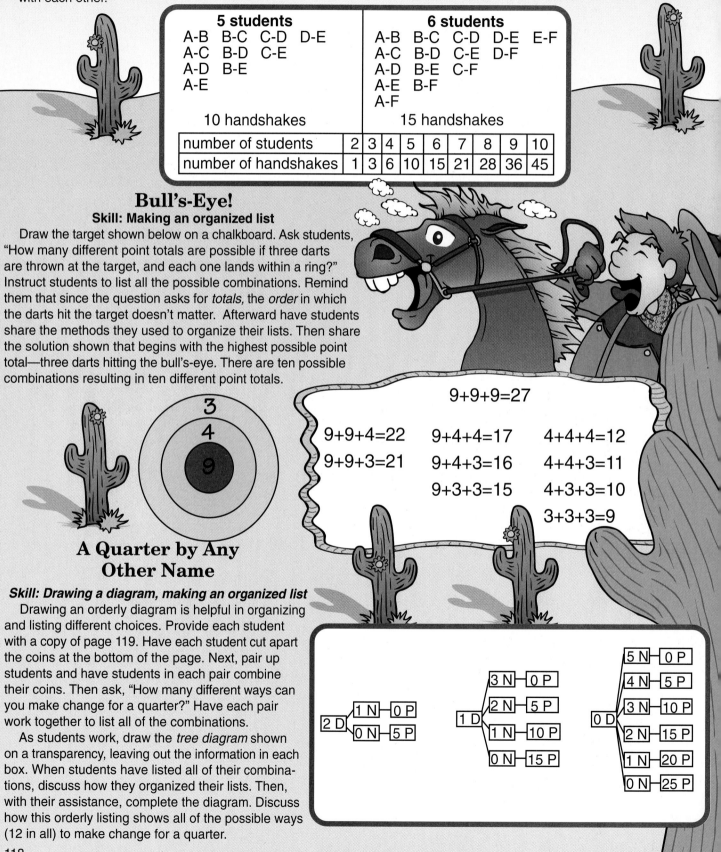

5 students

A-B B-C C-D D-E
A-C B-D C-E
A-D B-E
A-E

10 handshakes

6 students

A-B B-C C-D D-E E-F
A-C B-D C-E D-F
A-D B-E C-F
A-E B-F
A-F

15 handshakes

number of students	2	3	4	5	6	7	8	9	10
number of handshakes	1	3	6	10	15	21	28	36	45

Bull's-Eye!

Skill: Making an organized list

Draw the target shown below on a chalkboard. Ask students, "How many different point totals are possible if three darts are thrown at the target, and each one lands within a ring?" Instruct students to list all the possible combinations. Remind them that since the question asks for *totals,* the *order* in which the darts hit the target doesn't matter. Afterward have students share the methods they used to organize their lists. Then share the solution shown that begins with the highest possible point total—three darts hitting the bull's-eye. There are ten possible combinations resulting in ten different point totals.

9+9+9=27

9+9+4=22   9+4+4=17   4+4+4=12
9+9+3=21   9+4+3=16   4+4+3=11
            9+3+3=15   4+3+3=10
                        3+3+3=9

A Quarter by Any Other Name

Skill: Drawing a diagram, making an organized list

Drawing an orderly diagram is helpful in organizing and listing different choices. Provide each student with a copy of page 119. Have each student cut apart the coins at the bottom of the page. Next, pair up students and have students in each pair combine their coins. Then ask, "How many different ways can you make change for a quarter?" Have each pair work together to list all of the combinations.

As students work, draw the *tree diagram* shown on a transparency, leaving out the information in each box. When students have listed all of their combinations, discuss how they organized their lists. Then, with their assistance, complete the diagram. Discuss how this orderly listing shows all of the possible ways (12 in all) to make change for a quarter.

118

Rounding Up Lists

Why is making a list a good way to solve some math problems? An organized list helps you show all the possible answers. You can list all of the different answers and then find the one that works. Sometimes you may have to count all of the answers.

Solve each problem below by making an organized list. Show your work for problems 1–5 on another sheet of paper.

1. How many different three-letter words can you make using only the letters *A, B,* and *C?* The words may be nonsense words, but you *cannot* repeat a letter within a word.

_____ words

2. How many different three-letter words can you make using only the letters *A, B,* and *C* if you *can* repeat a letter within a word?

_____ words

3. Four cowpokes—Dex, Lex, Rex, and Tex—are going to ride a mechanical bull. How many different ways can they line up?

_____ ways

4. Lucky Leon is holding three cards. Their total value is 12. All of the cards are hearts, and he has no face cards. If the value of an ace is *1,* how many different combinations of cards could Leon possibly have?

_____ combinations

5. Look at the map below. How many different ways can one travel from Tombstone to Dodge City—passing through Dry Gulch along the way? Use the letters and numbers to name the routes.

_____ ways

6. Mitch Cassidy (the shortest cowpoke in the West) could see only legs when he looked into the corral—42 legs in all. He knows there is a total of 15 cowboys and horses in the corral. Continue the table to find out how many cowboys and how many horses Mitch saw.

horses	number of legs	cowboys	number of legs	cowboys & horses	legs in all
1	4	14	28	15	32
2	8	13	26	15	34
				15	
				15	
				15	
				15	
				15	
				15	

©The Education Center, Inc. • *The Best of* The Mailbox® *Math • Book 2* • TEC1492 • Key p. 160

Note to the teacher: Use the coin patterns with "A Quarter by Any Other Name" on page 118.

119

MISSION: Possible!
Math Projects to Improve Problem-Solving Skills

Your mission—should you choose to accept it—is to use one or more problem-solving strategies to complete a variety of investigative math projects. Will your students accept this mission? You bet! Challenge your young problem solvers with this collection of fun hands-on math projects.

by Irving P. Crump

It's in the Files

MISSION: MAKE A PLAN

What's the problem? That's the first question problem solvers ask themselves when they set out to solve a problem. Next, they choose one or more strategies. If a strategy doesn't work, they try a different one. The last step is checking the results. Help your students organize for problem solving by providing each of them with a copy of the outline on page 123. Have each student cut out the file folder art and then attach it to the inside cover of his math folder, composition book, or journal. Remind students to refer to this plan when solving any kind of problem.

If you choose to accept this mission, you'd better make a plan.

Take a Hike!

MISSION: DRAW A PICTURE, WRITE ABOUT MATH

In math, a picture *can* be worth a thousand words! Use the following activity to help students discover how helpful drawing a picture can be in solving a problem. First, share the following story with your class:

> Katie began her hike at the family campsite. The trail goes eight miles north to a stream and then continues four miles west to a waterfall. From the waterfall, the trail goes south six miles to a large boulder, where it turns southeast and winds along seven miles back to the campsite. Which landmark was Katie closest to after she had hiked 14 miles?

Ask students which problem-solving strategy would be helpful in finding the answer to the above question *(drawing a picture)*. Then direct each student to draw and label a picture, including each landmark, as you slowly reread the story. When everyone has drawn the last leg of the hike, ask the question again *(answer: waterfall)*. Remind students that drawing pictures and diagrams is a helpful way to solve many types of problems.

Next, have each student make up a story like the one you read, including a question at the end. The story may include city streets, a playground, stores in a mall—any kind of trip described with directional words, distances, and landmarks. When everyone has completed his story, pair up students and have them exchange stories with each other. Give each student a 12" x 18" sheet of white construction paper. Have the student attach his partner's story to one half of the sheet. Then have him draw a picture and answer the story's question on the other half. Display the completed projects on a bulletin board titled "Take a Hike!"

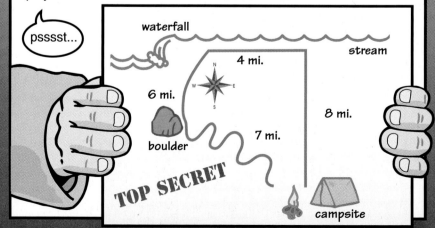

Graphing Cents

MISSION: COLLECT, DISPLAY, AND INTERPRET DATA

Problem solving often involves collecting lots of data and then analyzing that data. Send your students on a data graphing mission with this easy-to-prepare project. First, divide students into pairs. Give each twosome 50 pennies. Have the pair sort the pennies into decades according to the mint year on each one. Then provide each pair with a copy of page 124, a 12" x 18" sheet of white construction paper, a glue stick, a ruler, a calculator, and markers or crayons. Have each pair complete the reproducible as directed.

Rub-a-dub-dub, Compare These Tubs!

MISSION: GUESS AND CHECK, WRITE ABOUT MATH

Challenge your "spy-tacular" problem solvers with this simple-to-set-up center activity! First, collect five small margarine tubs with lids. Fill each tub with a different amount of gravel so that when any two of them are placed on a pan balance, the balance tips to one side. Code the tubs with letters; then make a key that lists the containers from lightest to heaviest. Place the tubs and a pan balance at a math center.

Challenge pairs of students to work together in the center to rank the five tubs from lightest to heaviest, using only the balance. Have each pair describe in a paragraph its strategy for ranking the tubs, using the tubs' letters in making comparisons, such as A > B, B > E, etc. When every pair has finished the activity, discuss the strategies used. Share with students that it is possible to correctly rank five different weights by making a minimum of ten comparisons; then share the key.

The tubs are here... but they're DIFFERENT WEIGHTS!

horses	ducks	total
1 = 4 legs	4 = 8 legs	12 legs
2 = 8 legs	3 = 6 legs	14 legs
3 = 12 legs	2 = 4 legs	16 legs

5 animals
26 legs
How many dogs?
How many beetles?

At the Zoo

MISSION: MAKE A TABLE, GUESS AND CHECK

Get problem-solving strategies out on the table with this nifty idea! Share with students the following puzzler: You have five pets; some are horses and the rest are ducks. Altogether the animals have 16 legs. How many horses and how many ducks do you have?

Brainstorm with students the best problem-solving strategy to use, leading them to conclude that recording guesses in a table would work well. Then draw the table shown, completing each line as students assist you, until you reach the solution: three horses and two ducks.

Extend this activity by giving each student a 9" x 12" sheet of light-colored construction paper. On her paper, have the student draw or glue cutout magazine pictures of two or three different animals, each having two, four, six, or eight legs. Then have the student label her poster with a problem similar to the one above. Have the student write her problem's solution on the back of her poster. Display the mini-posters in your math center or on a bulletin board. Invite students to examine the posters and draw tables to answer several of the questions on them.

Let's Count to a Million!

MISSION: ESTIMATE, USE A CALCULATOR

How long would it take you to count to one million? After students have thought about this question, have each one write down an estimate. Then, based on an average of about 2.5 seconds needed to say one number, have students use calculators to determine the solution. After each calculation, have the student round up each quotient to the next whole number. Share the solution shown. Then challenge students to find out how long it would take them to count to a billion. Since most calculators can't display large numbers, students will need to perform some calculating by hand. Challenge students to solve other large calculations, such as the ones below. For each calculation, have the student describe and list his strategies.

- How many pennies would be in a stack one mile high?
- How much money is a mile of quarters laid side by side?
- How many eight-inch bricks would it take to outline a football field?

2,500,000 SECONDS

41,667 MINUTES

695 HOURS

29 DAYS

Golly!

122

One-Three-Six

MISSION: GUESS AND CHECK, MAKE EQUALITIES

This "sands-sational" hands-on activity is similar to "Rub-a-dub-dub, Compare These Tubs!" on page 121. First, prepare three weights: one-pound, three-pound, and six-pound. Place them in three similar containers labeled as shown. Also provide a pan balance, a bucket of sand, several large and small plastic zippered bags, and a cup for scooping the sand. Challenge a pair of students to determine how they can measure out exact amounts of sand from one pound to ten pounds using only the pan balance, the sand and plastic bags, and the three different weights. Have students experiment with the weights and the sand, and record each solution and how they arrived at it on a sheet of paper. (See possible solutions at the right.)

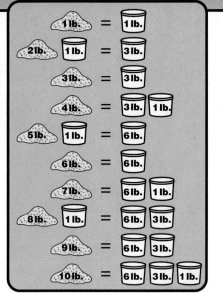

Give Me Four...in 3-D

MISSION: THINK VISUALLY, HAVE FUN!

Invite students to stretch their observation and thinking skills by trying a 3-D version of the popular Connect 4! game. Fold an eight-inch paper square in half four times and then unfold it to reveal 16 squares. Share with students the following directions for playing the game. Then place the game and 64 checkers (32 red and 32 black) in your math center.

1. Divide the checkers. Player 1 takes all of the red ones; Player 2 takes all of the black ones.
2. Player 1 places a red checker in any square on the gameboard.
3. Player 2 places a black checker on the gameboard—either on top of Player 1's red checker or on any other square.
4. No more than four checkers can be stacked on top of each other.
5. Play continues until a player has four checkers in a row either vertically, horizontally, or diagonally in any direction on the gameboard.

(Example: Suppose a player placed a red checker in one corner of the gameboard. He could possibly make four in a row in seven different ways as shown in the illustration.)

○ diagonal
◉ horizontal
● vertical

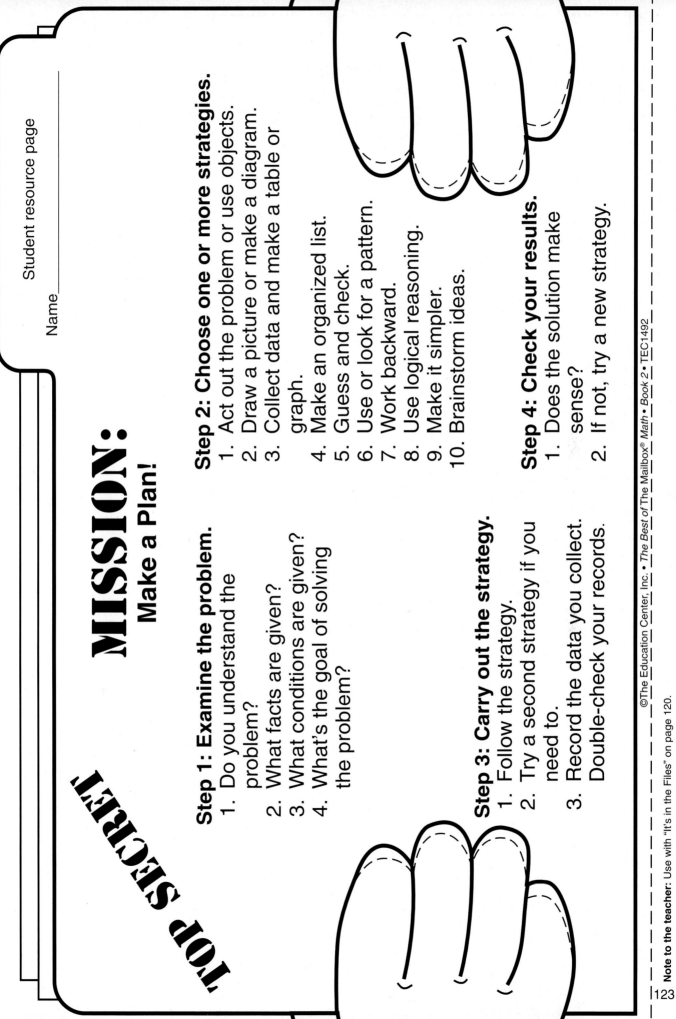

MISSION:

Make a Plan!

Name _____

Student resource page

TOP SECRET

Step 1: Examine the problem.

1. Do you understand the problem?
2. What facts are given?
3. What conditions are given?
4. What's the goal of solving the problem?

Step 2: Choose one or more strategies.

1. Act out the problem or use objects.
2. Draw a picture or make a diagram.
3. Collect data and make a table or graph.
4. Make an organized list.
5. Guess and check.
6. Use or look for a pattern.
7. Work backward.
8. Use logical reasoning.
9. Make it simpler.
10. Brainstorm ideas.

Step 3: Carry out the strategy.

1. Follow the strategy.
2. Try a second strategy if you need to.
3. Record the data you collect. Double-check your records.

Step 4: Check your results.

1. Does the solution make sense?
2. If not, try a new strategy.

Note to the teacher: Use with "It's in the Files" on page 120.

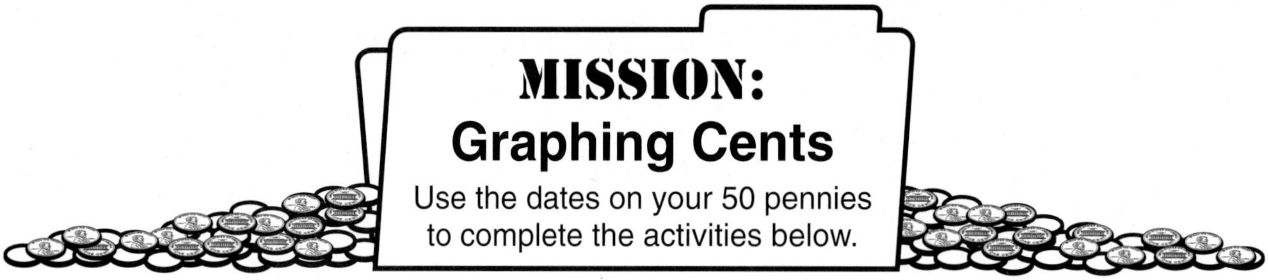

MISSION:
Graphing Cents
Use the dates on your 50 pennies
to complete the activities below.

1. First, organize your data. Make a tally mark beside the date in the box for each penny that
    has that date. If you have pennies that were minted before 1962, add those dates to the
    chart. (Check: Count the total number of tally marks you have made. Do you have 50?)

1962	1968	1974	1980	1986	1992	1998
1963	1969	1975	1981	1987	1993	1999
1964	1970	1976	1982	1988	1994	2000
1965	1971	1977	1983	1989	1995	2001
1966	1972	1978	1984	1990	1996	2002
1967	1973	1979	1985	1991	1997	2003

2. Fold your sheet of construction paper in half; then unfold it. Glue this page to the left half of
    the sheet.

3. On the right half of your sheet of construction paper, make a bar graph that shows the
    number of pennies that were minted in each decade (1960–69, 1970–79, etc.):
    a. Give the graph a title.   c. Label the horizontal axis.
    b. Label the vertical axis.   d. Color the bars.

4. Using a calculator, find the *average* year in which your pennies were minted. _____

5. Which year is the *median,* the middle year in your set of data? _____

6. Which year is the *mode,* the year that appears most often in your set of data? _____

7. What is the *range,* the difference between the earliest and most recent mint years in your set
    of data? _____

8. Describe another way that you could display your data besides a bar graph. _____

    _____

    _____

9. Write three facts based on what you observe in your graph.

    a. _____

    b. _____

    c. _____

Bonus Box: Combine your pennies with those of another pair of classmates. Repeat Step 1 above. Then find the
average, median, mode, and range of your data.

Note to the teacher: Use with "Graphing Cents" on page 121. Provide each pair of students with 50 pennies, a copy of this reproducible,
a 12"x 18" sheet of white construction paper, a glue stick, a ruler, a calculator, and markers or crayons.

MISSION: Telling Time

Telling time? Now *that* should be an easy mission!

Take a look at the two clocks below. The time on each one is shown in a digital display. The digits 0 through 9 are each formed by lighting different patterns of individual blocks. The time shown on the first clock is 3:56. The time on the second clock is 12:09.

Your mission: answer the questions below. (Don't include the colon in your answers.)

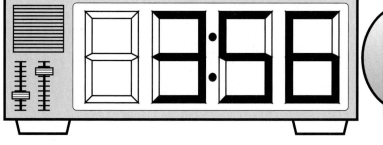

Part I: Easy-As-Pie Mission

1. How many blocks make up each place of a digital display? _____
2. How many blocks are in the entire display? _____
3. Which digit, when lit, uses the fewest blocks? _____
4. Which digit, when lit, uses the most blocks? _____
5. A digital display can also show the date. If the current month is shown on the left side of the colon and today's date is shown on the right side, how many blocks would be lit altogether?

   _____

Part II: Average Mission

1. What is the largest digit that can be shown in the first place of the digital display—beginning on the left? (Remember: this is a clock!) _____
2. What is the largest digit that can be shown in the second place of the digital display? _____
3. What is the largest digit that can be shown in the third place of the display? _____
4. What is the largest digit that can be shown in the fourth place? _____
5. If you flip the digit 2, what digit does it become? _____
6. What do the displays for the digits 4, 5, and 6 have in common? _____

   _____

Part III: Nearly Impossible Mission (But You Can Do It!)

1. How many blocks are lit at midnight? _____
2. At what time of day are the fewest blocks lit? _____ How many blocks are lit then? _____
3. At what time of day are the most blocks lit? _____ How many blocks are lit then? _____
4. The picture at the right shows the bottom half of a digital display. What *three* times could the clock possibly be showing? _____

Bonus Box: Write your birthday month and date in a digital display. How many total blocks would be lit to show your birthday?

A PROBLEM-SOLVING PARTY

A Festive Review of Math Problem-Solving Skills and Strategies

What is undoubtedly the single most important skill for survival in today's—and tomorrow's—ever-changing world? Most would agree that learning effective skills and strategies for problem solving is the key. Help students plan a math problem-solving party by including the following creative activities in your year-end teaching plans.

by Irving P. Crump

On this page and page 127, you'll find easy-to-do activities to help your students review and practice using problem-solving strategies. Page 128 includes an outline of activities in which small groups of students use their problem-solving skills to plan an end-of-the-year class party. Provide more fun problem-solving practice with the creative reproducibles on pages 129–131.

Plan to Solve
Skill: Understanding problem-solving steps

First review the steps shown in the box below for approaching and solving a problem. Make a chart or a transparency of these steps to share with your students. Then discuss with them the following additional information:

Step 1: Although the chart states "read the problem," don't stop after just one reading! Read the problem a second time more slowly, and then a third time if necessary. Reword the problem's question so that you truly understand it and know exactly what you're looking for.

Step 2: The facts needed to solve a problem are usually numbers: prices, measurements, quantities, etc. Sometimes there's not enough information included with a problem to solve it. And often a problem includes information that is unnecessary or irrelevant.

Step 3: Make an arithmetic plan. Simply say in words and then write as a math sentence exactly what you intend to do to solve the problem.

Step 4: Carry out the plan by performing the necessary computation to arrive at the solution.

Step 5: Check the answer. Does it make sense? If possible perform the math in a different way.

Tools for Solving
Skill: Recognizing problem-solving strategies

Next, remind students that the strategies they've already learned are tools to help them solve problems. They should remember that any one or a combination of these strategies can be used. Copy the list below on a chart or make a transparency to share with your students.

a. Make a table, chart, or graph.
b. Make an organized list.
c. Guess and check.
d. Look for a pattern.
e. Draw a picture or diagram.
f. Act out the problem.
g. Work backward.
h. Work a simpler problem.
i. Use logical reasoning and deduction.
j. Brainstorm ideas.

Problem-Solving Steps

1. Read the problem.
2. Find the facts that are needed.
3. Make a plan.
4. Carry out the plan.
5. Check the answer.

The Bare Facts

Skill: Understanding the relationships among data

Give students practice with understanding the relationships among data in a problem with this simple oral activity. Provide students with an arithmetic plan or math sentence; then ask them to provide problem situations in which that plan could be used. Begin with math sentences that students can easily relate to, such as:

- 12 + 14 = 26 *(Possible problem: There are 12 boys in our class and 14 girls. How many students are there in all?)*
- 26 x 4 = 104 *(Possible problem: If each of the 26 students in our class has 4 books, how many books is that in all?)*
- 12 ÷ 3 = 4 *(Possible problem: The boys in our class are divided into 3 teams. How many boys are on each team?)*

For additional practice with writing problems, provide each student with a copy of the reproducible on page 129.

Just a Few Facts

Skill: Understanding and using data

Extend "The Bare Facts" activity above with continued oral practice—but this time provide at least one bit of information for students to include in their problems. Help students understand that their problems must make sense and that the solution to the problem must be obtained with the data given. Begin with math sentences such as:

- 27 ÷ 3 teams = 9 *(Possible problem: There are 27 students in a class. If they are divided into 3 equal teams, how many students are on each team?)*
- 14 x 4 books = 56 *(Possible problem: There are 14 girls in a class. If each girl read 4 books, how many books is that in all?)*
- 27 nonfiction books + 38 = 65 *(Possible problem: A classroom library has 27 nonfiction books and 38 fiction books. How many books are there in all?)*

Sometimes There's Just Too Much Info...

Skill: Determining needed information

For practice with determining what information is needed to solve a problem, gather some old out-of-adoption math textbooks or workbooks. Read to your students several problems in which you've interjected additional information—information that is not needed to solve the problems. Begin by including in some problems information that is silly and obviously unnecessary to answer the questions. Read several problems in which students must identify the unnecessary information. Also read problems in which students must write math sentences that correspond to the problem's solution.

...And Sometimes Not Enough

Repeat the activity described above—but this time leave out some of the information that is vital to solving a problem. Have students raise their hands to volunteer the information, or have them write it on paper.

NOW IT'S PARTY TIME!

Skill: Using a variety of problem-solving strategies

Divide your students into small groups of four to five each. Have each group work together on one aspect of a party plan. (See the following suggested categories.) Ask each group to explain its problem-solving processes and strategies, plus determine the cost per pupil of any needed supplies. If the plans are good ones, schedule a year-ending party so that your students can showcase their math skills and problem-solving finesse!

Food

What kinds of food should be provided for a party? Chips? Dip? Cupcakes? Doughnuts? Cookies? Whole cakes that can be cut into slices? Determine the number of each item needed for the class. Determine the total cost of each item, plus the unit cost per student. Would it be more cost-effective to make some of the foods instead of buying them already prepared? Check out the costs of ingredients and compare. What should be the main considerations in determining the kinds and amounts of foods served at our class party?

Drinks

About how many ounces of drink should be provided for each student? How many ounces is that altogether? Should soft drinks or some other type of drink be purchased? If soft drinks are bought, what is the most economical size to buy? How many of that size must we buy? Are cups necessary? Ice? Should we provide each student with a canned drink or purchase large bottled drinks, along with cups and ice?

Decorations

What types of decorations would be best for the party? Party hats? Noisemakers? Balloons? Streamers? How about crepe paper to decorate the classroom? How much? What size rolls is it packaged in? Should each student be provided with a party favor? What kind? How much does one cost? What would be the total cost for the entire class?

Paper Goods

What kinds of paper goods do we need for the party? Napkins? Plates? Cups? Do we need any types of plasticware? Can we buy the right number of each item so that there are none left over or wasted? What is the unit price of each item that we need to purchase? What is the per-student cost and the total classroom cost for all paper goods?

Games

What kinds of games can we play? How long should we play each game? How will teams be determined? How will scoring be done? Should prizes be given to members of winning teams? Who will be in charge if judges or referees are needed? Is any special equipment required? Create a tentative schedule for the games, including their beginning and ending times.

And the Question Is...

The math sentence has been written. The computation has been done. The solution is correct. So what's the problem? The problem is the *problems* are missing! Write a math problem that can be solved by completing each equation below. Make sure that each problem fits its category. The first one has been done for you.

---

1. Category: party budget
   Answer: (26 x $3.50) – $78.50 = $12.50
   Problem: *Twenty-six students each gave $3.50 for party supplies. The total cost of the supplies was $78.50. How much money was left over?*

2. Category: party drinks
   Answer: 5 x $2.39 = $11.95
   Problem:

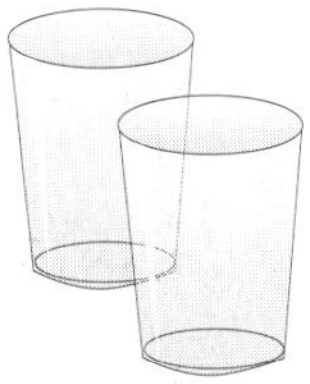

3. Category: party decorations
   Answer: 8 ft. x 6 = 48 ft.
   Problem:

4. Category: party snacks
   Answer: (7 x $1.29) + $4.95 = $13.98
   Problem:

5. Category: carpooling
   Answer: (2 x 4) + (3 x 3) + (4 x 2) = 25
   Problem:

6. Category: doughnuts
   Answer: (4 x 12) + (6 x 6) = 84
   Problem:

7. Category: balloons
   Answer: (2 x 15) + (3 x 16) + 12 = 90
   Problem:

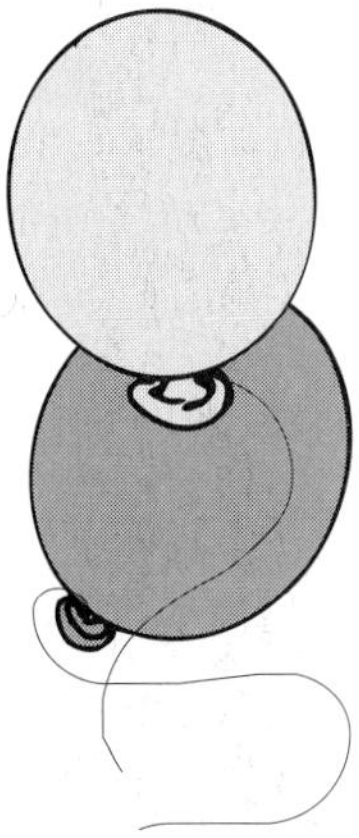

8. Category: time
   Answer: 30 + 30 + 45 + 15 + 30 = 150 = 2 hrs. 30 min.
   Problem:

BONUS

9. Category: paper goods— unit prices
   Answer: ($0.89 ÷ 50) + ($2.19 ÷ 100) + ($1.49 ÷ 30) = $0.09
   Problem:

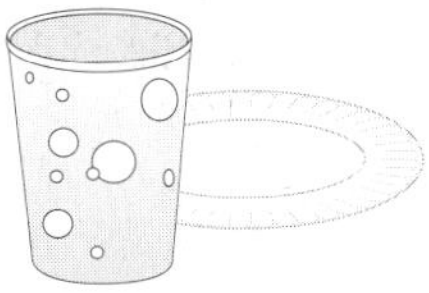

A Trio of Party Puzzles

A. It's party time! Four kids—Breann, Monte, Amelia, and Brandon—are sitting at a round table eating party snacks. Find the position of each student at the table by reading the clues below. Write the students' names in the blanks on the table.

   1. Brandon is opposite Amelia.
   2. Monte accidentally knocked over Brandon's drink with his left elbow.

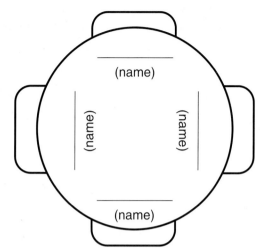

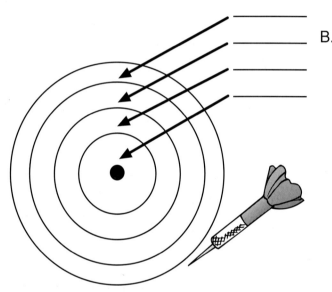

B. Breann, Monte, Amelia, and Brandon decided to play darts at the party. Each student carefully aimed and threw a dart. Luckily, all of the darts landed on the dartboard. Who had the best throw? The player's dart that is closest to the bull's-eye is the winner. Read the clues and write the students' names in the blanks.

   1. Monte's dart was closer than Amelia's but farther away than Breann's.
   2. Brandon's dart was one ring closer than Monte's.

C. Breann, Monte, Amelia, and Brandon—plus their classmates Bradley, Isaac, Jordan, Liz, Cher, Shandra, Jody, and Frankie—went outdoors after the party to play circle soccer. Can you find the position of each player? Read the clues below and write the students' names around the circle.

1. Monte is between Breann and Amelia.
2. Brandon stands between Shandra and Liz.
3. Cher is on Liz's right.
4. Jody is next to Breann with someone between him and Shandra.
5. Isaac is to the right of Bradley.
6. Amelia is on Frankie's right.

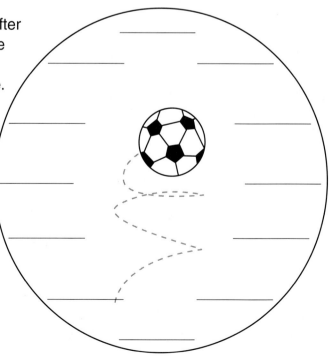

Bonus Box: On another piece of paper, design a logic puzzle like one of the examples above. Give it to a classmate to solve.

Game Sheet
Player 1

_____

1. ____ x ____ > 100

2. ____ x ____ < 50

3. ____ + ____ < 1

4. ____ x ____ is even.

5. ____ x ____ is odd.

6. ____ x ____ > 50 but < 100

7. ____ + ____ > 1 but < 2

8. ____ x ____ is a 3-digit number.

9. ____ ÷ ____ is a decimal number.

10. ____ − ____ − ____ < 10

11. ____ x ____ x ____ > 1,000

12. ____ x ____ − ____ < 100

13. (____ + ____) x 10 > 500

14. ____ x ____ > 100 but < 250

15. ____ + ____ > 5 but < 10

Guessing & Checking

Materials needed:
pair of scissors, 2 pencils, 2 calculators

Get ready:
Divide this page into three sections by cutting along the dashed lines. Each player takes a game sheet and writes his name in the blank. Place this section between the two players so that they can easily see it.

To play:
The object of the game is to fill in the blanks of each equation with numbers so that the equation is true.

1. Choose only from the numbers below to fill in the blanks. Example: "____ x ____ > 50." Filling in the blanks with 7 and 9 makes the equation true: 7 x 9 > 50.
2. You may use a number more than once.
3. Try to make good guesses—but don't work out the problems.
4. When both players are finished, exchange papers with each other.
5. Check your opponent's work with a calculator.
6. Who had more correct equations?

12   1.0

7

0.17   0.05   9

16   33

25   0.41   6

Game Sheet
Player 2

_____

1. ____ x ____ > 100

2. ____ x ____ < 50

3. ____ + ____ < 1

4. ____ x ____ is even.

5. ____ x ____ is odd.

6. ____ x ____ > 50 but < 100

7. ____ + ____ > 1 but < 2

8. ____ x ____ is a 3-digit number.

9. ____ ÷ ____ is a decimal number.

10. ____ − ____ − ____ < 10

11. ____ x ____ x ____ > 1,000

12. ____ x ____ − ____ < 100

13. (____ + ____) x 10 > 500

14. ____ x ____ > 100 but < 250

15. ____ + ____ > 5 but < 10

MATH ON THE GO!

Teaching Everyday Math Skills That Students Will Use for a Lifetime

Balancing a checkbook, comparing prices, planning a vacation—what do all these everyday activities have in common? If you answered "doing math," you're absolutely right! Use the following creative projects and reproducibles to help students better understand some of the answers to the common math class question, "When will I *ever* use this?"

by Beth Gress

Numbers All Around
Skill: Number concepts

Whether they realize it or not, kids see examples of math and numbers all around them. Highlight some of these numbers with this simple bulletin board idea. First, use a computer and a variety of fonts to print the following headings on colorful paper (one heading per sheet): *Number Expressions, Fractions, Decimals, Percents, Negative Numbers, Averages, Rates, Rankings, Ranges,* and *Prices.* Next, glue each heading to the top of a piece of poster board. Title a bulletin board "Numbers All Around" and attach the ten sheets to the board. Challenge each student to search in newspapers, magazines, advertisements, coupons, photos, and junk mail to find examples of each number concept. Then have him cut out each example and glue it onto the appropriate poster.

Each day, choose an example from the bulletin board. Then have students answer the following questions about it in their journals:

- Where do you think this number probably appeared?
- Express this number in some other form.
- Explain this number in such a way that a creature from outer space could understand it.
- Draw a simple illustration that explains the number.
- List three occupations that may use this kind of number.

Whee! A Shopping Spree!
Skills: Addition, estimation

Everyone dreams of winning big in the lottery. Bring that dream to life with this fun activity. Several days before the activity, begin gathering a variety of catalogs. Ask students to bring their favorites from home, and include some of your own as well as the newspaper's classified ads. Be sure to include ads that feature high-ticket items, such as cars, boats, and furniture.

After the catalogs have been collected, ask students, "What would you buy if you won the lottery? Where would you go?" Then invite your students to go on an imaginary spending spree with their lottery winnings! Divide the class into groups of three or four. Give each group several catalogs, a pair of scissors, and some glue; also give each student a large sheet of construction paper. Tell students that they have each won $25,000. Instruct each child to create a wish list of items that he would like to buy, listing the items and their prices on a sheet of notebook paper. Caution students not to go over their lottery winnings of $25,000. Next, direct each student to make a collage of his items on the construction paper, listing the price of each item beside its cut-out picture. Finally, have each student tape his wish list to one side of his poster. Display these colorful posters on a bulletin board titled "Shopping Spree!" with a border of play money.

For additional math skills reinforcement, have each student

- use a calculator to determine the sales tax on his items (such as 6% or 8%)
- order his items from least to most expensive
- compare his total to the other students' totals in his group
- find the average cost of his items

Check It Out!

Skills: Math writing, addition, subtraction

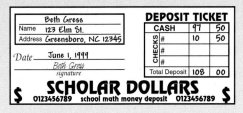

Help your students stretch their imaginations—and their dollars—while practicing real-life consumer skills. Photocopy pages 135 and 136 back-to-back and provide each student with a copy. (Tell students *not* to write on their copies.) In addition, make transparencies of the two pages to demonstrate this lesson. First discuss with students definitions of such banking terms as *transaction, deposit, withdrawal, debit, credit,* and *balance.* Then read the story below, while demonstrating on the transparencies how to fill out a deposit ticket, complete a checkbook transaction register, and write checks.

Last Friday night, I baby-sat for my neighbor's kids and was paid with a check for $10.50. On Saturday I took seven boxes of stuff to my aunt's house for her garage sale. I helped her all day and made $67.50 in cash. My aunt gave me a $10 bill for helping out! On Sunday I was lazy! After church, I watched TV, read books, and played video games all afternoon. Then I did my homework after supper. On Monday after school, I mowed the lawn and helped Dad clean out the attic. He rewarded me with a $20 bill. Wow! On Tuesday after school, I rushed to the bank to deposit my stash of cash. *(Stop here to demonstrate how to fill out the deposit ticket and transaction register.)*

On Wednesday afternoon I went shopping with Mom at J-Mart. I bought a sweatshirt, a paperback book, and a CD. I wrote a check for $36.64. *(Stop here and demonstrate how to write check #1 and fill in the transaction register.)*

The next day I went to The Timeshop and bought a watch that I've wanted for months. That put me back another $29.95! *(Stop here and demonstrate how to write check #2 and complete the register.)*

Friday night I invited some friends over for a party. I wrote a check for $23.12 to Pizza Planet. Wow, what a week! *(Demonstrate how to write check #3, complete the register, and balance the account.)*

Now direct students to make up their own money stories—like the one above—describing how they might earn and spend money. Have students follow the directions on their copies of pages 135 and 136 for writing their stories and completing the checking account activities.

How About a Credit Card?

Skill: Computing interest

How many students would jump at the chance to have their very own credit cards? But do they know what it means to have to pay for credit card purchases…with interest added? Provide each student with a copy of page 137. Work the first few steps together on the chalkboard (or on a transparency of the page) until students grasp the basic steps. Then allow students to work in pairs and use calculators to complete the activity. Discuss with students the variables that can affect how much a charged item may end up costing in the long run, such as the interest rates and the amount of the monthly payment that is made. After checking the activity with students, assign the Bonus Box to be completed as classwork.

Savvy Shoppers

Skill: Using a calculator

For kids (as well as adults!), nearly anything to do with food provides a motivating incentive. Obtain a class set of grocery ad circulars from your local grocery store. Divide students into pairs. Then give each pair a circular and a calculator. Encourage students to work together to solve the following problems:

1. List three different items whose total comes closest to $10.00 without going over.
2. Which single item has the largest discount?
3. Find two items priced as a pair. What is the price of one item?
4. Find an item that is now 50 percent less than its original price.
5. Find an item priced by the pound. Find the cost of a two-ounce serving.
6. Choose five items and find their total cost.
7. Find the sales tax on the total of the five items in Problem 6. Use 6 percent.
8. Choose appropriate items to plan a meal for four. What is the total cost of the items?

Room for Improvement
Skills: Scale drawing, perimeter and area

Most kids' rooms have room for improvement—besides picking clothes up off the floor! Give students a taste for interior design by having them plan scale models of their dream rooms. For homework, have each student measure and record the sizes of the major items in his room, such as the bed, closet, desk, chair, rug, toy box, nightstand, table, etc. Remind students to measure both the length *and* width of each item. In class the next day, provide each student with two sheets of ½-inch graph paper, scissors, and glue. Then follow these steps:

1. Discuss the concept of *scale drawing*. Tell students that with this particular scale drawing, ½ inch on the graph paper equals one actual foot. Demonstrate how a 3' x 6' bed equals a 1½" x 3" rectangle on the graph paper.

2. Have each student plan and then draw the items he wants in his room on a sheet of graph paper. (Tell students not to worry at this point about placement, but just to draw the items.) Review with students what the term "bird's-eye view" means.

3. Have the student label each item and then color it with colored pencils.

4. Have each student cut out all the items.

5. Direct each student to arrange his items on his second sheet of graph paper. Students may move the items around to form any arrangement they desire. If necessary, an item may be omitted or a new one drawn. Also remind students to include the placement of windows, closets, and doors.

6. When finished, have each student glue each item onto the graph paper.

Follow up this activity with questions such as:
- How many square feet is your room?
- About how many square yards of carpet would your bedroom need? (Remember: 1 square yard = 9 square feet.)
- What is the perimeter of your room?
- How large is each closet?
- How far is it from your bed to the entry?

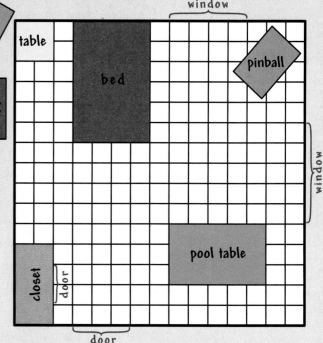

What I Wish I Could Do on My Summer Vacation
Skills: Budgeting, using a calculator

Spark your students' taste for adventure as they plan their own summer vacations. Ask students to bring to class any travel brochures that they may have at home. Divide students into pairs. Then provide each pair with a road map of the United States and a copy of the planning sheet on page 138. Explain to students that they get to plan a five-day excursion to the destination of their choice. Then discuss the following guidelines:

- The trip must have an itinerary detailing daily plans.
- Travel must be planned by mileage and by the time required to travel those miles.
- Use an estimate of 50 miles of travel each hour and an estimate of $1.00 per 25 miles traveled.
- Include visits to at least four points of interest during the trip. These places may be located along the route or at the destination. Use a variety of tourism and travel information sources, including the Internet.
- Include an itemized daily expense estimate for meals, entertainment, lodging, and any miscellaneous expenses.
- Present the trip to the class in a creative way.

Celebrate the conclusion of this fun project by holding a bon voyage party, complete with punch, cake, and other tasty treats.

Going to the Bank!

Stretch your imagination—and your dollars—with this math money activity! On another sheet of paper, write a money story like the one your teacher read to you. Follow these guidelines:

1. Begin by describing at least three ways you've earned money. Make up each amount, but be realistic. You should be paid in cash at least once and by check at least twice.
2. Complete the deposit ticket based on your earnings.

deposit ticket

Name		DEPOSIT TICKET		
Address		CASH		
		CHECKS #		
		#		
*Date*_____		#		
_____ *signature*		Total Deposit		

$ **SCHOLAR DOLLARS** $
0123456789   school math money deposit   0123456789

3. Enter the above deposit in your checkbook register at the bottom of this page. You already have a balance of $20.00 in your checking account.
4. Plan three ways to spend your money and describe them in your story. Remember: you can't spend more money than you have!
5. On the other side of this sheet, write a check for each expense that you described in Step 4.
6. Enter each withdrawal (check) in the register below.
7. Balance your checkbook.

checkbook register

		RECORD ALL CHARGES THAT AFFECT YOUR ACCOUNT			
NUMBER	DATE	DESCRIPTION OF TRANSACTION	PAYMENT/ DEBIT	DEPOSIT/ CREDIT	BALANCE $20 00
			$	$	

Name ______________________ Using a checking account: sample checks

Going to the Bank!

Name ______________________
Address ______________________
____

#001

Date ______________

Pay to the Order of ______________________ $ [ ] SCHOLAR DOLLARS

____

SCHOLAR DOLLARS CLASSROOM CHECK

On-The-Go Bank

MEMO ______________ Signature ______________

Name ______________________
Address ______________________
____

#002

Date ______________

Pay to the Order of ______________________ $ [ ] SCHOLAR DOLLARS

____

SCHOLAR DOLLARS CLASSROOM CHECK

On-The-Go Bank

MEMO ______________ Signature ______________

Name ______________________
Address ______________________
____

#003

Date ______________

Pay to the Order of ______________________ $ [ ] SCHOLAR DOLLARS

____

SCHOLAR DOLLARS CLASSROOM CHECK

On-The-Go Bank

MEMO ______________ Signature ______________

 Note to the teacher: Photocopy pages 135 and 136 back-to-back. Use them with “Check It Out!” on page 133.

Name ____________________ Percents, computing interest, using a calculator

Going for a Credit Card!

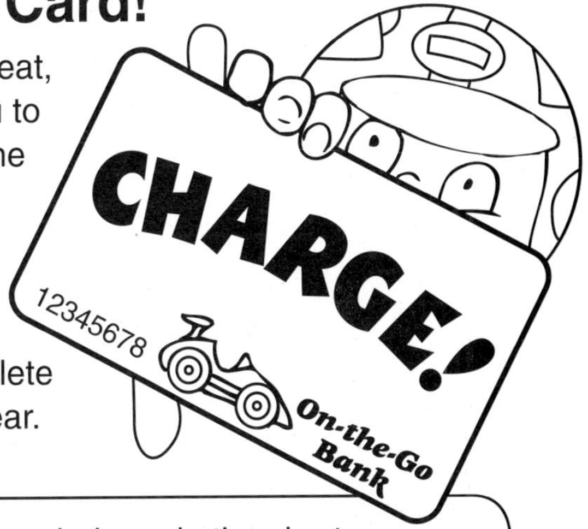

How would you like your very own credit card? Sounds great, huh? But have you ever wondered why businesses want you to have credit cards? Because you pay them extra money for the use of their cards. This extra money is called *interest.* The higher the interest rate and the lower the amount you pay each month, the more extra money (besides the cost of the items you charged) you'll have to pay.

And just how much can that be? Use a calculator to complete the chart below. This credit card charges 10% interest per year. Follow these steps:

1. Suppose you charge an item that costs $100. See *new balance* in the chart.
2. You make the first monthly payment of $15.00.
3. Subtract $15.00 from $100.00 to get a *balance* of $85.00.
4. Use a calculator to determine the *interest* on that balance: $85.00 x 10% = $8.50 per year.
5. Divide $8.50 by 12 to find the interest for one month: 0.7083333. Round 0.7083333 up to the next cent: $0.71.
6. Add the interest to the balance to get the *new balance*: $85.71.
7. Now make your next monthly payment: repeat Steps 2–6.
8. Continue making monthly payments until your balance equals 0.
9. Add the total amount of the payments you made. What was your total payment for this $100 item?

monthly payment	amount	balance	interest	new balance
	——	——	——	$100.00
1	$15.00	$85.00	$0.71	$85.71
2	$15.00			
3	$15.00			
4	$15.00			
5	$15.00			
6	$15.00			
7	$_____			
	__________ = total payment			

Bonus Box: Use the same procedure above to find the total payment on a $100.00 charge if you pay $10.00 per month and the interest rate is 20%. Show your work on the back of this sheet.

Note to the teacher: Use with "How About a Credit Card?" on page 133.

Name _____   Budgeting time & money, using a calculator

Going on a Vacation!

or bust!

Use this sheet to plan your five-day vacation.

D a y 1

Travel: Depart from _____ and arrive at _____ at _____ (time).
mileage (about 50 miles per hour): _____ mileage costs (about $1.00 per 25 miles): _____
Meals: breakfast: _____ lunch: _____ dinner: _____
Entertainment: _____
_____
Lodging: _____ **Miscellaneous expenses:** _____

D a y 2

Travel: Depart from _____ and arrive at _____ at _____ (time).
mileage (about 50 miles per hour): _____ mileage costs (about $1.00 per 25 miles): _____
Meals: breakfast: _____ lunch: _____ dinner: _____
Entertainment: _____
_____
Lodging: _____ **Miscellaneous expenses:** _____

D a y 3

Travel: Depart from _____ and arrive at _____ at _____ (time).
mileage (about 50 miles per hour): _____ mileage costs (about $1.00 per 25 miles): _____
Meals: breakfast: _____ lunch: _____ dinner: _____
Entertainment: _____
_____
Lodging: _____ **Miscellaneous expenses:** _____

D a y 4

Travel: Depart from _____ and arrive at _____ at _____ (time).
mileage (about 50 miles per hour): _____ mileage costs (about $1.00 per 25 miles): _____
Meals: breakfast: _____ lunch: _____ dinner: _____
Entertainment: _____
_____
Lodging: _____ **Miscellaneous expenses:** _____

D a y 5

Travel: Depart from _____ and arrive at _____ at _____ (time).
mileage (about 50 miles per hour): _____ mileage costs (about $1.00 per 25 miles): _____
Meals: breakfast: _____ lunch: _____ dinner: _____
Entertainment: _____
_____
Lodging: _____ **Miscellaneous expenses:** _____

Note to the teacher: See "What I Wish I Could Do on My Summer Vacation" on page 134 for information on how to use this reproducible.

Picture Books and Math— ANOTHER DYNAMIC DUO!

Using Picture Books to Teach Math Skills

Picture books and math—a dynamic duo? You bet! Use the following suggestions to make picture books a powerful part of your math lessons!

Math Curse
written by Jon Scieszka and illustrated by Lane Smith

Skill: Writing equations

Just when you think it's safe to go to school, your teacher puts a math curse on you! At least that's what the child in this hilarious, high-speed picture book thinks as she finds out that "...you can think of almost everything as a math problem." Read this book to your students after a lesson on equations. After a discussion about how math can be found in everyday life, instruct each student to list ten problems (along with their solutions) based on his activities for that day. The student displays or illustrates his problems on a sheet of construction paper as creatively as possible. Your kids will love comparing their work with one another. The equations also make a creative student-centered display. *Diane W. Lupia—Gr. 6, Mechanicsburg Area Intermediate School, Mechanicsburg, PA*

How Many Feet? How Many Tails?: A Book of Math Riddles
written by Marilyn Burns and illustrated by Lynn Adams

Skill: Division

Part of the Hello Math Reader series, this book by renowned educator Marilyn Burns is the perfect springboard to review division skills. In the book, a grandfather challenges his grandkids with riddles such as "What has twelve feet, three tails, and sleeps under the porch?" *(one mother cat and two kittens)*. After reading this book to students, have each child make up his own series of riddles using larger numbers. For example, a student might ask, "What has 48 feet, 12 tails, and 24 ears, and lives in India?" *(12 tigers)*. Challenge students to try to include information currently being studied in other subjects in their problems. For example, if you're studying invertebrates, a student might ask, "What has 36 legs, 18 body parts, and 12 antennae?" *(6 ladybugs)*. Bind the students' riddles into a class math-riddle book. *Kelly A. Lu, Berlyn School, Ontario, CA*

Jim and the Beanstalk
written and illustrated by Raymond Briggs

Skill: Measurement

For a picture book that measures up to all of its math potential, you can't beat this updated version of the famous bean stalk tale! In this story, Jim climbs a mysterious bean stalk only to find a giant with lots of problems—all involving measurement—that need solving. After sharing this book with students, challenge them to create a suit for the book's gigantic character (to go with the new wig, glasses, and teeth, which Jim helps him get in the story). First, choose one student to use as a model. After taking this student's measurements, decide as a class whether to double or triple them for a giant's outfit. Then divide students into groups, giving each team a large piece of butcher paper, measuring tools, and other art supplies. Each group then measures, draws, colors, and cuts out its giant-size outfit. It's a math project that's always a gigantic success! *Kelly A. Lu*

Eating Fractions
written and illustrated by Bruce McMillan

Skills: Addition, multiplication of fractions, multiplication facts

In this photo-illustrated book, two children learn about simple fractions while whipping up some yummy foods. In the back of the book, the author gives recipes for the pictured foods. After sharing this book with your class, challenge the students to double or triple the recipes to make larger serving sizes. Then make some of the dishes using the rewritten recipes. Who would have thought that math practice could be so delicious? *Kelly A. Lu, Berlyn School, Ontario, CA*

Pam Crane

1,000,000,000 BUNNIES!!

Bunches and Bunches of Bunnies
written by Louise Mathews and illustrated by Jeni Bassett

Skill: Multiplication

Showing that multiplication is really a form of addition, bunches of bunnies cavort across the pages of this engaging picture book. Share the book with students; then discuss that the bunny bunches represent the numbers from one to twelve multiplied by themselves. Next, divide students into small groups or pairs. Have each group rewrite the story using even larger numbers of bunnies. Provide oversize paper for students to illustrate their rewrites. The fun, and learning, are sure to multiply like rabbits! *Kelly A. Lu*

Anno's Magic Seeds
written and illustrated by Mitsumasa Anno

Skill: Patterning

In this multilayered tale, a wizard gives Jack two mysterious seeds: one to eat and one to plant. And from that day forth, Jack's fortunes grow as rapidly as his magic seeds. After reading this book to students, search together for a pattern to determine how many seeds Jack has over a ten-year period. Once the pattern is determined, use it to predict the number of seeds over longer periods of time, such as 15, 20, and 50 years. Once students understand the pattern, change the number of seeds Jack starts with and add circumstances that might affect the number eaten each year. *Stacey Roggendorff— Gr. 6, Union Sixth Grade Center, Tulsa, OK*

How many ways can you get to 25?
25+0,...24+1,...
23+2,...22+3,...
21+4,...

12 Ways to Get to 11
written by Eve Merriam and illustrated by Bernie Karlin

Skill: Writing equations

Bright illustrations of cut paper show that there's more than one way—12, to be exact—to illustrate an addition sentence for the number 11. After sharing this preschool book with your students, group them into pairs and assign each pair a number greater than 20 (depending on the ability levels of your students). Also give each pair a sheet of chart paper and a marker. Have the pair title its chart paper "How many ways can you get to [assigned number]?" Then challenge each pair to list as many equations for their number as possible on their chart paper. As a follow-up, have each group transform its chart into an illustrated picture book. *Kelly A. Lu*

People
written and illustrated by Peter Spier

Skills: Data collection, graphing, probability

For a book that's populated with a variety of math opportunities, take a look at *People* by Peter Spier. One section of this book looks at the variety of facial features found on people around the world. After sharing this section, have students collect data on the heights, eye colors, and hair textures of people; then graph the data together. To explore probability, give students a handout illustrated with three pairs of eyes, three noses, three pairs of ears, three mouths, three face outlines, and three hairstyles. Then challenge the students to compute the probability of any two classmates putting together the same face from those illustrations. Besides all the opportunities for math exploration, this terrific book emphasizes the ways people are all alike while being uniquely different. *Phyllis Ellett—Grs. 3 & 4, Earl Hanson Elementary, Rock Island, IL*

Recycle!: A Handbook for Kids
written and illustrated by Gail Gibbons

Skills: Data collection, graphing, writing story problems

In this small handbook, readers are given a comprehensive yet simple background on recycling. After reading and discussing this book, have the class complete these two integrated activities:

Activity 1: Have each student estimate the amount of each recyclable item mentioned in the book (paper, glass, aluminum, plastic, polystyrene) in his home. Record all estimates on a class chart. For homework, have each student tally the number of items he finds at home in each category. The next day, discuss students' findings, and divide the class into groups. Instruct each group to compile its data, displaying it on a graph. After the group graphs are completed, compare them; then display the graphs on a bulletin board, along with index cards labeled with some of the facts in the book.

Activity 2: Have each child use the facts in the book—most of which deal with numbers—to create story problems for classmates to solve. Give each student several large index cards. Have the student fold each card greeting card–style. Then have her write a problem on the front of the resulting card and the answer inside. Post the problems on the bulletin board with the graphs created in Activity 1. *Lisa Miecznikowski—Gr. 5, Hylen Souders Elementary, Galena, OH*

Domino Addition
written by Lynette Long
designed by Diane M. Earley

Skill: Multiplication

It's easy to spot the fun in this book that uses dominoes to teach simple addition facts. After sharing the book with your class, give each pair of students a set of dominoes. Then challenge each pair to create multiplication equations in the same way that the book illustrates addition equations. For example, instead of using a domino to illustrate 2 + 6 = 8, the student multiplies the two halves of a domino to make the equation 2 x 6 = 12. For more difficult problems, have students place two dominoes side by side and write an equation as shown in the example. Bind the students' equations together to make a class "Domino Multiplication" book. *Kelly A. Lu, Berlyn School, Ontario, CA*

$$65 \times 12$$

Making the Writing-in-Math Connection

Eager to integrate writing and math, but unsure about how to make the connection? Plug in to the following creative ideas and reproducibles to electrify your students' skills in two of the three Rs!

by Peggy W. Hambright

Why Write in Math?

According to the new math standards released by the National Council of Teachers of Mathematics (NCTM), students are now expected to *communicate* their understanding of math concepts. In order to know whether students can communicate their understanding, they are being asked to explain concepts in their own words. Writing allows students to clarify their thinking and summarize what they're learning. Save yourself some planning time and strengthen two important skills at once by having students practice writing while doing math. The easy ideas that follow will help you make the connection with ease!

Daily Math Journals

Skill: Problem solving, expository writing

Keep 'ritin' and 'rithmetic skills sharp with the help of daily math journals. Each Monday have students follow the steps shown to make simple flip books. Following each day's math lesson, write a prompt (a problem to solve and explain) on the board. Have each student copy the prompt onto the corresponding journal page and write his response (see the example). Each Friday collect the books to assess students' understanding.

Directions:

Step 1: Stack three sheets of paper so that the top edges are one-half-inch apart.

Step 2: Fold over the top half to form six layers.

Step 3: Staple the book at each side near the top of the fold.

Step 4: Label the top flap "[your name]'s Math Journal" and illustrate it.

Step 5: Label the space on each remaining flap with a different day and date.

Step 6: Copy the day's prompt from the board in the space above the date. Then solve and explain the problem.

Step 1:

Step 2:

Steps 3–5:
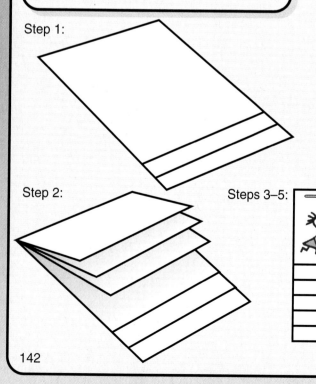

Erin's Math Journal

Monday, Sept. 14
Tuesday, Sept. 15
Wednesday, Sept. 16
Thursday, Sept. 17
Friday, Sept. 18

Step 6:
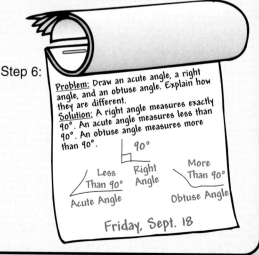

Problem: Draw an acute angle, a right angle, and an obtuse angle. Explain how they are different.
Solution: A right angle measures exactly 90°. An acute angle measures less than 90°. An obtuse angle measures more than 90°.

90°

Less Than 90°
Acute Angle

Right Angle

More Than 90°
Obtuse Angle

Friday, Sept. 18

"Math-Maginations"

Skills: Finding perimeter and area, descriptive writing

Pull out all the stops—and the pattern blocks—for this fun-filled math lesson that doubles as a descriptive-writing exercise! Give each student a zippered bag of pattern blocks (minus the white and orange pieces), a sheet of drawing paper, colored pencils, and the directions below.

1. Construct a shape, such as an animal or an object, with the pattern blocks on your drawing paper. Trace the blocks; then color the drawing.
2. On a sheet of lined paper, record the number of blocks of each kind you used to make your shape.
3. Use the side of a green triangle as one unit to find your shape's perimeter. Record it on the lined paper.
4. Use the area of a green triangle as one unit to find your shape's area. Record it on the lined paper.
5. On the lined paper, write a descriptive paragraph about your shape. Tell what it is, its name, its color, the kinds of blocks you used, its size (perimeter and area), and what it can and cannot do, along with any other important characteristics.
6. Edit your paragraph; then copy it in the extra space on your drawing.

Display students' papers in the classroom. For additional ways students can incorporate math with descriptive writing, see the list below.

P = 48
A = 66

Writing + Math

Describe:
- yourself using math sentences and math terms.
- a geometric design you made by drawing line segments on poster board.
- a geometric design you created by overlapping the tracings of circles or polygons.
- a shape you created from tangram pieces (described from top to bottom or side to side).
- any symmetrical shape.
- a design you created by connecting ordered pairs of numbers on a grid.
- any shape without naming it.
- how well your group worked together to solve an assigned problem.

Same or Different?

Skills: Finding attributes of polygons, classificatory writing

Many math topics lend themselves to classificatory writing. Draw a Venn diagram on the board. Label the left circle "Square" and the right circle "Rectangle." Have students compare and contrast the two polygons as you record their comments in the appropriate spaces of the diagram. Next, direct each student to describe the similarities of squares and rectangles in one paragraph and their differences in another. Then give each student a copy of the pattern at the bottom of page 148 to use for comparing and contrasting one of the topics on the right. Display students' cutout patterns on a bulletin board titled "We've Got a Yen for a Venn!"

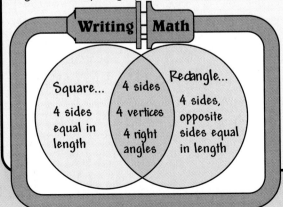

Writing + Math

Square...

4 sides equal in length

4 sides
4 vertices
4 right angles

Rectangle...

4 sides, opposite sides equal in length

Writing + Math

Compare and Contrast:
- an English ruler and a metric ruler
- any two different periods in a place-value chart, such as ten thousands and ten millions
- any fraction with its equivalent decimal, such as $3/4$ and 0.75
- any two sets of multiples
- an acute angle and an obtuse angle
- a bar graph and a line graph
- two inverse operations, such as multiplication and division or addition and subtraction
- using mental math instead of a calculator
- a line and a ray

As Easy As 1, 2, 3!

Skill: Reviewing math concepts, expository writing

Expository writing is as easy to integrate into the math curriculum as 1, 2, 3! Try one of the following activities:

- Pair students; then give each pair colored markers and a sheet of white poster board. Have the pair create a math game that's correlated to another subject, writing directions on the gameboard or on an index card clipped to the board. Allow students to trade and play their games.
- Duplicate page 147 for each student to complete as directed. Then follow up by having students make flow charts of favorite "arithmetricks," such as the one shown, or other simple math problems. Give each student a sheet of white poster board, colored markers, scissors, a hole puncher, and yarn. Direct him to create his flow chart by labeling and connecting poster board pieces (shaped according to the legend on the reproducible) with yarn as shown. Display the flow charts. For additional ideas on expository math writing, see the list below.

START

Think of a number.

Add 10.

Multiply by 4.

Add 200.

Divide by 4.

Subtract the original number.

Did you get 60?

Yes? Great! Try another number.

No? Check your work.

Writing | Math

Write directions for:

- dividing a Geoboard to show fractional parts of a whole.
- drawing the missing part of a symmetrical design.
- creating a bar graph that shows favorite Saturday-morning TV shows.
- solving a problem with the working-backward strategy.
- setting up a table that shows the total wheels on 16 bicycles and seven tricycles.
- making change from a particular bill for a certain amount of purchases.
- doubling or tripling a recipe's ingredients for a party.
- measuring the dimensions of a box.

Do It My Way!

Skill: Problem solving, persuasive writing

There's more than one way to solve most problems. Challenge pairs of students to think of a problem that could be solved in different ways (for example, acting out the problem instead of drawing a picture). Direct one student to use biased wording to write a persuasive paragraph favoring one method while her partner writes about the other. Remind students to support each reason they provide with a logical explanation or an example. Finally, instruct each pair to fold a large sheet of construction paper in half vertically. Have one student in the pair glue her paragraph and an illustration on the top half of the paper, while her partner does the same on the bottom half. Display the projects on a bulletin board titled "I'd Do It My Way!"

Writing | Math

Persuade a partner to:

- find the cost of three packs of gum using mental math instead of a calculator or paper and pencil.
- find the weight of three new pencils using metric instead of English measurement.
- find the number of feet from her desk to the nearest trash can using estimation instead of an exact measurement.
- find the length of an object using a nonstandard unit, such as a paper clip, rather than a standard unit, such as an inch.
- agree that your favorite team should be in first place. Use statistics to support your opinion.

Once Upon a Math Time...

Skill: Checking understanding, narrative writing

Want to make sure your students understand new math concepts? Turn them into math storytellers! Pick a picture book that complements a math unit the class is currently studying (see the books suggested below or ask your media specialist for help). After sharing the book, give each student a copy of the story-planning guide on page 148 to complete as directed. Then combine the students' completed stories into a class book. At the end of math class each day, share several of the stories aloud. Talk about a great ending!

Writing Math

PICTURE BOOKS TO CONNECT MATH AND NARRATIVE WRITING

Addition and Subtraction
Elevator Magic by Stuart J. Murphy
Ten Sly Piranhas: A Counting Story in Reverse (A Tale of Wickedness—and Worse!) by William Wise

Multiplication
Anno's Mysterious Multiplying Jar by Mitsumasa Anno
Bunches and Bunches of Bunnies by Louise Mathews
How Many Feet? How Many Tails? A Book of Math Riddles by Marilyn Burns
One Grain of Rice: A Mathematical Folktale by Demi
One Hundred Hungry Ants by Elinor J. Pinczes
Too Many Kangaroo Things to Do! by Stuart J. Murphy

Division
A Remainder of One by Elinor J. Pinczes
The Doorbell Rang by Pat Hutchins

Large Numbers
The King's Chessboard by David Birch

Fractions
Gator Pie by Louise Mathews

Measurement
Counting on Frank by Rod Clement
How Big Is a Foot? by Rolf Myller
Jim and the Beanstalk by Raymond Briggs
Spaghetti and Meatballs for All! by Marilyn Burns
The Librarian Who Measured the Earth by Kathryn Lasky (a biography, but still a good one to share with students)
Twelve Snails to One Lizard: A Tale of Mischief and Measurement by Susan Hightower

Geometry
Grandfather Tang's Story: A Tale Told With Tangrams by Ann Tompert
Sam Johnson and the Blue Ribbon Quilt by Lisa C. Ernst
The Greedy Triangle by Marilyn Burns

Money
Alexander, Who Used to Be Rich Last Sunday by Judith Viorst
Pigs Will Be Pigs: Fun With Math and Money by Amy Axelrod

Patterns
Anno's Magic Seeds by Mitsumasa Anno

Data Collection, Graphing, Probability, and Statistics
The Best Vacation Ever by Stuart J. Murphy

Miscellaneous
Alice in Pastaland: A Math Adventure by Alexandra Wright
Math Curse by Jon Scieszka

Make the Math and Writing Connection!

Want to make a positive connection every time you must write in math?
Then get some practice with math writing by completing ____ of the
following activities. Color the outlet when you complete its activity.

Write clues to help a classmate guess a given number.

Write clues to help a classmate solve a logic-grid problem.

Read or listen to a fairy tale; then write five math word problems related to the tale.

Write about a day during which you could use no math at all.

Look at a magazine picture; then write a math word problem related to the picture.

In writing, explain a shortcut for solving a math problem. For example, to explain how to subtract by adding, you might write: "In the problem 107 – 85, 107 is 7 more than 100, and 85 is 15 less than 100. Since 7 + 15 = 22, then 107 – 85 = 22."

Write a letter to an absent classmate explaining what the day's math class was about.

Write a phrase to help others remember a math concept. For example, use "**Dad**, **Mom**, **Sister**, **Brother**" to help someone remember these long-division steps: **Divide, Multiply, Subtract, Bring down.**

Study a chart, map, or graph; then write at least five questions a classmate could answer by using it.

Write a math riddle to share with the class.

Write an explanation of how to solve the last problem in tonight's math homework.

Write an "If…then" problem for a classmate to solve. For example: *If* Brett eats four pieces of pizza each week for a year, *then* how many pieces will he eat in ten years?

Make a Word Bank for a current math unit; then write a story using as many words from the bank as possible.

Write a math word problem your teacher could include on the class's next math test.

©The Education Center, Inc. • *The Best of The Mailbox® Math • Book 2* • TEC1492

Goin' With the Flow!

Graphic organizers, such as flow charts, can help you solve math problems. Study the flow chart below. It explains how to subtract 756 from 1,642. Follow its steps to help you solve the problem.

Next, write the steps explaining how to subtract 2,408 from 5,117 on the lines provided. Use the flow chart as a guide. Be as specific with your steps as you can.

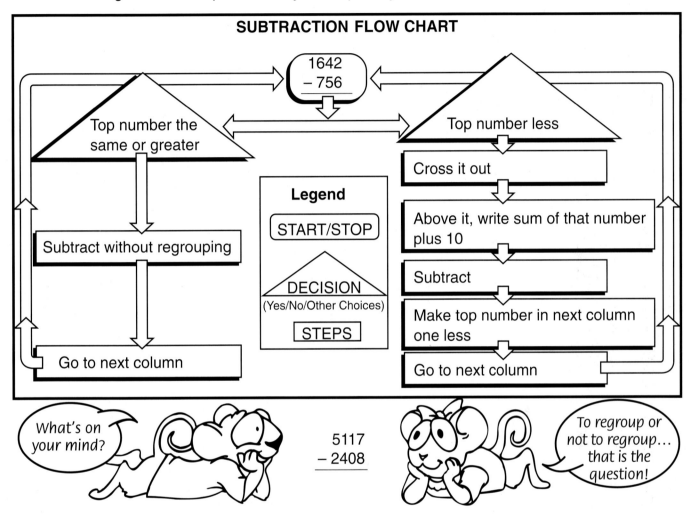

SUBTRACTION FLOW CHART

1642
− 756

Top number the same or greater

Top number less

Cross it out

Above it, write sum of that number plus 10

Subtract

Make top number in next column one less

Subtract without regrouping

Go to next column

Go to next column

Legend

START/STOP

DECISION
(Yes/No/Other Choices)

STEPS

What's on your mind?

5117
− 2408

To regroup or not to regroup... that is the question!

_____

_____

_____

_____

_____

_____

_____

Bonus Box: Write a different subtraction problem on another sheet of paper. Ask a classmate to write the steps that explain how to solve it. Then check his or her work.

Name ____________________ Math story-planning sheet

A Math Story From Scratch

The yummiest foods can come from mixing together just the right combination of ingredients. Likewise, coming up with just the right mixture of story elements is what makes a great story. Use the recipe card to plan your own made-from-scratch story that includes a concept you're studying in math. Then write and illustrate your story on another sheet of paper.

Title: ____________________

Setting: ____________________

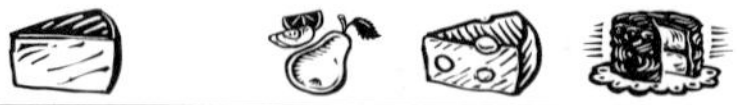

Main character: ____________________

Other characters: ____________________

Main character's goal: ____________________

Math concept in my story: ____________________

Plot (problem/conflict): ____________________

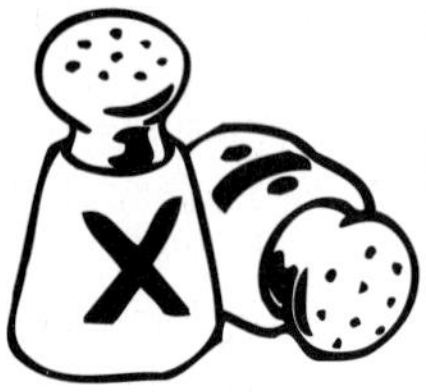

Event 1: ____________________

Event 2: ____________________

Event 3: ____________________

Climax: ____________________

Resolution: ____________________

Note to the teacher: Use with "Once Upon a Math Time…" on page 145.

Pattern Use with "Same or Different?" on page 143.

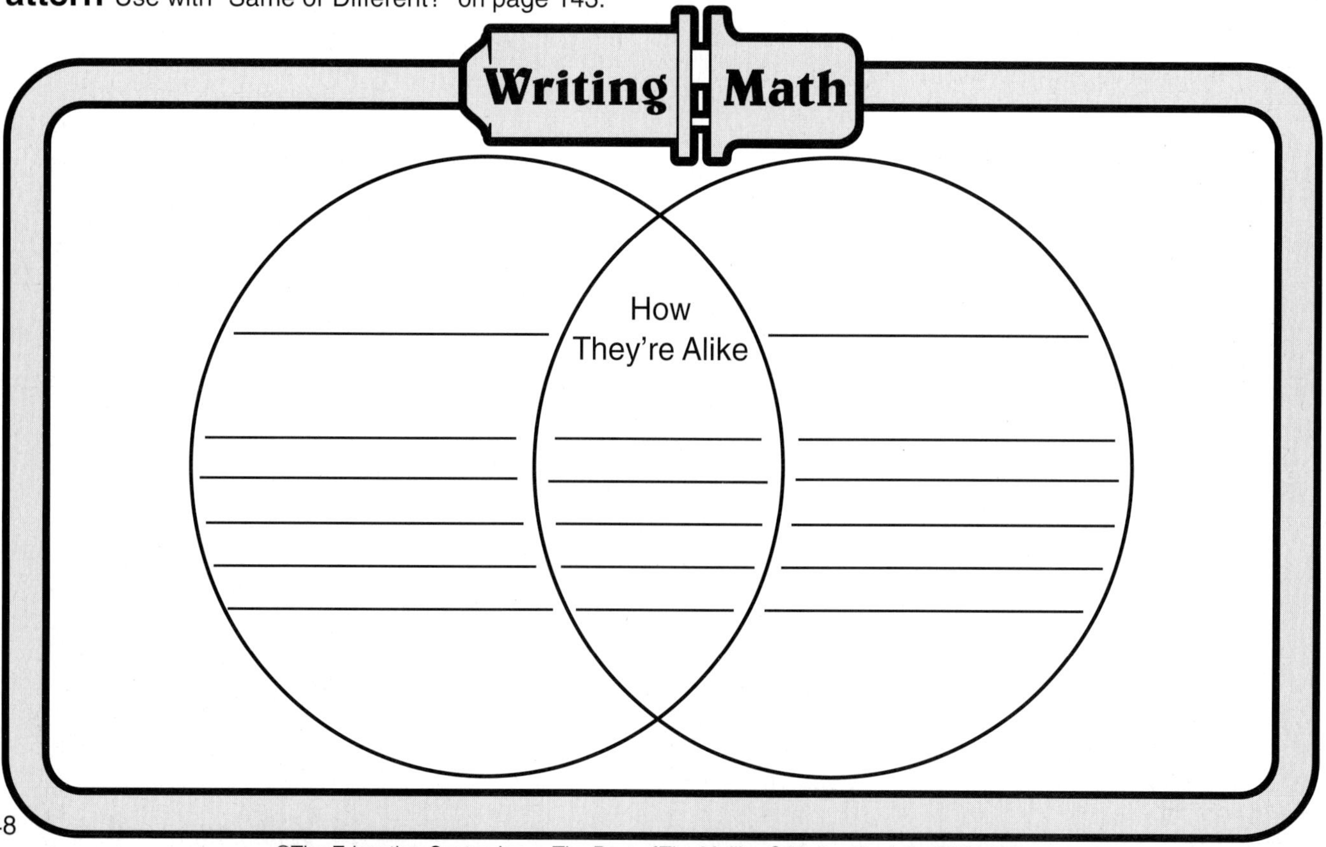
Writing
Math
How They're Alike

DIGGIN' DOMINOES AND DICE

A Chart-Topping Combo for Teaching Math Skills

They're hot! They're versatile! And they've been at the top of the math charts for years. Who are these talented sensations? Dominoes and dice! Use these centuries-old games to provide your students with a variety of fun math activities.

by Irving P. Crump

In the Spotlight: The Dynamic Dice

Dice have been around for thousands of years. Today dice are used in a variety of games. But it's random chance—not skill—that determines which numbers appear when dice are rolled. Reinforce basic math skills with the quartet of dice games that follow below and on page 150. First, provide each student with a copy of the reproducible on page 152. Introduce one game a day as a whole-class activity. Then, on the fifth day, have a gamefest by providing each pair of students with a new copy of the reproducible and three dice. Invite students to play the four games in any order that they wish.

Game 1: Target 15
Skills: Addition and subtraction facts, mental math

This game of strategy gives students practice with mental computation as they review basic facts. The object is to make and circle a horizontal, vertical, or diagonal row of three numbers whose sum is 15. To begin play, roll two dice and announce the numbers showing. Jot down your rolls to use as a key to check students' answers. Direct each student to either add or subtract the two numbers and write the answer in any square on his grid.

Roll the dice a second time and announce the two numbers showing. Again, each student adds or subtracts the numbers and writes the answer in any square on his grid. Continue rolling the dice and calling out numbers until a student circles three numbers in a row whose sum is 15. Have the lucky student call out, "Fifteen!" Continue play until the grid is filled with numbers. The player who circles the most rows wins.

Game 2: Target 30
Skills: Addition, subtraction, and multiplication facts; mental math

Target 30 reinforces addition, subtraction, and mental math—and adds a third operation: multiplication. The object is to make and circle a horizontal, vertical, or diagonal row of three numbers whose sum is 30. Follow the same directions described for playing Target 15, adding the additional option of multiplying the two numbers. After a student announces, "Thirty!" continue play until the grid is filled with numbers. The player who circles the most rows wins.

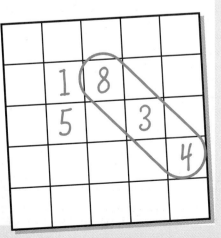

149

Game 3: Mayday! Mayday!
Skill: Plotting points on a graph

To play this game of skill and decision making, have each student randomly write four *M*s (missiles), three *A*s (aircraft carriers), two *J*s (jetfighters), and one *D* (ammunition depot) in the grid squares. Roll a pair of dice and call out the numbers. Have each student use the two numbers as coordinate pairs: for example, a roll of 5 and 1 will be (5, 1) and (1, 5). If a double is rolled, there is only one possible pair. The student locates the grid boxes that correspond to those pairs. If each box includes a target letter, the student chooses the one of greater value according to the code below the grid and makes an X through it. If only one box has a target, the student marks through it; if there is no target in either box, the student does not make a strike. Roll the dice ten times; then have each student add her points to determine her score. (When student pairs play the game, instruct one child in each pair to label the grid with targets before play begins.)

Game 4: Making Connections
Skills: Addition, subtraction, multiplication, division

The guess-and-check strategy is a solid hit when students play Making Connections. Roll three dice and announce the numbers. Have each student jot down these numbers. Allow students two minutes to add, subtract, multiply, and divide the three numbers in any way to get the largest possible answer that touches the circled 23. Direct the student to circle this number with a marker. (If the student cannot make a connection, he must wait for the next roll of the dice.) Then roll the three dice a second time. Have students use the three numbers showing to make an equation with an answer that connects to one of the two circled numbers. Continue play for ten rounds; then direct each student to find the total of his circled numbers, excluding the 23. (When student pairs play, have students take turns rolling the three dice. If a player cannot make a connection, he loses his turn. After ten turns each, each student adds to find the total of his circled numbers.)

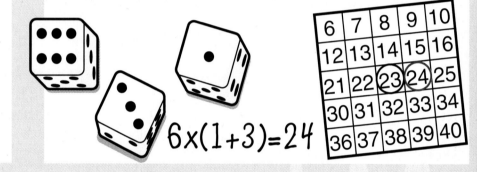

$$6 \times (1+3) = 24$$

6	7	8	9	10
12	13	14	15	16
21	22	㉓	㉔	25
30	31	32	33	34
36	37	38	39	40

Presenting: The Fabulous Dominoes

Dominoes have also been around for a long time. In fact, a set was discovered in King Tutankhamen's tomb when it was opened in 1922! Duplicate page 153 on tagboard for each student. Have students cut apart the first two columns of dominoes to make a double-six set. For a double-nine set, have each student cut apart the 27 dominoes in the right two columns and combine them with the 28 double-six dominoes.

They're the Pips!
Skills: Introduction to dominoes, patterns, vocabulary

Introduce dominoes by first having each student lay out his 28 double-six tiles on his desk. Have students find and describe at least three different patterns. During this exploratory time, discuss the following facts about dominoes:

- There are 28 *tiles,* or pieces, in a set of double-six dominoes. The highest tile is the double-six. The lowest is the double-blank.
- Domino tiles are also called *stones, bones,* or *men.*
- The spots on a domino are called *pips.*
- The end of a domino that has no pips is called a *blank.*
- A domino with an equal number of pips on each end is called a *double.*
- There are seven suits in a set of double-six dominoes: sixes, fives, fours, threes, twos, ones, and blanks.

Have students describe the different patterns they observed. Also ask them how dominoes and dice are alike.

On the Lookout for a Pattern
Skills: Making a bar graph, noting patterns

After examining the double-six dominoes, have each student make a graph that shows each domino's total number of pips. First, ask students what type of graph would best show such information *(a bar graph or pictograph)*. Then ask them how many different sums are represented in a set of 28 double-six dominoes *(13 different sums: 0–12)*. Have students sort the dominoes by their sums and then use that data as the horizontal axis of a bar graph. Instruct students to determine the vertical axis of the graph as well.

For a follow-up, have students repeat the activity using the set of double-nine dominoes. Ask them to describe the pattern this graph makes and how it's similar to the graph for a set of double-six dominoes.

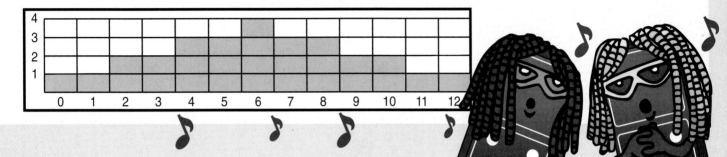

Domino Rummy
Skills: Recognizing patterns, categorizing

This partner game, similar to the card game rummy, provides practice in making patterns with dominoes. First, divide students into pairs. Have the students in each pair spread out one set of double-six dominoes facedown between them. To begin play, follow the directions:

← pattern
← same value

 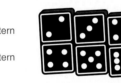
← pattern   ← pattern
← pattern   ← pattern

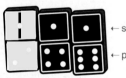
← same value
← pattern

1. Each player draws seven dominoes and turns them faceup and vertical. Each player looks at her dominoes and tries to make sets of three in which the three top faces have the same value or form a pattern, and the three bottom faces have the same value or form a pattern. See the examples. If either player has a set of three, she lays it aside, faceup.
2. Player 1 then draws one domino from the pile.
3. Player 1 checks to see if she can make a set of three. If so, she lays it aside. If not, she adds the domino to the ones she already has.
4. A player may, during her turn, place one domino onto a set of three already played—if it continues that set. Then she takes her turn by drawing one domino.
5. Player 2 then takes a turn.
6. The winner of the game is the first player to get rid of all of her dominoes.

Magic Squares
Skills: Addition, creative thinking

Challenge students to make magic squares using dominoes from their double-six set. A domino magic square consists of four dominoes placed in a square pattern (see the sample shown) so that the sum of pips on each side of the square is the same. Have each student use the sets of dominoes listed below to make magic squares. For the solutions, see the key on page 160.

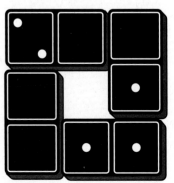

1. 0/0, 0/1, 0/2, 1/1: each side equals 2
2. 0/1, 0/2, 0/3, 1/2: each side equals 3
3. 0/1, 0/2, 1/3, 2/2: each side equals 4
4. 1/1, 1/2, 1/3, 2/2: each side equals 5
5. 1/2, 0/3, 2/3, 3/3: each side equals 6

6. 1/3, 2/3, 3/3, 2/2: each side equals 7
7. 1/6, 3/6, 0/3, 2/4: each side equals 9
8. 2/3, 2/5, 2/6, 3/5: each side equals 10
9. 0/6, 5/6, 6/6, 1/5: each side equals 12
10. 4/4, 4/5, 4/6, 5/5: each side equals 14

Game 1: Target 15

materials:
2 dice
2 pencils (for writing numbers)
2 different-colored markers (for circling rows of numbers)

object:
Circle three numbers in a row (across, down, or diagonally) whose sum is 15. The winner is the player who circles the most rows.

Game 2: Target 30

materials:
2 dice
2 pencils (for writing numbers)
2 different-colored markers (for circling rows)

object:
Circle three numbers in a row (across, down, or diagonally) whose sum is 30. The winner is the player who circles the most rows.

Game 3: Mayday! Mayday!

6						
5						
4						
3						
2						
1						
0	1	2	3	4	5	6

materials:
2 dice
pencil (for writing letters in the grid)
2 different-colored markers (for striking out targets)

object:
Win the most points by striking out targets.
D (ammunition depot) = 4 points each
J (jetfighter) = 3 points each
A (aircraft carrier) = 2 points each
M (missile) = 1 point each

Game 4: Making Connections

6	7	8	9	10
12	13	14	15	16
21	22	(23)	24	25
30	31	32	33	34
36	37	38	39	40

materials:
3 dice
2 pencils (for computing)
2 different-colored markers (for circling numbers)

object:
Win the most points by circling numbers that are connected to each other.

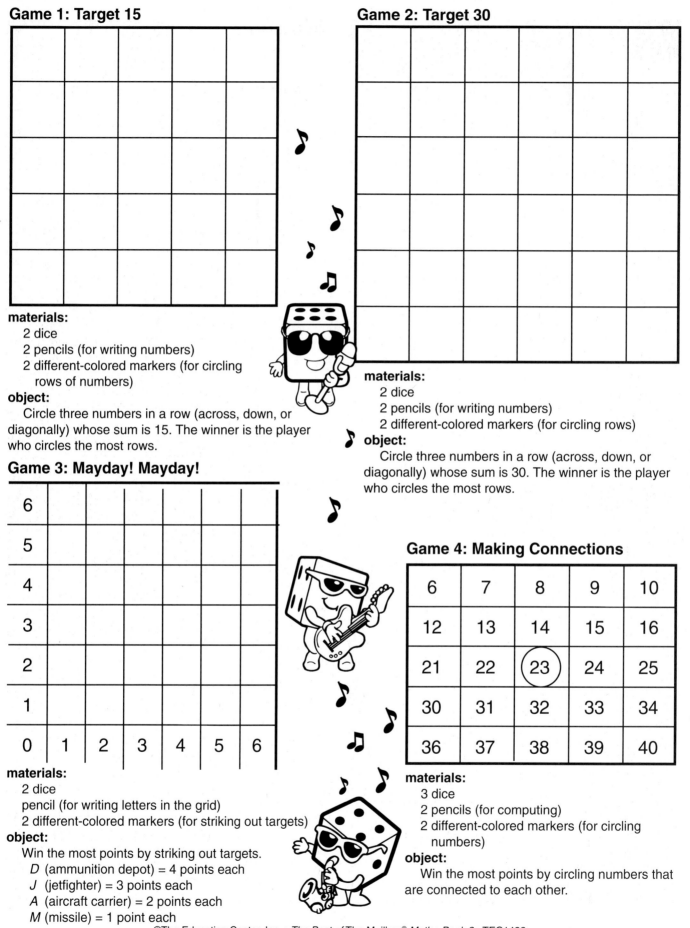

Double-Nine Dominoes

©The Education Center, Inc. • *The Best of* The Mailbox® *Math* • *Book 2* • TEC1492

Note to the teacher: See page 150 for information on using this page.

153

Game Plans

X-Out

Strengthen basic computational skills with a game of X-Out. Copy the gameboard shown in the illustration onto the chalkboard. Divide your class into four or five teams. Have Team 1 roll three dice; then have it add, subtract, multiply, or divide the numbers until the solution is one of the numerals on the gameboard. Have one member of Team 1 record that number of points and cross out that numeral on the gameboard. Next, allow Team 2 to use the same three numbers rolled by Team 1 to arrive at a different solution. Continue rotating turns until all possible solutions have been found for those three numbers; then have Team 2 roll the dice for three new numbers. When all the numerals on the gameboard have been crossed out, tally each team's score. Declare the team with the most points the winner.

Patricia Clancy—Gr. 5, Peter Noyes School, Sudbury, MA

①	②	③	④	⑤	⑥
⑦	⑧	⑨	⑩	⑪	⑫
⑬	⑭	⑮	⑯	⑰	⑱
⑲	⑳	㉑	㉒	㉓	㉔
㉕	㉖				

Basic Facts Card Game

This fun multiplication review will have your students mastering their basic facts in no time! Begin by making several sets of multiplication flash cards—recording a different problem on the front of each card. Next, divide your class into groups of two to four players. Give each group a set of cards. Select one child in each group to be the dealer, evenly distributing the cards in his deck to his group members. Have the player to the left of the dealer begin play by laying down a card from his hand. Direct the next player to lay down a card with a product equal to or greater than the card played before him. Explain that if a player does not have such a card, he doesn't get to lay down a card and he loses that turn. Direct students to continue until a player gets rid of all his cards or no player is able to lay down a card. Then have the last student to play a card collect all the fact cards and begin the game again.

Melinda Salisbury—Grs. 4–6, Baldwin North Intermediate School Quincy, IL

Luck of the Draw

Teaching place value is a breeze when you play Luck of the Draw! Remove all face cards, aces, and tens from a standard deck of playing cards. Then have each student set up a game grid with blanks (example: __,__ __ __). The number of blanks in the grid will vary depending on the ability levels of the students playing. Inform students that the objective of the game is to create the number with the largest place value possible. Play begins when the dealer pulls a card from the deck and announces the number on the card. Players must decide in which blank to put the drawn number. This procedure continues until all blanks have been filled. The player whose final number has the highest value receives a point. Students will look forward to getting their chance to test the "luck of the draw."

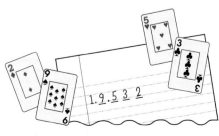

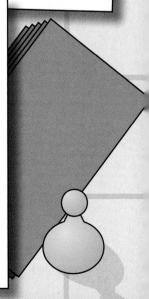

Kristin Adamson—Gr. 4, Landis Elementary, Houston, TX

Coordinate Grid Tic-Tac-Toe

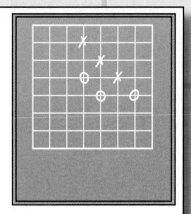

Reinforce the basics of coordinate graphing with this fun variation of tic-tac-toe. On the chalkboard or overhead projector, draw a 7 x 7 grid as shown. Place a dot at one of the graph's intersections to indicate the origin (x, y = 0, 0). Then divide your class into two teams. Have the teams take turns giving you a coordinate pair. Mark an X for Team 1 and an O for Team 2 at the intersection indicated by the coordinate pair given by the group. When a team gets four marks in a row vertically, horizontally, or diagonally, circle that row and award the team a point. Continue marking Xs and Os on the grid and awarding points until it is no longer possible for a group to get four in a row. Tic-tac-toe was never more "math-tastic"!

Game Variations:
- Don't explain to students how to find a coordinate pair location on the grid. Instead, have them figure out how to indicate the coordinates by studying where each mark falls on the grid.
- Have the grid blocks represent increments of two, five, or ten rather than one.
- Move the origin up and to the right to incorporate an area of negative integers.
- Laminate sheets of grid paper; then place dry-erase markers and the grids at a learning center so students can play in their free time.

Beth Gress—Gr. 6, Mt. Gilead, OH

Erase It!

This mental math game will have your students racing against the clock! Write the numbers 1–25 on the board, as shown, and record the exact time the game starts. Challenge your students to create an equation using the digits 1, 2, 3, and 4 with a solution equivalent to one of the numbers on the board. Explain that the equation can include addition, subtraction, multiplication, and division, but must use each digit only once. When a student shares a correct equation, erase its solution from the board. For example, if a student says, "$3 \times 4 \div 2 + 1 = 7$," erase the number 7 from the board. The game ends when each of the 25 numbers has been erased. Check the clock again and calculate the amount of time it took to finish the game; then write the numbers 1–25 on the board again and have students play another round, trying to beat the time of the first round.

Once students have mastered numbers 1–25, have them solve 26–50 and 51–75 using the digits 1–5. For an even greater challenge, have students solve 76–100 using the digits 1–6.

Nancy Paley—Grs. 5–6, Clara Barton Elementary, Cherry Hill, NJ

Integer Challenge

Let the fun roll when students practice adding integers with this challenging game. Give each pair of students a die and a sheet of paper. Then guide students through the steps below, challenging them to become the player closer to zero after five rounds.

1. Roll the die. The student rolling the higher number becomes Player 1.
2. Before Player 1 rolls, Player 2 calls out either "positive" or "negative." Then Player 1 rolls and records his roll on the paper. For example, if Player 2 calls out "negative" and Player 1 rolls a five, Player 1 records "–5" on the paper.
3. Player 1 calls out either "positive" or "negative." Then he rolls the die again and adds that number to the first number he rolled. For example, if Player 1 calls out "positive" and rolls a six, he records "+6" as shown and then adds to get "+1" (his score for Round 1).
4. Player 2 follows Steps 2 and 3 to take her turn in Round 1 using the back side of the paper.
5. Continue play in this manner for five rounds or until time is called. Add the scores for all rounds together to get a final score. The winner is the player whose final score is closer to zero.

Integer Challenge
Name: Mandy
Round 1: _-5_ + _+6_ = _+1_
Round 2: ___ + ___ = ___
subtotal: ___
Round 3: ___ + ___ = ___
subtotal: ___
Round 4: ___ + ___ = ___
subtotal: ___
Round 5: ___ + ___ = ___
final score: ___

Lois J. Lalley—Gr. 5, Kyrene Monte Vista School, Phoenix, AZ

Answer Keys

Page 7

1. 148; 158; 168; <u>178</u>; 188; 198; <u>208</u> *(add 10)*
2. 605; 705; 805; <u>905</u>; <u>1,005</u>; 1,105; 1,205 *(add 100)*
3. 6,734; 5,734; 4,734; <u>3,734</u>; <u>2,734</u>; 1,734; <u>734</u> *(subtract 1,000)*
4. 76,485; 81,485; 86,485; <u>91,485</u>; 96,485; <u>101,485</u>; 106,485 *(add 5,000)*
5. 18,000; <u>20,000</u>; <u>22,000</u>; 24,000; 26,000; 28,000; <u>30,000</u> *(add 2,000)*
6. 156; 166; 266; 276; 376; <u>386</u>; <u>486</u>; <u>496</u>; 596 *(add 10, add 100)*
7. 85; 185; 285; 385; 1,385; 2,385; 3,385; <u>13,385</u>; <u>23,385</u>; 33,385 *(add 100; add 100; add 100; add 1,000; add 1,000; add 1,000; add 10,000; add 10,000; add 10,000)*
8. 12,612; 12,617; 12,667; 13,167; <u>18,167</u>; 68,167 *(add 5; add 50; add 500; add 5,000; add 50,000)*
9. 1,487,329; 487,329; 387,329; 377,329; 376,329; <u>376,229</u>; <u>376,219</u> *(subtract 1,000,000; subtract 100,000; subtract 10,000; subtract 1,000; subtract 100; subtract 10)*
10. 512,479; 512,478; 512,468; 512,368; <u>511,368</u>; 501,368; <u>401,368</u> *(subtract 1; subtract 10; subtract 100; subtract 1,000; subtract 10,000; subtract 100,000)*
11. 614,375; 614,376; 614,386; 614,486; 615,486; <u>625,486</u>; <u>725,486</u> *(add 1; add 10; add 100; add 1,000; add 10,000; add 100,000)*
    Bonus Challenge: 364,237; 364,240; 364,300; 365,000; <u>370,000</u>; 400,000 *(Each value is added to create 0 in the next placeholder: add 3; add 60; add 700; add 5,000; add 30,000.)*

Page 11

1. Add a + sign and an = sign.
a. 6 + 8   5 = 9   1
b. 1   7 + 9 = 2   6
c. 6   3 + 2   7 = 9   0
d. 5   8 + 2   7 = 8   5
e. 8   6 + 9   5 = 1   8   1

2. Add a – sign and an = sign.	3. Add a x sign and an = sign.
a. 4 7 – 9 = 3 8	a. 9 x 8 = 7 2
b. 6 2 – 7 = 5 5	b. 1 6 x 5 = 8 0
c. 9 1 – 1 9 = 7 2	c. 4 x 2 4 = 9 6
d. 1 0 6 – 8 = 9 8	d. 5 4 x 7 = 3 7 8
e. 1 4 3 – 5 6 = 8 7	e. 1 7 x 2 1 = 3 5 7

4. Add a ÷ sign and an = sign.	5. Add either a +, –, x, or ÷ sign and an = sign.	6. Add *two* signs and an = sign. Add parentheses if needed. The first one is done for you.
a. 1 8 ÷ 6 = 3	a. 7 2 ÷ 1 2 = 6	a. (6 x 8) + 5 = 5 3
b. 5 6 ÷ 7 = 8	b. 4 6 – 3 9 = 7	b. (7 + 3) x 6 = 6 0
c. 6 0 ÷ 4 = 1 5	c. 9 + 5 7 = 6 6	c. (9 – 5) + 8 = 1 2
d. 1 2 0 ÷ 1 0 = 1 2	d. 7 x 1 4 = 9 8	d. (2 0 ÷ 5) + 3 = 7
e. 4 3 5 ÷ 1 5 = 2 9	e. 2 7 – 2 5 = 2	e. 5 x 6 x 3 = 9 0

Page 12

Score: 50 (10 problems missed)

Add:

65 + 21 = 86 (correct)

107 + 95 = 202 (correct)

456 + 327 = 783 (incorrect: The Big Four did not add the regrouped 1 in the 10s column.)

205 + 806 = 1,011 (correct)

398 + 273 = 671 (incorrect: The Big Four did not add the regrouped 1 in the 100s column.)

Subtract:

73 – 20 = 53 (correct)

164 – 25 = 139 (incorrect: The Big Four did not subtract in the 100s column.)

212 – 96 = 116 (correct)

1,010 – 253 = 757 (correct)

862 – 149 = 713 (incorrect: The Big Four did not have to regroup in the 100s place.)

Page 12 (Continued)

Multiply:

12 x 8 = 96 (incorrect: The error is that 2 x 8 = 16, not 12.)

63 x 10 = 630 (correct)

17 x 7 = 119 (incorrect: The error is that 7 x 7 = 49, not 56.)

86 x 3 = 258 (correct)

107 x 9 = 963 (incorrect:The Big Four forgot to add the regrouped 6 in the 10s place; 0 + 6 = 6.)

Divide:

28 ÷ 2 = 14 R0 (correct)

87 ÷ 6 = 14 R3 (incorrect: The remainder is too large; 27 ÷ 6 = 4 with a remainder of 3.)

81 ÷ 4 = 20 R1 (correct)

783 ÷ 5 = 156 R3 (incorrect: The Big Four brought down the 8 twice instead of the 3 in the ones place.)

1,062 ÷ 7 = 151 R5 (incorrect: The first digit of the quotient was written in the wrong place; the 1 should have been written in the 100s place above the 0.)

Page 18

Part I:

1. N = 7
2. E = 24
3. L = 9
4. W = 0
5. B = 15
6. R = 3
7. O = 5
8. T = 1
9. T = 5
10. S = 15
11. E = 9
12. E = 0
13. H = 37
14. S = 0
15. T = 2
16. O = 23
17. E = 5
18. N = 0
19. T = 51

Part II:

- property of one: E, T, H
- order property: N, B, O, S, O, T
- zero property: W, E, S, N
- grouping property: L, R, T, E, T, E

Part III:

THE BOSTON NEWS-LETTER

Bonus Box: 1704

Page 19

1. $140
2. $168
3. $38
4. $356
5. $60
6. $24.75
7. $96
8. $126
9. $71.75; ($7.50 + $6.85) x 5 = $71.75
10. $59.50; ($5.50 x 4) + ($7.50 x 5) = $59.50
11. $180, $2,160; $540 ÷ 3 = $180; $180 x 12 = $2,160
12. $96.25; ($5.25 + $8.50) x 7 = $96.25
13. $40; $16 x 15 = $240; $240 – $200 = $40
14. $6,480; $540 x 12 = $6,480
15. $50.25; ($5.25 + $5.25 + $6.25) x 3 = $50.25

Bonus Box: $42 (regular price: 2 x $85 = $170, Brandon's price: 4 x $32 = $128, $170 – $128 = $42)

Page 23

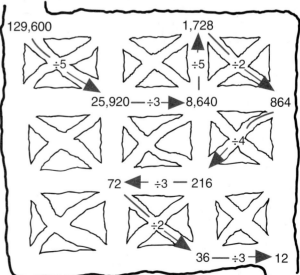

Page 28

1. $33 \div 3 - 3 = 8$
2. $5 + 55 \times 5 = 280$
3. $9 \div 9 + 99 = 100$
4. $(77 - 7) \times 7 = 490$
5. $(10 + 10) \div 10 + 10 = 12$
6. $(29 \times 29) + (29 + 29) = 899$
7. $(12 \div 12) \times 12 + 12 = 24$
8. $(72 \times 72) + (72 \div 72) = 5,185$
9. $100 + (100 \times 100) \div 100 = 200$
10. $505 \div 505 + 505 + 505 = 1,011$

Bonus Box: $(3 \times 3)^2 \div 3 + 3 = 30$

Page 34

Gameboard 1		
$\frac{1}{2}$	$\frac{1}{8}$	$\frac{1}{8}$
$\frac{1}{3}$	$\frac{1}{4}$	$\frac{2}{3}$
$\frac{2}{3}$	$\frac{1}{2}$	$\frac{3}{4}$

Gameboard 2		
$\frac{3}{4}$	$\frac{1}{4}$	$\frac{2}{3}$
$\frac{1}{3}$	$\frac{1}{8}$	$\frac{1}{4}$
$\frac{1}{3}$	$\frac{1}{2}$	$\frac{1}{2}$

Gameboard 3		
$\frac{1}{4}$	$\frac{1}{3}$	$\frac{1}{2}$
$\frac{2}{3}$	$\frac{2}{3}$	$\frac{1}{2}$
$\frac{1}{8}$	$\frac{3}{4}$	$\frac{1}{8}$

Gameboard 4		
$\frac{1}{8}$	$\frac{3}{4}$	$\frac{2}{3}$
$\frac{1}{2}$	$\frac{1}{4}$	$\frac{2}{3}$
$\frac{1}{2}$	$\frac{1}{4}$	$\frac{1}{3}$

Page 35

1.

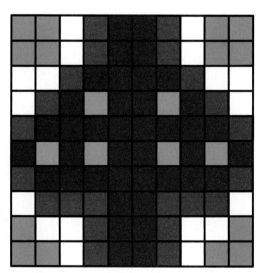

2. R = .22
   Bl = .06
   G = .14
   B = .40
   W = .18
3. $.22 + .06 + .14 + .40 + .18 = 1.00$
   The sum represents one whole.
4. R + Bl = .28; G + B = .54; R + G + W = .54
   Bl + B = .46; B – W = .22; R – G = .08
   (B + Bl + G) – (R + W) = .60 – .40 = .20
5. B > R
   R > W
   G < W
   G > Bl
   W > Bl

Bonus Box: black (.40), red (.22), white (.18), green (.14), blue (.06)

Page 39

1. $5\frac{1}{4}$, $5\frac{7}{8}$
   Rule: add $\frac{5}{8}$
2. 9, $10\frac{1}{2}$
   Rule: add $1\frac{1}{2}$
3. 15, $17\frac{1}{3}$
   Rule: add $2\frac{1}{3}$
4. $11\frac{1}{5}$, 13
   Rule: add $1\frac{4}{5}$
5. $17\frac{1}{8}$, $20\frac{3}{8}$
   Rule: add $3\frac{1}{4}$
6. $18\frac{5}{6}$, $24\frac{5}{6}$
   Rule: add 1, add 2, add 3, add 4, etc.
7. $6\frac{1}{2}$, $5\frac{1}{4}$
   Rule: add $2\frac{1}{2}$, subtract $1\frac{1}{4}$
8. 20, $25\frac{1}{2}$
   Rule: add $\frac{1}{2}$, add $1\frac{1}{2}$, add $2\frac{1}{2}$, add $3\frac{1}{2}$, etc.
9. $11\frac{7}{10}$, $13\frac{9}{10}$
   Rule: add $1\frac{1}{5}$, add $1\frac{2}{5}$, add $1\frac{3}{5}$, add $1\frac{4}{5}$, etc.
10. $10\frac{2}{3}$, $12\frac{1}{2}$
    Rule: subtract $\frac{2}{3}$, add $1\frac{5}{6}$

Bonus Box: $23\frac{5}{8}$ ($1\frac{1}{8} + 2\frac{2}{8} + 3\frac{3}{8} + 4\frac{4}{8} + 5\frac{5}{8} + 6\frac{6}{8}$ or in simplest terms: $1\frac{1}{8} + 2\frac{1}{4} + 3\frac{3}{8} + 4\frac{1}{2} + 5\frac{5}{8} + 6\frac{3}{4}$)

Page 41

Measurements are to the nearest eighth.

1. $7\frac{1}{4}$ in.
2. 5 in.
3. $5\frac{1}{8}$ in.
4. $6\frac{1}{4}$ in.
5. $4\frac{3}{8}$ in.
6. 2 in.
7. $10\frac{3}{4}$ in.
8. $7\frac{3}{4}$ in.
9. $5\frac{1}{4}$ in.
10. $9\frac{3}{4}$ in.
11. $8\frac{1}{8}$ in.
12. $2\frac{3}{8}$ in.
13. $\frac{1}{8}$ in.
14. $1\frac{3}{4}$ in.
15. $2\frac{1}{2}$ in.
16. $1\frac{1}{2}$ in.
17. $13\frac{1}{8}$ in.
18. $10\frac{3}{8}$ in.
19. $15\frac{3}{4}$ in.
20. $12\frac{1}{4}$ in.
21. 11 in.
22. $15\frac{7}{8}$ in.
23. $16\frac{1}{2}$ in.
24. $11\frac{3}{8}$ in.
25. $17\frac{3}{8}$ in.

Bonus Box: A–G–I–E–C = $11\frac{7}{8}$ in. A–B–E–C = $16\frac{7}{8}$ in.
A–G–I–E–C is shorter by 5 in.

Page 47

1. 68
2. 100
3. 75
4. $65.00
5. $4.56
6. 108
7. 15
8. 2
9. $37\frac{1}{2}$
10. 12

My proverb:
An old mouse does not run twice into the snare.

Bonus Box: 285%

Page 51

Part II:
A = 7; B = 9; C = 8; D = 0; E = 6; F = 1; G = 3; H = 5; I = 4; J = 2

Explanations

1. F = 1 (Identity property: The only number times J that equals J is 1.)
4. J = 2 (F + F)
5. I = 4 (J + J)
6. D = 0 (If E were 1, D could represent any digit. But 1 has been used.)
7. G = 3 (I – F, or 4 – 1)
8. H = 5 (H could be 4, 5, or 6. Only 5 will work: 3 x 5 = 15.)
9. B = 9 and E = 6 (The remaining digits are 6, 7, 8, and 9. The two that work are 9 and 6: 9 – 3 = 6.)
3. C = 8 and A = 7 (C – A = 1)

Page 52

Input-output numbers are listed from top to bottom.
Part I
2. rule: + 7; I-O: 12, 17, 14
3. rule: x 4; I-O: 2, 32
4. rule: ÷ 5; I-O: 2, 4, 9
Part II
6. rule: + 6, ÷ 2 (or ÷ 2, + 3); I-O: 14, 7
7. rule: x 3, + 5; I-O: 5, 10
8. rule: – 4, x 2; I-O: 34, 5
Part III
9. rule: + 1, ÷ 3; I-O: 6, 29
10. rule: x 2, + 5; I-O: 7, 45
Bonus Box: Students' answers will vary.

Page 53

1. $\frac{4}{z}$
2. $5(p - q)$
3. $m - 6$
4. $3f$
5. $16 - y + 5$
6. $b + 5$
7. $\frac{4y}{2}$
8. $2k + 4$
9. $10 + j$
10. $12 - w$
11. $5(6 + u)$
12. $8s$
13. $\frac{n}{2}$
14. $6(c + d)$
15. $3p - 5$
16. $2\left(\frac{3}{x}\right)$

Answer to riddle: gator hole

Page 56

1. f
2. d
3. h
4. e
5. c
6. b
7. a
8. g
9. a, c, e
   b, d, f
10. a. 2 triangles and 3 rectangles
    b. 1 square and 4 triangles

Bonus Box: cone, cylinder, and sphere

Page 64

Pizza	Circumference	Diameter	Circumference ÷ Diameter
Pepperoni	9.5"	3"	3.17
Black olive	5"	1.5"	3.33
Cheese	3"	1"	3
Anchovy	1.5"	.5"	3
Green pepper	6.5"	2"	3.25
Mushroom	7.5"	2.5"	3

Bonus Box: Students' sentences will vary but should mention that the circumference is about three times the diameter.

Page 65

Part 1: Answers may vary slightly.

1. a. 33 whole squares, 10 partial squares
   b. 5 sq. units
   c. 38 sq. units
   d. 152 sq. units

2. a. 56 whole squares, 13 partial squares
   b. 7 sq. units
   c. 63 sq. units
   d. 252 sq. units

Part 2: Accept all reasonable estimates:
For a radius of 5 sq. units: estimated area = 76 to 84 sq. units
For a radius of 6 sq. units: estimated area = 112 to 120 sq. units
For a radius of 3 sq. units: estimated area = 24 to 32 sq. units

Bonus Box: Answers will vary. If a student didn't use the method outlined in Part 1, he might have used this method:

1. Count all of the whole squares in the circle.
2. Count the partial squares and divide by 2.
3. Add the answers to 1 and 2 together.

Page 66

Part 1:

1. sausage and extra cheese
2. 4 different combinations: pepperoni and anchovies; pepperoni and mushrooms; mushrooms and anchovies; pepperoni, mushrooms, and anchovies

Part 2: Students' choices of two and three toppings for the overlapping pizzas will vary.

Page 75

"Looking for Gold!"

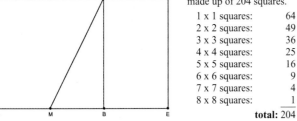

"A Puzzling Pair"

Puzzle 1: The checkerboard is made up of 204 squares.

1 x 1 squares:	64
2 x 2 squares:	49
3 x 3 squares:	36
4 x 4 squares:	25
5 x 5 squares:	16
6 x 6 squares:	9
7 x 7 squares:	4
8 x 8 squares:	1
total:	**204**

When sharing this solution with your students, have them note a pattern: The totals are equal to the squares of the numbers 1–8. Based on this pattern, ask students to determine the number of squares that would make up a checkerboard that is 5 x 5. *(55 squares)* 10 x 10? *(385 squares)*

Puzzle 2: The shape has 16 triangles:
a, b, c, d, e, f, bc, ed, af, fab, abc, bcd, cde, def, efa, and abcdef.

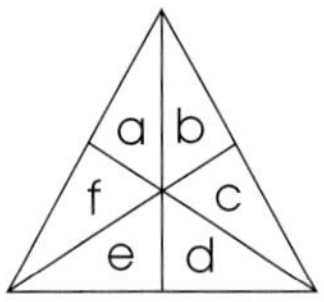

Page 77

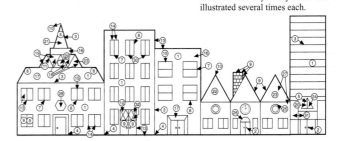

Answers will vary. Many terms are illustrated several times each.

Bonus Box: Answers may vary. Suggested answers include:
- 2nd building (rectangle) is similar to 3rd building (rectangle)
- circular doorknobs are similar to clock and circle on each side of clock
- 1st building door is similar to its door frame
- 4th building roofs (three equilateral triangles) are all similar to the triangle above the 5th building's door
- 1st building windows (rectangles) are similar to rectangular front of the building

Page 82

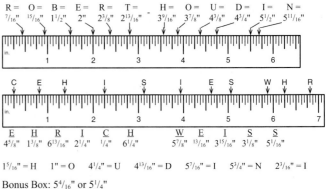

R = 7/16"   O = 15/16"   B = 1 1/2"   E = 2"   R = 2 3/8"   T = 2 13/16"   H = 3 9/16"   O = 3 7/8"   U = 4 3/8"   D = 4 3/4"   I = 5 1/2"   N = 5 11/16"

C   E   H   I   S   I   E   S   W   H   R

E 4 5/8"   H 1 3/8"   R 6 13/16"   I 2 1/4"   C 1/4"   H 6 1/4"   W 5 7/8"   E 13/16"   I 3 15/16"   S 3 1/8"   S 5 1/16"

1 5/16" = H   1" = O   4 1/4" = U   4 13/16" = D   5 7/16" = I   5 3/4" = N   2 3/16" = I

Bonus Box: 5 4/16" or 5 1/4"

Page 83

12 cm = P	5 cm = G
40 mm = R	17 cm = I
22 cm = E	10 mm = T
35 mm = S	90 mm = A
8 cm = T	15 cm = T
25 cm = I	70 mm = I
10 cm = D	18 cm = O
5 mm = I	25 mm = N

Answer: prestidigitation

Page 86

Part 2: The square and three rectangles are shown below. Accept two other possible rectangles as well: 10 cm x 2 cm (A = 20 sq. cm) and 11 cm x 1 cm (A = 11 sq. cm). The largest shape is the square with an area of 36 sq. cm.

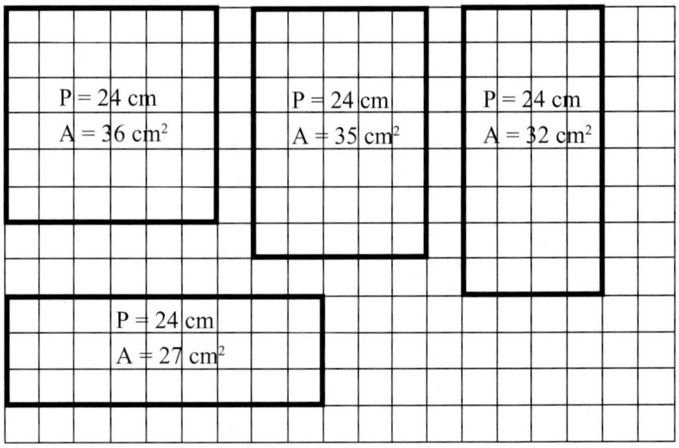

P = 24 cm
A = 36 cm²

P = 24 cm
A = 35 cm²

P = 24 cm
A = 32 cm²

P = 24 cm
A = 27 cm²

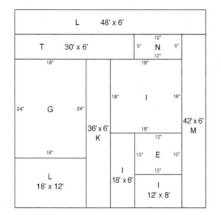

The crime:	
perimeter/area	letter
84 ft./216 ft.²	K
40 ft./96 ft.²	I
60 ft./216 ft.²	L
108 ft./288 ft.²	L
48 ft./108 ft.²	I
36 ft./72 ft.²	N
84 ft./432 ft.²	G
84 ft./96 ft.²	
72 ft./180 ft.²	T
72 ft./324 ft.²	I
96 ft./252 ft.²	M
44 ft./120 ft.²	E

Bonus Box: **P = 192 ft.** (4 x 48); **A = 2,304 ft.²** (48 x 48)

Page 88

1. **P = 48 ft.** Since the area of the rug is 80 sq. ft., the area of each section is 16 sq. ft. If the area of each small section is 16 sq. ft. and each section is a square, then each side is 4 ft. 4 ft. x 12 sides = 48 ft.

2. The largest possible garden is a 9 ft. x 9 ft. square with an area of **81 sq. ft.**

3. **72 cards:** 36 ÷ 4 = 9; 48 ÷ 6 = 8; 9 x 8 = 72 or 36 ÷ 6 = 6; 48 ÷ 4 = 12; 6 x 12 = 72

4. **P = 60 in.** Since the area of the square sheet is 400 sq. in., each side must be 20 in. Then the dimensions of each rectangle are 20 in. x 10 in. Perimeter = 20 in. + 10 in. + 20 in. + 10 in., or 60 in.

5. **A = 1,400 sq. ft.** There are several ways to solve this problem. One way is to subtract the area of the small rectangle, the pool (80 x 50 = 4,000 sq. ft.), from the area of the large rectangle (90 x 60 = 5,400 sq. ft. Ten feet is added to each dimension to include the width of the sidewalk.). Another way is to divide the sidewalk into sections and find the area of each section, as shown below.

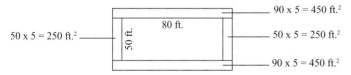

6. **P = 20 yd.** Since the area of the square is 144 sq. yd., each side is 12 yd. long. The length of each rectangle is 6 yd. (half of 12) and the width of each rectangle is 4 yd. (one-third of 12). So the perimeter of each rectangle is 2 (6 yd. + 4 yd.).

7. **A = 100 sq. ft.** By cutting out each section of the garden and placing them together, a square is formed. Since each side of the square is 10 ft., 10 ft. x 10 ft. = 100 sq. ft.

8. **P = 48 ft.; A = 108 sq. ft.**

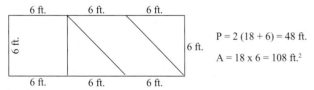

P = 2 (18 + 6) = 48 ft.

A = 18 x 6 = 108 ft.²

Bonus Box: A square whose area and perimeter are the same must have sides that are each 4 units long; then P = 4 x 4 = 16 units and A = 4 x 4 = 16 sq. units.

Page 90

"Nothing But Perimeter?": Answers will vary according to the different candy bars used. Students' answers should reflect a consideration of the candy bar's weight as well as its perimeter.

Page 93

"The Right Combination"

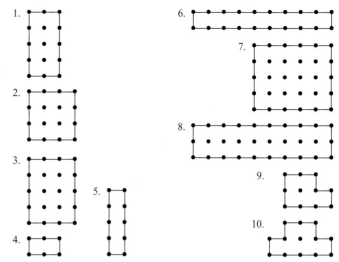

Page 94

"Positively Perimeter": The length of a raisin box (1½-ounce size) is approximately three Gummy Worm candy segments. Its width is two Gummy Worm candy segments, making the box's perimeter approximately 10 units. The length of the raisin box is approximately 1 pretzel stick. The width of the box is also approximately 1 pretzel stick. Thus, the raisin box's perimeter in pretzel sticks is approximately 4 units. Rounding to the nearest whole centimeter, the length of the raisin box is 7 cm, and its width is 5 cm, making its perimeter 24 cm.

"Making Circumference Make Sense": A length of Twizzlers Pull-N-Peel candy measures approximately 27 cm. Depending on the brand used, the circumference of a chocolate chip cookie is approximately 15 cm, and its diameter is 5 cm. The circumference of a rice or popcorn cake is approximately 27 cm, and its diameter is 9 cm. The circumference of a York Peppermint Pattie candy is approximately 18 cm, and its diameter is 6 cm. The circumference of a Ritz cracker is approximately 12 cm, and its diameter is 4 cm.

Bonus Box: Students should arrange the snacks in the following largest-to-smallest order: popcorn or rice cake, York Peppermint Pattie candy, chocolate chip cookie, Ritz cracker. Answers may vary depending on the brands of popcorn/rice cakes and cookies.

Page 95

"Zooming In on Volume": The actual number of raisins in students' boxes will vary but should number approximately 90. To fill a 1½-ounce raisin box with cubic centimeters, students need to fit 7 cm³ together to make a row and continue until they have made two layers of five rows each, giving a total of 70 cm³. Seven cm³ per row x five rows x two layers = 70 cm³.

"Squaring Off With Area": Students will use approximately 42 pieces of Corn Chex cereal when covering the flattened surfaces of their raisin boxes. They will probably estimate that it will take approximately six more pieces (rounded to the nearest piece) to cover the box completely, making a total estimated area in cereal pieces of 48 square units. After tracing the box onto centimeter-grid paper, students should count about 142 whole squares and about 38 partial squares. Since 38 divided by two is 19, the estimated surface area of the raisin box is 142 + 19, or about 161 cm².

Page 101

Step 1: 5, 7, 9, 12, 12, 14, 15, 17, 18, 20, 22, 23, 24, 27, 27, 27, 31, 33, 38, 39, 41, 43, 45

Step 2: Titles will vary.

Stems	Leaves
0	5, 7, 9
1	2, 2, 4, 5, 7, 8
2	0, 2, 3, 4, 7, 7, 7
3	1, 3, 8, 9
4	1, 3, 5

Step 3:
1. 40
2. 23
3. 27

Bonus Box:
1st doghouse: 22; 2nd doghouse: 21; 3rd doghouse: 36; 4th doghouse: 14

Page 116

1. likely	5. unlikely	9. 1	13. $^8/_{37}$
2. unlikely	6. unlikely	10. $^5/_{37}$	14. 0
3. likely	7. unlikely	11. 1	15. $^{12}/_{37}$
4. unlikely	8. likely	12. 0	16. $^1/_{37}$

Page 119

1. Since the three letters cannot be repeated, there are only **6** possible combinations:

   ABC, ACB   BAC, BCA   CAB, CBA

2. Since a letter can be repeated within a word, there are a total of **27** possible words. (Tell students that *a tree diagram* would be a good organizer for this problem.)

AAA	ABA	ACA	BAA	BBA	BCA	CAA	CBA	CCA
AAB	ABB	ACB	BAB	BBB	BCB	CAB	CBB	CCB
AAC	ABC	ACC	BAC	BBC	BCC	CAC	CBC	CCC

3. There are **24** different ways that the four cowpokes can line up:

Dex-Lex-Rex-Tex	Lex-Dex-Rex-Tex	Rex-Dex-Lex-Tex	Tex-Dex-Lex-Rex
Dex-Lex-Tex-Rex	Lex-Dex-Tex-Rex	Rex-Dex-Tex-Lex	Tex-Dex-Rex-Lex
Dex-Rex-Lex-Tex	Lex-Rex-Dex-Tex	Rex-Lex-Dex-Tex	Tex-Lex-Dex-Rex
Dex-Rex-Tex-Lex	Lex-Rex-Tex-Dex	Rex-Lex-Tex-Dex	Tex-Lex-Rex-Dex
Dex-Tex-Lex-Rex	Lex-Tex-Dex-Rex	Rex-Tex-Dex-Lex	Tex-Rex-Dex-Lex
Dex-Tex-Rex-Lex	Lex-Tex-Rex-Dex	Rex-Tex-Lex-Dex	Tex-Rex-Lex-Dex

4. There are **7** different combinations of cards that equal 12 (with the ace counting as 1):

   9-2-A, 8-3-A, 7-4-A, 7-3-2, 6-5-A, 6-4-2, 5-4-3

5. There are **10** different routes possible:

   1-J, 1-K, 1-L, 1-M, 1-N, 2-J, 2-K, 2-L, 2-M, 2-N

6. There are **6** horses (24 legs) and **9** cowboys (18 legs) for a total of 42 legs:

horses	number of legs	cowboys	number of legs	cowboys & horses	legs in all
1	4	14	28	15	32
2	8	13	26	15	34
3	12	12	24	15	36
4	16	11	22	15	38
5	20	10	20	15	40
6	24	9	18	15	42
				15	

Page 125

Part I
1. 7 blocks
2. 28 blocks
3. 1
4. 8
5. Answers will vary.

Part II
1. 1
2. 2
3. 5
4. 9
5. 5
6. The number of blocks that make up each digit equals that digit: 4 has 4 blocks, 5 has 5 blocks, and 6 has 6 blocks.

Part III
1. 19 blocks
2. 1:11; 6 blocks
3. 10:08; 21 blocks
4. 2:01; 2:04; or 2:07

Bonus Box: Answers will vary.

Page 130

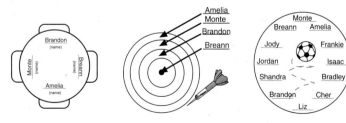

Note: In puzzles A and C, all the names may be rotated to other positions. However, the names must remain in the order shown.

Page 137

monthly payment	amount	balance	interest	new balance
	—	—	—	$100.00
1	$15.00	$85.00	$0.71	$85.71
2	$15.00	$70.71	$0.59	$71.30
3	$15.00	$56.30	$0.47	$56.77
4	$15.00	$41.77	$0.35	$42.12
5	$15.00	$27.12	$0.23	$27.35
6	$15.00	$12.35	$0.11	$12.46
7	$12.46	0		
	$102.46	= total payment		

Bonus Box:

monthly payment	amount	balance	interest	new balance
1	$10.00	$90.00	$1.50	$91.50
2	$10.00	$81.50	$1.36	$82.86
3	$10.00	$72.86	$1.22	$74.08
4	$10.00	$64.08	$1.07	$65.15
5	$10.00	$55.15	$0.92	$56.07
6	$10.00	$46.07	$0.77	$46.84
7	$10.00	$36.84	$0.62	$37.46
8	$10.00	$27.46	$0.46	$27.92
9	$10.00	$17.92	$0.30	$18.22
10	$10.00	$8.22	$0.14	$8.36
11	$8.36	0	—	
	$108.36 = total payment			

Page 147

```
  0  15  13  12          4  11   0  17
  X   6   X   2          8   X   X   7
-      7   5   6        -      2   4   0   8
  ------------          ----------------
      8   8   6          2   7   9   9
```

The wording of students' answers may vary.

1. Compare the digits in the ones column. Since 7 is less than 8, cross out the 7. Above it write 17, the sum of 10 + 7. Subtract 8 from 17 to get 9. Cross out the 1 in the tens column and write a 0 above it.

2. Compare the digits in the tens column. Since the digits are the same, subtract 0 from 0 to get 0.

3. Compare the digits in the hundreds column. Since 1 is less than 4, cross out the 1. Above it write 11, the sum of 10 + 1. Subtract 4 from 11 to get 7. Change the 5 in the thousands column to 4.

4. Compare the digits in the thousands column. Since 4 is greater than 2, subtract 2 from 4 to get 2. The difference is 2,709.

Page 151

1. Each side equals 2:
6. Each side equals 7:
2. Each side equals 3:
7. Each side equals 9:
3. Each side equals 4:
8. Each side equals 10:
4. Each side equals 5:
9. Each side equals 12:
5. Each side equals 6:
10. Each side equals 14: